To RALPH
OUR #1 "CONTEMPORARY"
ARCHITECT

Laura Templeton

Al

Al

Celeste Silveira

"Remember Ralph"
(The Slogan for 1992/1993"
April

Michele Choate

**100** CONTEMPORARY ARCHITECTS

SELECTED BY BILL LACY

# 100 CONTEMPORARY ARCHITECTS

## Drawings & Sketches

HARRY N. ABRAMS, INC., PUBLISHERS, NEW YORK

Editor: Ruth A. Peltason
Designer: Elissa Ichiyasu

Library of Congress Cataloging-in-Publication Data
Lacy, Bill.
100 contemporary architects : drawings & sketches
/ selected by Bill Lacy.
p.   cm.
ISBN 0–8109–3661–5
1. Architectural drawing—20th century—Themes, motives.
I. Title.   II. Title: One hundred contemporary architects.
NA2700.L26   1991   91–10155
720′.22′222—dc20   CIP

Page 2

**LEBBEUS WOODS**

**'BERLIN-FREE-ZONE' PROJECT, BERLIN, GERMANY. 1990**

**MEDIUM: PEN AND INK, COLORED PENCIL**

Page 5

**MARIO BOTTA**

**HOUSE IN BREGANZONA, TICINO, SWITZERLAND. 1988**

**MEDIUM: PENCIL ON SKETCHING PAPER**

Pages 6-7

**GERHARD KALLMAN/MICHAEL MCKINNELL**

**AMERICAN ACADEMY OF ARTS AND SCIENCES,**

**CAMBRIDGE, MASSACHUSETTS. 1981**

**MEDIUM: PEN AND INK**

# CONTENTS

ACKNOWLEDGMENTS  8

FOREWORD  9


THE ARCHITECTS


RAIMUND ABRAHAM  12

EMILIO AMBASZ  14

ANTHONY AMES  16

TADAO ANDO  18

JOHN ANDREWS  20

ARQUITECTONICA  22

GAETANA AULENTI  24

EDWARD LARRABEE BARNES  26

KAREN BAUSMAN/LESLIE GILL  28

THOMAS BEEBY  30

GUNNAR BIRKERTS  34

RICARDO BOFILL  36

GOTTFRIED BÖHM  38

MARIO BOTTA  40

JEAN PAUL CARLHIAN  44

PETER CHERMAYEFF  48

DAVID CHILDS  50

HENRY N. COBB  54

COOP HIMMELBLAU  56

CHARLES CORREA  60

BALKRISHNA VITHALDAS DOSHI  64

ANDRES DUANY/
ELIZABETH PLATER-ZYBERK  68

PETER EISENMAN  70

ARTHUR ERICKSON  72

NORMAN FOSTER  74

ULRICH FRANZEN  76

JAMES INGO FREED  78

FRANK GEHRY  80

ROMALDO GIURGOLA  82

CHARLES GRAVES  84

MICHAEL GRAVES  88

ALLAN GREENBERG  92

CHARLES GWATHMEY  94

ZAHA HADID  96

HUGH HARDY  98

GEORGE HARTMAN/WARREN COX  100

JOHN HEJDUK  102

HERMAN HERTZBERGER  104

STEVEN HOLL  106

HANS HOLLEIN  108

MICHAEL HOPKINS  112

ARATA ISOZAKI  114

HUGH NEWELL JACOBSEN  116

HELMUT JAHN  118

CARLOS JIMENEZ  120

JOHN JOHANSEN  122

PHILIP JOHNSON  124

E. FAY JONES  126

SUMET JUMSAI  128

Shady Hill transformed.

**GERHARD KALLMANN/
MICHAEL MCKINNELL** 130

**RAM KARMI/ADA KARMI-MELAMEDE** 132

**JOSEPH PAUL KLEIHUES** 136

**REM KOOLHAAS** 138

**KISHO KUROKAWA** 140

**RICARDO LEGORRETA** 142

**DANIEL LIBESKIND** 144

**WILLIAM S. W. LIM** 146

**MARK MACK** 148

**FUMIHIKO MAKI** 150

**IMRE MAKOVECZ** 152

**RICHARD MEIER** 156

**RAFAEL MONEO** 158

**ARTHUR COTTON MOORE** 162

**CHARLES MOORE** 164

**MORPHOSIS** 166

**OSCAR NIEMEYER** 168

**JEAN NOUVEL** 170

**WILLIAM PEDERSEN** 172

**I. M. PEI** 174

**CESAR PELLI** 176

**RENZO PIANO** 178

**REIMA PIETILÄ/RAILI PIETILÄ** 180

**JAMES STEWART POLSHEK/
JAMES GARRISON** 184

**ANTOINE PREDOCK** 186

**JAQUELIN T. ROBERTSON** 188

**RICHARD ROGERS** 190

**ALDO ROSSI** 192

**PAUL RUDOLPH** 196

**MOSHE SAFDIE** 198

**ADÈLE NAUDÉ SANTOS** 202

**MACK SCOGIN** 204

**HARRY SEIDLER** 206

**KAZUO SHINOHARA** 208

**CATHY SIMON** 210

**SITE** 212

**ALVARO SIZA** 214

**ETTORE SOTTSASS** 216

**ROBERT A. M. STERN** 218

**JAMES STIRLING** 220

**KENZO TANGE** 222

**BENJAMIN THOMPSON** 224

**STANLEY TIGERMAN** 226

**BERNARD TSCHUMI** 228

**WILLIAM TURNBULL** 230

**O. M. UNGERS** 232

**ROBERT VENTURI** 234

**HARRY M. WEESE** 236

**TOD WILLIAMS/BILLIE TSIEN** 238

**HARRY C. WOLF** 240

**LEBBEUS WOODS** 244

**BIOGRAPHIES** 248

**CREDITS** 272

# ACKNOWLEDGMENTS

This book is concerned with a certain kind of drawing, one that expresses the earliest thoughts of an architect as he or she begins to think about a design problem. It would not have been possible without the support of a legion of dedicated friends and colleagues who either shared my passion for the drawn line or who were willing to humor that obsession as the price of our friendship. I am grateful to all of them for their assistance.

Paul Gottlieb, the President of Harry N. Abrams, Inc., and the muse of artists, poets, and other sundry creative types who yearn for the legitimacy of the printed page, first discussed the idea with me and has been unflagging in his enthusiasm for the project since its inception. Ruth Peltason, Senior Editor at Abrams, shared my keen interest in the book and it was she who skillfully guided the project to completion. It was her encouragement, patience, and persistence that got me across the finish line with the gentle admonition that became my mantra, "Don't despair—but don't delay." Her many contributions to the manuscript and her assistance in selection of drawings went well beyond the normal bounds of editorial duties.

Lita Talarico and Judy Carmichael were relentless in their pursuit of materials and served superbly in their role as project managers. Charles Miers provided early advice and direction on the concept of the book. Nora Richter Greer played a key role in developing the essays, and Karen C. Chambers Dalton, Ellen Shapiro, and Andrea Oppenheimer Dean worked tirelessly and cheerfully to assemble the materials that gave final form to the book. My appreciation also goes to Patti Vogt and David Yellin who provided invaluable assistance in the logistical tasks of soliciting and receiving the drawings. Elissa Ichiyasu brought the drawings to life with her sympathetic and sensitive design for the book, making the book the creative amalgam of art and architecture that I had envisioned.

I am also indebted to Dr. Kurt Forster, Director, the J. Paul Getty Center for the History of Art and the Humanities, for his personal encouragement and for the use of the library and research facilities as a visiting scholar, and to Julia Bloomfield, Director of Publications, for her assistance and firm belief in the validity of the book.

There were times when the frustration of seeking drawings from peripatetic architects was overwhelming; when I thought perhaps ten architects would suffice instead of one hundred architects. There were other times, however, upon spotting yet another talented architects' work when I wished that the book could have included one thousand architects. My final word of appreciation, then, goes to the architects represented in the book. They are an unusually gifted group who gave freely of their talent, time, and drawings to make the publication a reality.

Bill Lacy, FAIA
New York City

**A**t a memorial service for the talented architect and industrial designer Eliot Noyes in 1978, the writer John Hersey described various things about him which he remembered with pleasure. He spoke of his fascination with the capable hands of Noyes that were able to tackle any task set before them. In one passage he described Eliot's drawing ability, and his words have remained with me ever since. "Best of all, we've seen those hands explaining an idea on paper. The pad in one hand, the felt-tipped pen skating in the other, and the clarity of the concept jumping out at us as lines cried out to other lines their conspiracy of meaning—so obvious when the sure hand has swept them all into place." That eulogy sums up in many respects the power of the sketch and the central theme of this book.

I have always been fascinated by the magic of a drawn line on a piece of paper. This book is an acknowledgment, a celebration, of a profession of men and women who still draw on pads and yellow tracing paper in an age that no longer attaches great importance to this particular skill. At one time in the history of the United States the ability to communicate one's thoughts by drawings was considered an essential part of the education of a person, just as playing the piano was a mark of cultural development. In 1870 a law mandated by the Massachusetts legislation required that cities and towns with populations of more than 10,000 people must offer free drawing lessons.

Architects still follow the tradition of drawing and often as not begin their careers by taking an art course or a mechanical drawing course in high school. In college this new means of expressing (and experiencing) one's thoughts in imagery rather than in words is further reinforced and developed, and by the time the fledgling architect is graduated, he has acquired this ability to give ideas form through linear representations that stand for buildings and spaces. Architects and artists are among only a few professionals who retain the visual curiosity and knowledge that most of us possessed as infants. Pictographic skills which took thousands of years of human evolution to develop are possible now within a single lifetime. The architect is not that far removed in his impulse for thinking in visual terms from post—Cro-Magnon ancestors who made drawings in the caves at Niaux, France, some 25,000 years ago.

Architects use drawings to give visual form to their ideas. In the non-verbal world of architecture lines on paper play a central role. Architects' sketches are not the same as those by artists who depict people, places, and objects that already exist. The architect thinks visually about buildings that he "sees" well before they exist. Whereas a mathematician might use numbers and algebraic notations, and a musician, notes and bars, the architect employs a personal calligraphic shorthand of lines and shadings to describe the earliest images that form in his mind's eye.

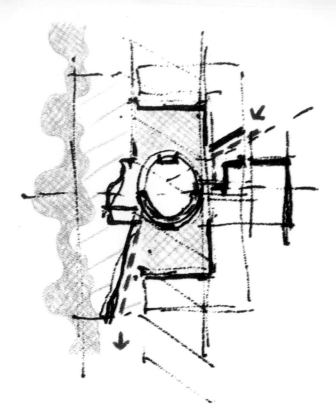

The drawings included here are not the kind that architects make to guide the contractor in constructing the building, nor are they representational renderings and perspectives simulating, as in a painting, the fully realized product. These drawings are more in the nature of preliminary sketches of a project, snatched from the drawing table at that moment when the genesis of the design is first revealed. Central to many architects' method is the time-tested and somewhat old-fashioned procedure of making an initial drawing—a hypothesis on tracing tissue, testing it by placing another piece of tracing paper over that iteration, correcting, revising, and testing further thoughts. Usually this is done many times, as sheets mount into a thick sheaf of ideas that spring from mind and eye onto blank paper. Lesser ideas sink to illegibility as other fresher ones clamor for the top sheet's position of primacy. Architects approach the design of buildings in a number of ways. Some begin with floor-plan sketches; noodlings of lines that

attempt to define the horizontal circulation patterns on each floor level and the size of the rooms. Others think first in slices cut through the building to decide on floor heights and means of vertical access. Still others may be interested in the overall view—how the building relates to its site and to the adjacent buildings. And there are architects who seem to have a full-blown image at the outset of how their building will look as one approaches it from a pedestrian eye level. These early thoughts in line are a special kind of artistic impression, and each architect develops an individual set of complex personal hieroglyphics that are represented in his or her drawings, in what critic John Russell has called an "alphabet of seeing." A squiggle, a dot, a smudge all have come to bring particular meaning to the architect whose style has evolved over years of solving problems in this time-tested manner.

It is a cliché that the first conceptual sketch often occurs on the back of an envelope or on a napkin in a restaurant, but there is more than a grain of truth in these tales. Architects are well known for carrying their

sketchbooks and journals with them wherever they go in order to record fleeting ideas and impressions. Often the first impulse sketch is the last time the architect will be freed from all the constraints of time, budget, program, and politics. It is the moment when only the problem and its possible design solution exists, the moment when, as Vittorio Lampugnani describes it, "creativity appears in its purest form." This encapsulation of the final solution to the problem will be followed by months and sometimes years of refinement and revision, but in that first tiny sketch, like the one James Stirling made for the Staatsgalerie Museum in Stuttgart, crude and brilliant, all the elements of an enormously complicated project are clearly present.

Architects with their sketchbooks as their constant companions are in some respects like writers who jot down notes of characters and scenes they encounter, which years later become part of a novel. Similarly, architects revisit their sketchbooks and journals and discover thoughts and

observations that have current design application and which when viewed from a different perspective in time are themselves different and intriguing. Architects like Frank Gehry carry this quality of that first sketch into their final design. "I am interested in the work not appearing finished, with every hair in place, every piece of furniture in its spot ready for the photograph. I prefer the sketch quality, the tentativeness, the messiness if you will, the appearance of 'in progress' rather than the presumption of total resolution and finality." Or as another architect, Reima Pietilä, has noted about what he refers to as these "process sketches" and their role in his arrival at a creative design solution, "These sketches allow us insight into how architecture emerges from 'scrap'; of how architecture emerges from that indefinite anything." Referring to his own working method, Pietilä said, "I lay sketch upon sketch perhaps up to ten times, carefully holding the previous one as a basis for the following sketch until I feel 'it is there.'" Pietilä describes his sketches as "conceptual tools on the way to becoming objects."

Pursuing this idea further I was curious to see how Philip Johnson started to think about his now-famous Glass House in New Canaan; whether there might be a similarity between Johnson's first sketches (being strongly influenced by his close association with Mies) and those of Niemeyer's early studies for his equally renowned curvilinear house outside of Rio. Johnson, in Miesian tradition, stayed close to a narrowly focused rectilinear idiom, and Niemeyer drew in an almost naive fashion that echoed his major influence, Le Corbusier. At one end of this book's inventory of drawing personalities are the explosive and avant-garde drawings by Libeskind, Woods, Zaha Hadid, Morphosis, Coop Himmelblau, and others who invest their lines with an intensity that goes well beyond the realm of conventional architectural symbolism. In another grouping one can see a pure artistry in the way that Rossi, Ambasz, Holl, and Hollein approach a design problem. It is easy to imagine that this bent of architects might, like a photographer who having

seen the picture in his lens has no need to actually snap the shutter, could live happily with the architecture that they have already experienced through their colorful sketches without seeing it built.

I have watched many of the architects included here develop over the years, while others are new discoveries for me. I was attracted to this younger generation by their first buildings and rewarded by the sketches that had prompted those works. This book is an eclectic selection of architects and certainly not comprehensive in its scope. It represents the casting of a net fashioned by years of my selecting architects for commissions, awards, fellowships, and prizes, and the choices were necessarily restricted by the limitations of time and space. This book is only about a small percentage of the world architectural community, a selection of those who have noticeably distinguished themselves by word, deed, or building. The choice was based on professional contributions and also reflects in some instances the author's passion for certain drawings.

At times it seems that architecture of the past twenty years has been as concerned with words as with deeds, with the promotion of careers being more important than the buildings created. Each new issue of the proliferating worldwide architectural publications brings a new "ism," a new "post" or "neo," a raging debate over whether Post-modernism is dead or merely sleeping, or never existed at all. What once was a profession of form givers and master builders has become one of structuralists, functionalists, deconstructivists, and rationalists. I have tried in the essay on each architect to give something of the flavor and background of this continuing debate and the contribution made to it by each architect, but the primary purpose of the book was an attempt to capture that initial moment of conceptual thought as expressed in early drawings by a variety of architects, young and old, men and women, at different points in their careers and dealing with different cultural contexts.

"A sheet of drawing paper is the Utopian's true medium," according to Wolfgang Pehnt and the history of architecture is rich with examples of architects whose drawings, rather than the actual buildings, have influenced the course of architecture. One that springs most readily to mind is the young Italian futurist Antonio Sant 'Elia who died at twenty-eight, but who, along with Fillipo Marinetti, founded a movement that gave form to a modern industrial-oriented architecture many years before its actual realization. Sant 'Elia's bold drawings for the Milan Railway station in 1914 and his Città Nuova apartment building the same year evoked images that have retained their currency throughout the century. The drawings in this book are a part of this architectural heritage, this inextricable weaving of lines into buildings.

José Ortega y Gasset has said, "He who wishes to tell us a truth, should not tell it to us, but simply suggest it with a brief gesture. . . ." In primitive cultures drawings were regarded as magical. I still consider them so.

Bill Lacy

# RAIMUND ABRAHAM

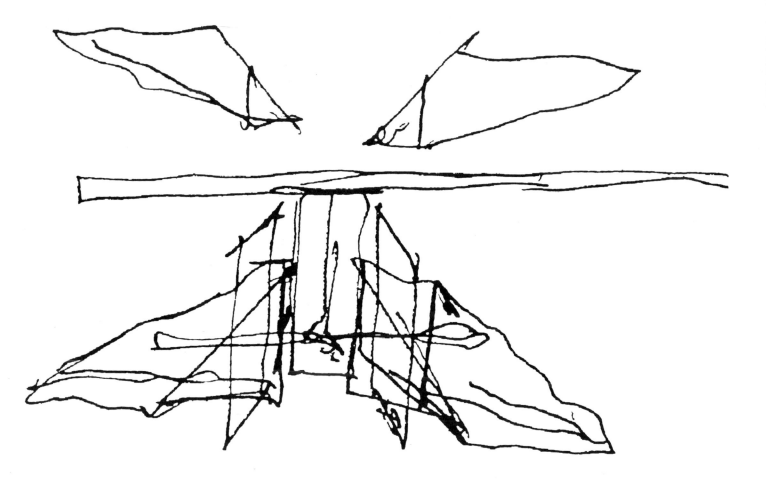

**T**he educational system of learning the trade, craft, or profession of architecture has traditionally relied heavily on the apprentice method, which perhaps explains in part why so many architects have a strong affinity for the teaching of architecture as well as its practice. Raimund Abraham is such an architect, having taught with distinction and dedication at The Cooper Union in New York City since 1971. He has challenged generations of students there to design well and in the doing has honed his own skills for poetic solutions to different problems.

Until only recently, with a series of commissions in Berlin and Eastern Europe, Abraham had not had the opportunity to test his compelling and highly imaginative designs with the reality of execution. Until the Berlin project, Abraham had to content himself with the visionaries' role of unrealized works represented in exquisitely crafted models and drawings. But like another visionary and academic professor, Louis Kahn, his simulations of actual buildings seem complete objects, not "standing for" something else but existing in their own right as completed entities.

As Abraham explains, "A drawing for me is a 'model' that oscillates between the idea and the physical or built reality of architecture. It is not a step toward this reality and in this respect it is autonomous." Raimund Abraham's work rejects historicism as its inspiration and moves more in the direction of the metaphysical rather than the modern. All of his projects are typified by a timeless, yet current, use of materials and forms, and are always heavily laden with symbolism and architectural connotations.

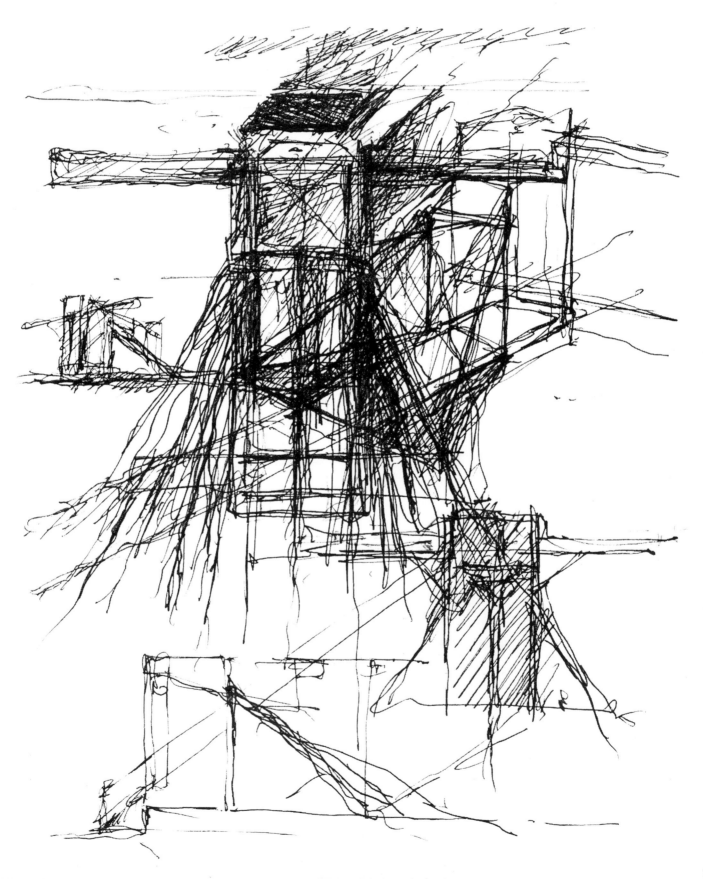

# EMILIO AMBASZ

In a speech at the International Design Conference in Aspen in 1989, Emilio Ambasz attempted to make his work more understandable to the audience by saying that there were really two persons responsible for it. He contended that there was *Emilio* who was a writer, poet, and critic, and who had held the position of Curator of Design at the Museum of Modern Art in New York from 1970 to 1976. It was during this time that with characteristic brilliance of vision and execution he had organized a number of highly influential exhibitions on architecture and industrial design. Three of these achieved landmark status as presentations that altered the thinking on design—"Italy: The New Domestic Landscape," 1972, "The Architecture of Luis Barragán," 1974, and "The Taxi Project," 1976. *Emilio*, the wunderkind from Argentina, breezed in genius-fashion through Princeton's undergraduate curriculum and graduate studies for a master's degree in architecture in two years time. He quickly achieved a reputation among his academic peers for his prolific outpouring of published articles and criticisms and for his lectures on the many varied aspects of architecture and product design.

Enter *Ambasz*, who has nothing to do with the theorist and wordsmith *Emilio*. *Ambasz* does not make exhibitions nor write essays about other designers' work; he designs his own products. His architecture is featured in exhibitions; prizes are awarded for his graphic designs. Perhaps no other architect in this century—with the possible exception of Charles Eames—has managed to excel at the range of design activities as Ambasz. His Vertebra chair, according to Mario Bellini, one of Italy's most distinguished and talented designers, "dated everything that had been done before. It was, and is, the reference point for everything that has been designed in its field since."

Whether Ambasz turns his head to lighting fixtures, electric shavers, or fountain pens, his brilliance as an industrial designer gives objects qualities of simple elegance and timeless styling, but always firmly within the bounds of the best available technology. His design for the Cummins N13 diesel engine rivals any of Louise Nevelson's sculptures in sheer aesthetic appeal and yet is the result of rigid engineering specifications and functional requirements.

The unique nature of Ambasz's architecture successfully defies being placed in any of the categories into which late twentieth-century architecture can be organized. His imagination is fueled by visions that incorporate the mystic genius of Magritte and the dreamy poetic landscapes of Barragan. Add to that an understanding of the technological possibilities, which Mies van der Rohe understood as well, and one approaches a frame of reference for the buildings that Ambasz, the other half of the design partnership of "Emilio/Ambasz," represents.

It is often the case with visionary architects that the built realization is much less than the idea which is incorporated into our imagination as part of its design. Until recently, Ambasz's architecture existed mainly as exquisite drawings and striking renderings in Dali-like settings that seemed more of another planet and place than of this earth. The Lucille Halsell Conservatory in San Antonio, Texas, is the notable exception where a series of dramatic greenhouse structures thrust out of the ground although the circulation spaces are submerged under shaded patios. With this building the fascinating "partnership" of Emilio and Ambasz are joined, the vision and the realization.

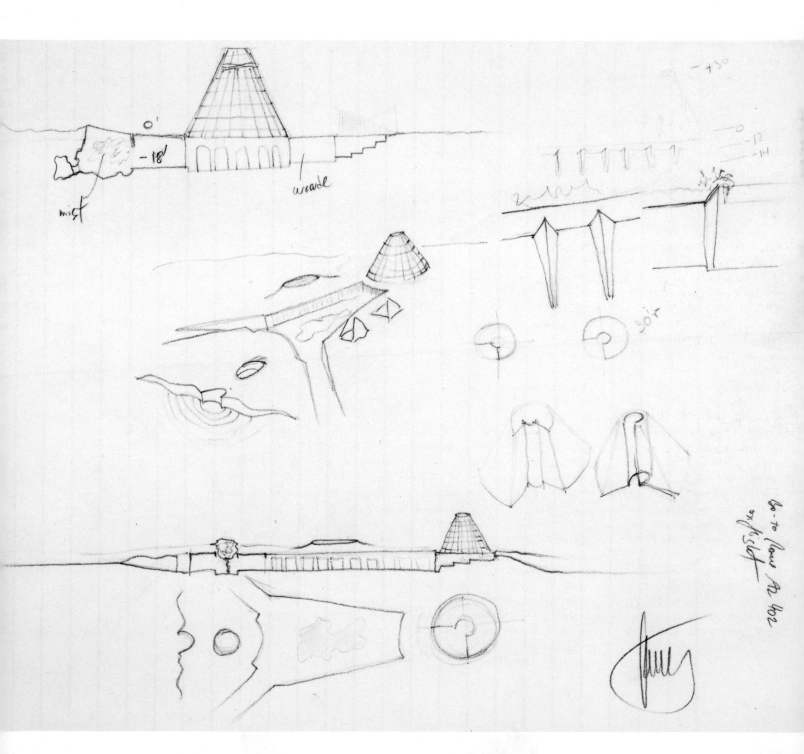

# ANTHONY AMES

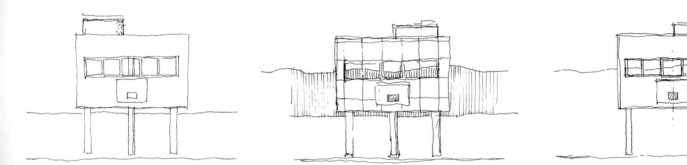

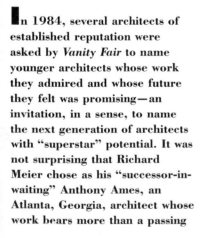

In 1984, several architects of established reputation were asked by *Vanity Fair* to name younger architects whose work they admired and whose future they felt was promising—an invitation, in a sense, to name the next generation of architects with "superstar" potential. It was not surprising that Richard Meier chose as his "successor-in-waiting" Anthony Ames, an Atlanta, Georgia, architect whose work bears more than a passing resemblance to Meier's buildings. Just as Meier's work is derivative of but different from Le Corbusier's, so are Ames' designs "Meieresque" but original, acknowledging a debt both to the great French architect and to Meier.

Ames's own house is one of the primary examples of his design theory and of his body of work to date. Like Corbusier's early houses, it relies on simple white planar geometry and a purity of line and volume.

In an unusual acknowledgment of form following fancy, architect Ames has given prominence to a sports activity in his treatment of the primary facade of the house by placing a carefully designed (and composed) basketball backboard in the center of the front elevation. By featuring an element normally banished to rear service yards, the architect has given a distinctly humorous and American touch to an otherwise classically modern composition.

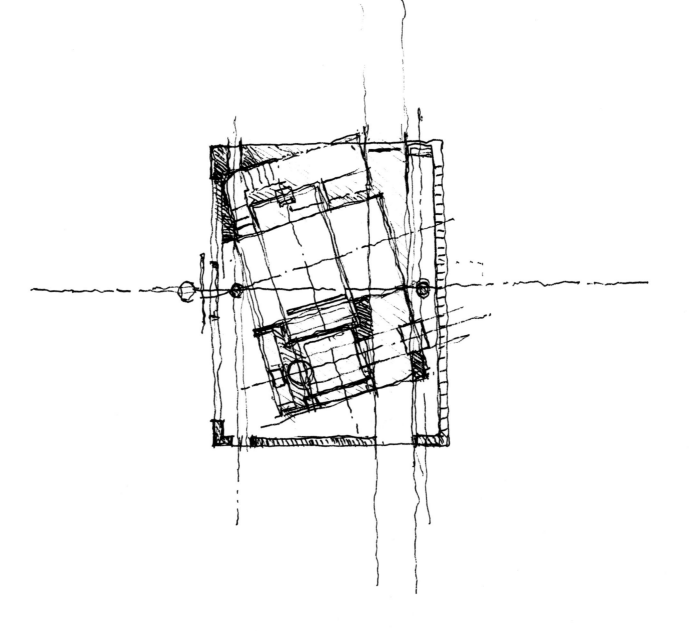

# TADAO ANDO

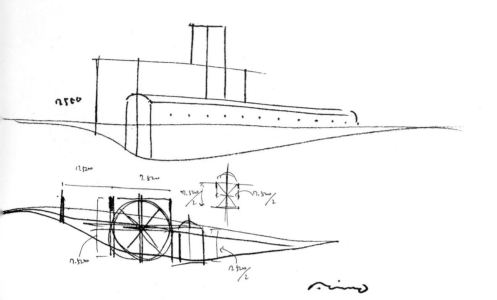

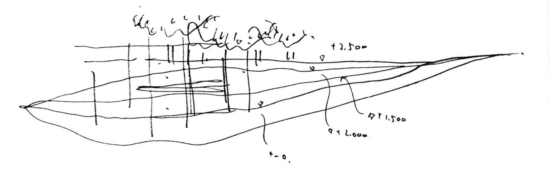

In the field of architecture, as in other fields, Japan has moved to a position of preeminence since World War II. At first the new buildings were impressive only in their size and seemed faltering in their search for a cultural identity and underpinning. Modern Japanese architecture emulated traditional architecture in a slavish manner resulting in concrete structures that attempted to look like similar wooden structures of earlier historic periods.

This period of uncertain work gave way quickly, however, to successive generations of a more sophisticated and refined architecture. There was variety, to be certain, but there was also a distinctive character to Japanese architecture that emerged with the work of Tange, Maki, Isozaki, and others. A representative of a generation younger than these, Tadao Ando, born in 1941, captured the imagination of the younger architects in Japan and became known worldwide for his philosophy and his beautifully rendered buildings. About his architecture, Ando has written:

I am interested both in Japanese aesthetics which places importance on parts and the application of reason which gives order to the whole. To give a stable order to the building as a whole, I use geometry.

However, my concern is not geometric forms in themselves but the spaces to which they give birth. When natural light is introduced into the building and makes apparent the space that is there, geometric order recedes into the background. Patterns of shadow are thrown against the evenly finished concrete surface which softly envelop the space. I am always conscious of the nature of these times and of the needs of human beings, and my wish is to interpret in new ways and using contemporary materials and methods Japanese aesthetics, which is being forgotten.

Ando's buildings, like Louis Kahn's, are about concrete and light, but as he shows in his exquisite monastery chapel on Mt. Rokko for the Cistercian Order, he can expand this palette to include stone, steel, and glass to serve his intentions. The small church is otherworldly in its serene grassy setting, at the highest point in the Osaka area, and Ando has skillfully framed distant views of Osaka Bay by the long inclined colonnade that parallels and leads to the chapel. The strength of this small chapel and all of Ando's very powerful buildings lies in the use of basic materials—usually concrete—and simple time-tested geometric permutations of the square, the rectangle, and the circle.

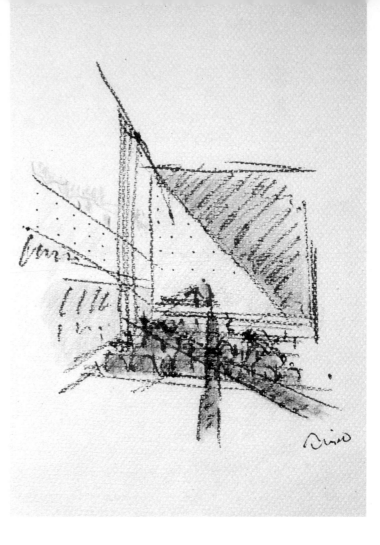

# JOHN ANDREWS

One of Australia's leading architects, John Andrews, gained international renown for his design for Scarborough College in Toronto, Canada, in the early 1960s. This project set the tone from which the architecture of John Andrews would emerge. It is a bold and rugged building—"confident and convincing like the man himself," in the words of Andrews' biographer Jennifer Taylor. It also firmly established the methodical approach that Andrews would apply to every design problem.

Andrews is a self-proclaimed pragmatist who begins with an "intuitive definition" of the problem. His projects evolve around: (1) a detailed analysis of a site and its relationship to the surrounding area; (2) human needs; (3) seeing a building not as a container for inert objects but a place where human beings move and work and play together; and (4) a perpetual dialogue with users of the building. From there the design evolves in a rational and systematic manner. "Only the forms that start to want to happen," in his words, are manipulated into compatible orders.

The organization of Scarborough College (and later the Bellmere Primary School in 1985, also in Toronto) set the pattern for projects to come. In Scarborough College it was an open-ended lineal structure that dictated the design solution and at Bellmere it was the school's centralized but expandable cellular matrix. In both the buildings are low in height and organize themselves in a geometrical pattern that allows for diversity without disintegration.

The focal point of any Andrews design is in providing an appropriate setting for human action and experience. Instead of creating a beautiful object (although his buildings *are* beautiful objects), the architecture is meant as a stage for social contact, so much so that one critic has suggested, "These buildings without their occupants have a stark, empty air like a deserted stage."

A visit to Intelsat Headquarters in Washington, D.C., confirms this appraisal. The design, winner of an international competition in 1980, consists of a series of low-rise, crystalline, futuristic-looking office pods that diagonally march up a steep hill and down again. Inside each pod the work spaces are wrapped around a tremendous atrium. These atriums—or stages—are furnished with ponds, plantings, and centrally positioned elevators. They are designed to encourage maximum social contact; during nights or weekends the lack of such activity gives the atriums an almost surreal quality.

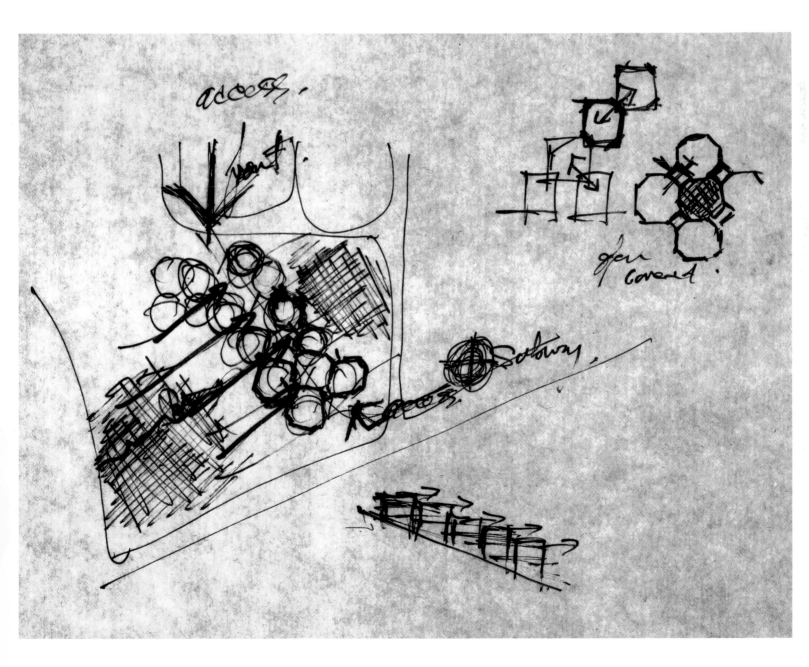

# ARQUITECTONICA
# BERNARDO FORT-BRESCIA, LAURINDA SPEAR

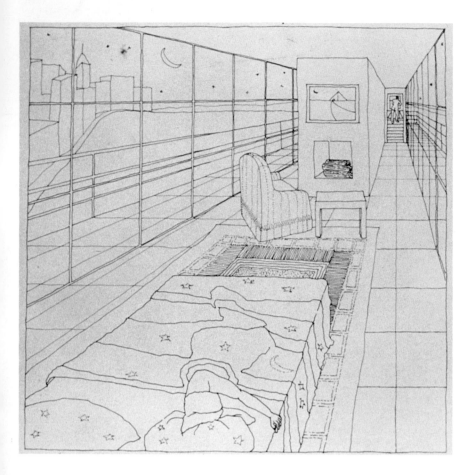

**B**ernardo Fort-Brescia, Laurinda Spear, and three others founded Arquitectonica of Coral Gables, Florida, in 1977. Spear is arguably the most prolific woman working in architecture today. During the first twelve years of the firm's existence she designed over sixty buildings with a combined construction value somewhere in the neighborhood of $500 million, according to a recent magazine article.

The firm's early Miami modernist high-rise buildings are especially recognizable. Most are marked by a giant rectangular void, pastel and bright colors, and deeply recessed openings. In fact, Arquitectonica's highly noticeable design put the firm and the Miami skyline on the map—as well as on the credits of the trendy television show *Miami Vice*.

More recently Arquitectonica, which has added offices in New York, Chicago, and San Francisco, has expanded its range and vocabulary to include visionary and high-tech-looking shopping centers, banks, and office buildings. Among the last is the Center for Innovative Technology in Herndon, Virginia, which from the adjacent highway looks like an inverted pyramid with sharply slanted walls that angle out as the building rises. It appears to rest miraculously on a single, narrow point, although it is actually a configuration of hard-edged, irregular shapes on a raised platform. The building "abandons tradition in search of 21st century forms," according to *Progressive Architecture*. Designer Fort-Brescia calls it "the machine in the forest."

# GAETANA AULENTI

**T**here are more theories about why there aren't more women architects than there are women architects. Many of the schools of architecture will certify that the enrollment of women students accounts for approximately half of their student body seeking degrees, and it is certainly not uncommon to find women as well as men bending over the drafting tables in today's architectural offices. Why then are there only a handful of female architects in the world who are name partners in firms and who have a national or international reputation? The answer most often given is that it takes time and that this will happen within the next ten to twenty years. There are a few role models like Gaetana Aulenti, or Gae (pronounced "guy," no pun intended), who are leading the way as successful architects.

Ms. Aulenti is one of the few women architects practicing today who enjoys equal billing with her male counterparts in a profession that has traditionally and historically been dominated by men. Born and educated in Italy, the early part of her career included several years of affiliation with each of the giant business concerns of Italy— Olivetti and Fiat—but she has maintained her own private practice since 1954 when she received her degree from the Milan Polytechnic School of Architecture. Her practice, like that of other prominent Italian architects, is wide-ranging and encompasses industrial design and interior design as well as architecture. Even with a busy schedule of commissioned works she has found time to lecture at universities and to serve on various editorial boards of the major professional journals in Italy.

The early years of every architect's practice, male or female, seem inevitably to include a number of private residences and Ms. Aulenti's case is no exception. But in the last thirty years she has moved from the design of houses and showrooms to large museum commissions such as the major renovation and redesign of the railroad station in Paris, the Gare d'Orsay station/museum. This project has been well received and critically acclaimed, resulting in Aulenti's selection for other similar undertakings in Barcelona and Berlin.

It is unimportant any longer to call attention to the fact that Gae Aulenti happens to be a woman, but she does serve as an exemplary model of a successful and talented architect to all who are engaged in this profession.

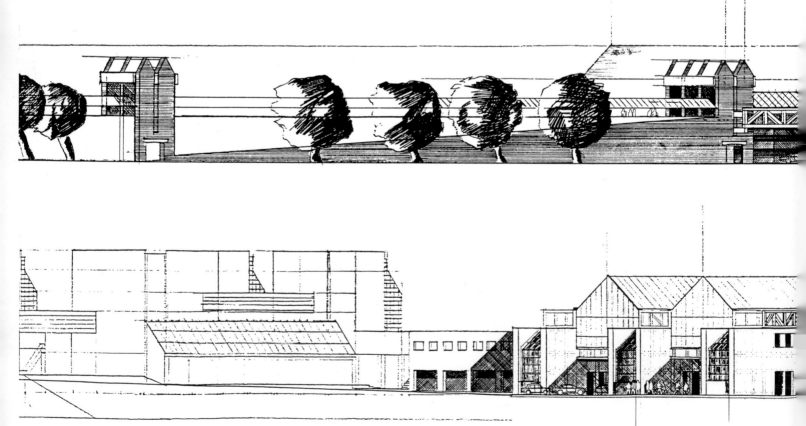

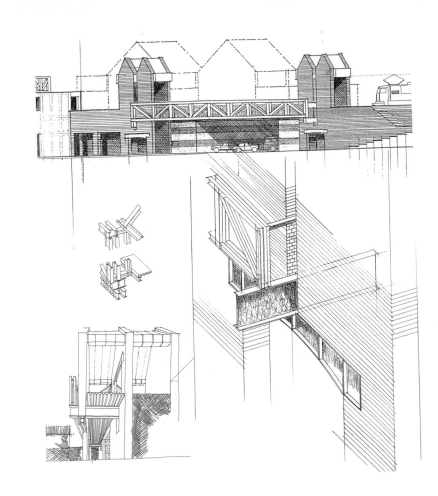

NEW RAILWAY STATION AND RAMP,
S. MARIA NOVELLA RAILWAY STATION, FLORENCE. 1988
MEDIUM: INK ON PAPER

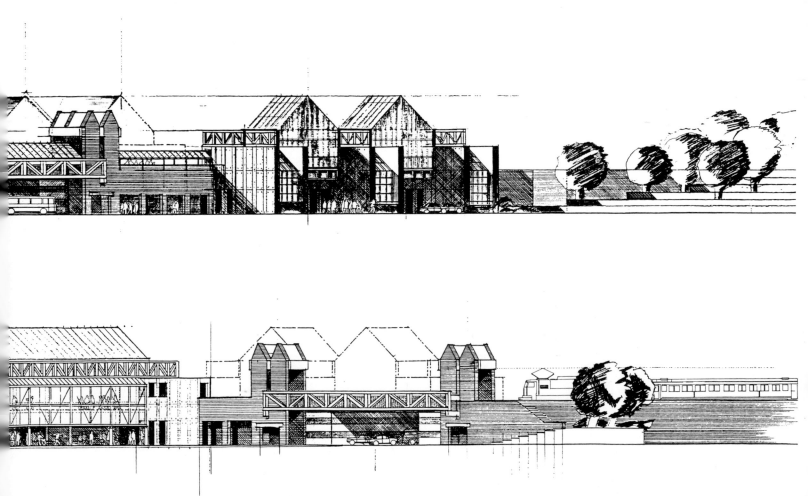

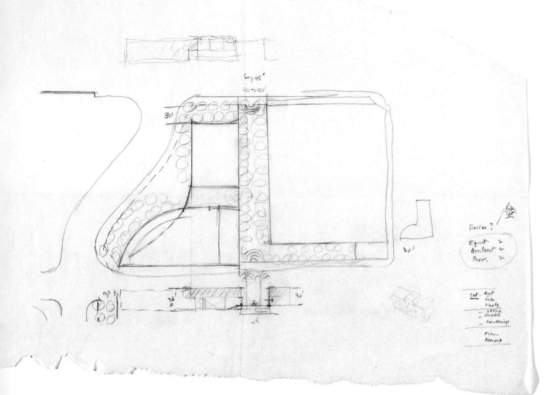

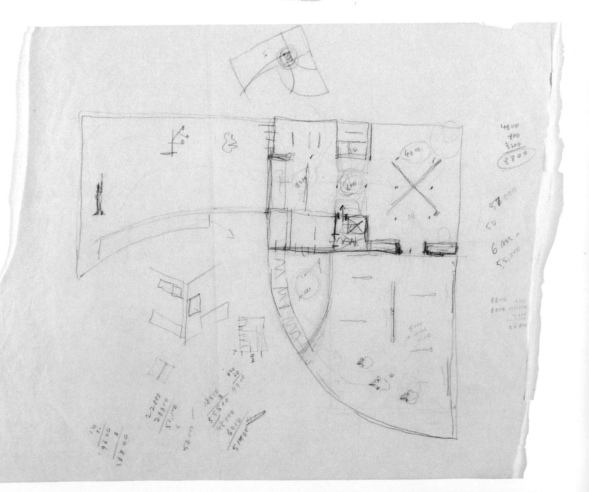

If Edward Larrabee Barnes had created only one building, the IBM tower in Manhattan, with its gracious and hospitable forecourt, it would have given him a high place in the annals of American architectural achievement. Among his other outstanding designs are the Walker Art Center in Minneapolis, the Dallas Museum of Art, the Asia Society in New York City, and numerous educational and residential buildings. Whether designing a high rise, corporate headquarters in Manhattan, a residence in Minnesota, or a museum in Texas, Ed Barnes brings a special dignity and gift to solving design problems.

A former student of the modern masters Gropius and Breuer, Barnes, like I. M. Pei, remained impervious to Post-modernism's departure from the mainstream of architectural theory in the 1970s. By the late 80s, however, even Barnes had taken a detour into classicism, as illustrated by his classically inspired, competition-winning Judiciary Office Building for Washington, D.C.'s Pennsylvania Avenue. Whatever his design vocabulary, Barnes is a masterful designer of monuments.

In a similarly flexible fashion, Barnes's design for a house completed in Texas in the mid-1980s evokes the renowned Mexican architect Luis Barragán, as well as Le Corbusier, Mykonos, and a twelfth-century abbey. Though the style is broadly and lyrically modernist, the house comes close to international regionalism, if there were such a thing. Barnes's architecture is typically, "clear, rational, and self-assured," as Dallas architecture critic David Dillon has remarked. It creates a unity of environment and building, a sequence of elegant, uncluttered, clear spaces, and balances between autonomy and restraint—a worthy perch.

# KAREN BAUSMAN / LESLIE GILL

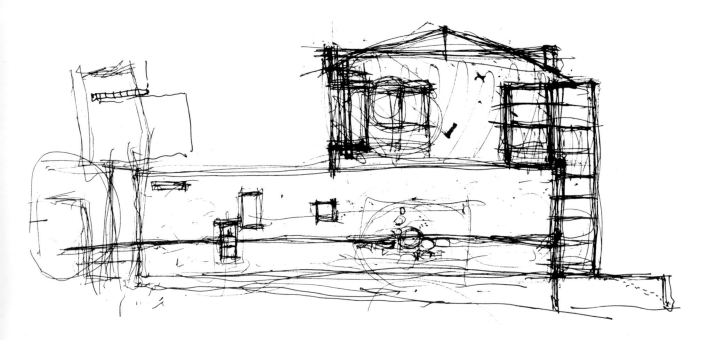

**A**rchitecture is not a professional calling to be undertaken without passion or commitment; to successfully reach the point at which one finally gets to exercise that "urge to build" that originally drew you to this endeavor, requires a five- or six-year education, a three-year apprenticeship in an office, and persuading a client to hire you for the job. Both the education and the practice require long and grueling hours with little monetary compensation. But it is perhaps the last of the acknowledged professions such as law and medicine where an individual's ideas can be expressed and realized. It is one of the few areas of human endeavor that encompasses the tangible and the aesthetic, the scientific and the artistic, the public and the private realms. As a consequence the study and practice of architecture still attracts bright and dedicated young people to it like Karen Bausman and Leslie Gill, who after graduating from Cooper Union in 1982, set to work immediately on projects and commissions that suited their particular interests—interests that show an uncommon artistic inclination.

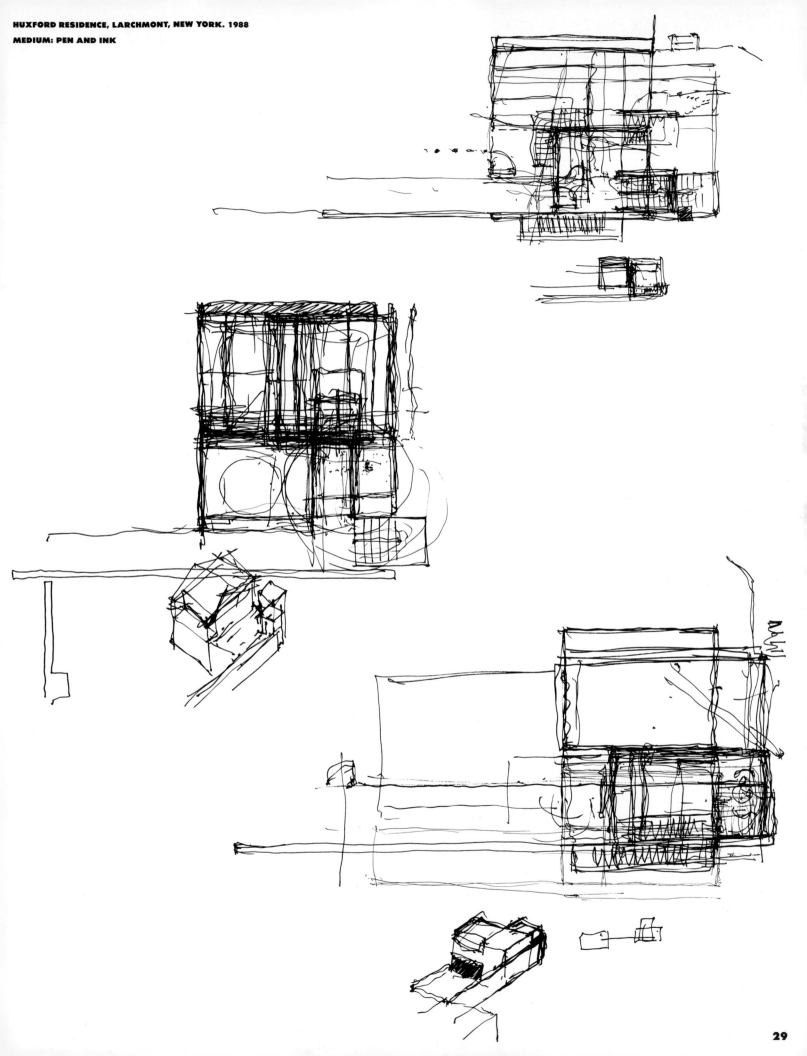

Chicago architecture is steeped in the tradition of Mies van der Rohe—the Chicago architect who perfected the art of taut, skillfully detailed functional glass and steel structures and father of the modern movement in architecture. In the 1970s, however, a new breed of architects known as the Chicago 7 grew in prominence. Their work evolved from modernism, incorporating vestiges of the Chicago vernacular.

Among the Chicago 7 was Thomas Beeby. Born in Chicago's nearby Oak Park—the first home and work-place of Frank Lloyd Wright—Beeby spent his formative years in Philadelphia and England. His mentors were Colin Rowe and John Hejduk at Cornell University, and Paul Rudolph, Vincent Scully, and Serge Chermeyeff at Yale University, architects who acknowledged Mies as the master he was but who stretched the scope of modernism. Nonetheless, Beeby returned to Chicago to the firm C. F. Murphy Associates, at that time one of the leading exponents of Miesian design.

In 1971 he joined James Hammond to eventually form the firm Hammond Beeby and Associates (and in 1977 Hammond Beeby and Babka). The experimenting began. He moved toward a balance in what he called "pure construction" and "picturesque romanticism," two concepts that are evident in his design of the Harold Washington Library in downtown Chicago. But Beeby is not tied to one style of architecture, for he approaches each job as a technician solving a technological problem. The form of the building is influenced by investigations into formal and vernacular history.

In the mid-80s Beeby wrote, "Our work between 1979 and 1984 focused on the meaning of form with the increased integration of historical precedent as a design method. The constructional methodology, including structure and detailing, has maintained modern techniques, but the imagery has shifted toward more easily understood models. There has been a decrease in the level of abstraction with the notion of an increased comprehensibility."

Beeby paints lush and evocative images. Through his art and his buildings, architecture critic Suzanne Stephens once wrote, "there is a desire for his architecture to 'spiritually integrate' man with nature and myth with life." Since 1985 Beeby has divided his time between his firm and his deanship at Yale University's School of Architecture.

# GUNNAR BIRKERTS

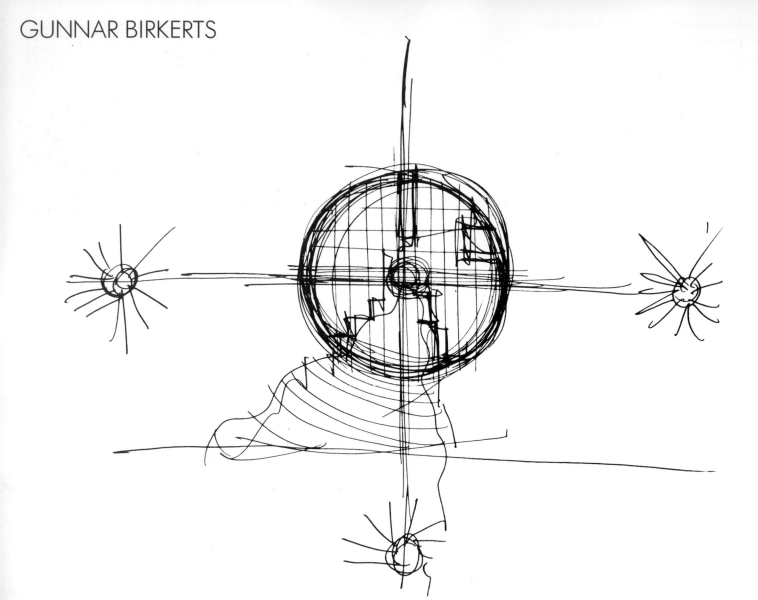

**B**orn in Latvia Riza and educated at the Technische Hochschule in Stuttgart, Gunnar Birkerts came to the United States in 1949 and worked with two important figures in the architectural scene of the 50s— Eero Saarinen (Dulles Airport, Washington, D.C., CBS Building, NYC) and Minoru Yamasaki (World Trade Towers, NYC). While at Saarinen's office he came into contact with other rising stars in the field, Kevin Roche, Cesar Pelli, and Robert Venturi, and worked on two significant projects—the glazed red brick GM Technical Center and the Milwaukee War Memorial. Both buildings seemed to exert special influence on the young Birkerts.

In the process of separating himself from the pragmatic influences of Saarinen and Yamasaki, Birkerts retained the boldness that characterized both. Of the impressive talent that populated the Saarinen office Birkerts arguably carried forward the audacious spirit that best inspired the historic office's designs. Once on his own, each of Birkerts's buildings resembled no other building that had gone before. The Contemporary Arts Museum in Houston was a great "aluminum sail" that housed exciting works to match the architecture. Situated across the street from Van der Rohe's Museum of Fine Arts, it appeared to be a brash iconoclastic challenge to modernism. At the same time, the shocking Federal Reserve Bank in Minneapolis established

Birkerts as the "loosest cannon on the architectural deck." The bank was a structural feat, equalling architecturally any of Evel Knievel's stunt-car feats—a dramatic half-moon facade which was the structural marvel of the period.

This was followed by one unexpected building after another—an underground law library flooded with light, a leaning corporate office tower for the Domino Pizza empire, and a geological layered U.S. Embassy for Caracas. In describing the law library, Birkerts's creative design approach is tailored to the specific design problem at hand:

The circle is the purest geometric form; it cannot be compromised. It is a fitting symbol for the profession of law since it expresses perfection, clarity, integrity, and geometric purity. The circle means concentration, study, and seclusion. It is the shortest circumference of any enclosure for a given space. It does not favor sides or exposures. It can only be changed by changing one's dimension—the radius. It can be deducted from, however. The perfect circle maintains its affinity with the universe and the law of the universe. It also seeks affinity with astrology and early architecture of Stonehenge. The building responds to the solar orbit with its orientation on earth.

Birkerts is a blithe spirit in the architectural landscape.

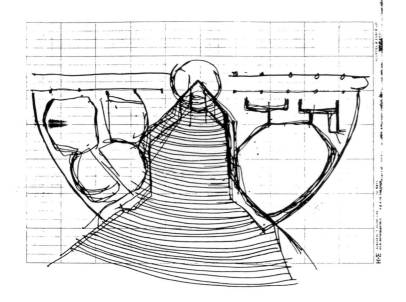

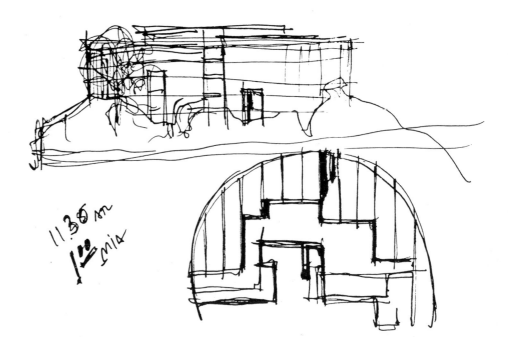

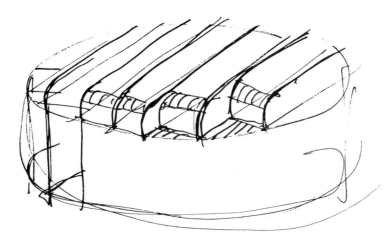

# RICARDO BOFILL

NY. nov. 87

Spaniard Ricardo Bofill is a master at creating architectural stage sets, in which the "experience of intimacy and protection is combined with a sense of a continuous, grand environment where zones of movement are juxtaposed with places of meeting and togetherness," in the words of architecture critic Christian Norberg-Schulz.

Bofill's buildings stand as gigantic models, articulated by a precise geometry and three dimensionality, perhaps a reflection of his predilection for designing from models and large perspective drawings. Architecture critic David Mackay calls it "an indifference to detail that sometimes makes his buildings seem like full-size models, with abundant redundancies." The genre is mostly classical, although Bofill borrows heavily from the Baroque belief that intermediate spaces change the experience of light. From the baroque he also learned to create dynamic spatial effects through expansion and contraction, subdivision and juxtaposition.

Taller de Arquitectura, the firm Bofill founded in 1962, is as unique as his buildings. "The atelier rapidly developed to include people from architectural, artistic, literary, musical, philosophical and mathematical fields," Bofill has written. This grouping was necessary, he added, "to regain the ignored quality and value of life." Throughout his career Bofill has attempted to demonstrate that "man requires a context for social activities that cannot be defined solely in terms of use," or, in other words, a turning away from the "functionalism" of the modern movement. To borrow from Adolf Loos, Bofill's "architecture provokes spiritual reactions in man . . . the mission of architects is to make these explicit." Of great concern to Bofill is providing a common, public space creating streets, squares, promenades, and forums.

The preservation and regeneration of existing urban fabrics is also of interest to Bofill. He cites the Taller's proposal for Les Halles in Paris as a "return to an ambience that could have existed originally when the neighborhood, Le Marais, was built." A stunning example of reuse are the offices of Taller de Arquitectura: a reinvigorated cement factory of exceptional grace.

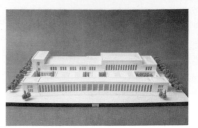

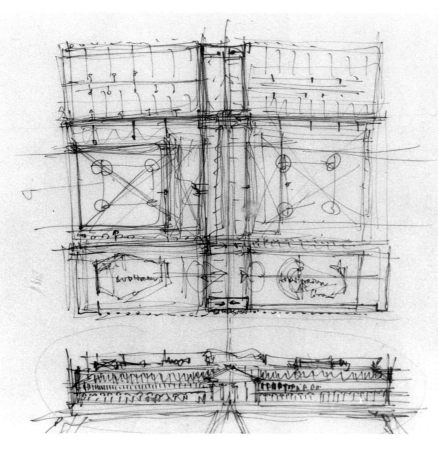

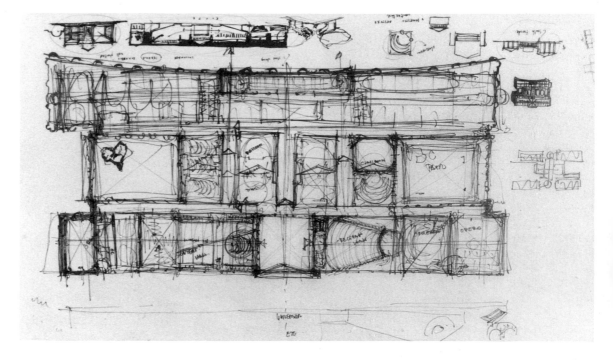

# GOTTFRIED BÖHM

**A**s the son and grandson of architects, Gottfried Böhm has a strong hereditary tie to the field of architecture. Although renowned in Germany, he was virtually unknown internationally until 1986 when he won the Pritzker Architecture Prize, the building arts' equivalent of the Nobel Prize. After announcement of the prize, which until then had been predictably bestowed on celebrities in the field, Böhm's strong and original body of work came to world attention.

His buildings have been called "romantic and intuitive fantasies." One of his first large commissions, the Church of the Pilgrimage at Neviges in 1964, shows Böhm's early preference for concrete construction and is ranked among the best contemporary-style ecclesiastical buildings of this century.

Böhm's recent directions are evident in his new town hall for the German city of Rheinberg. Comprised of new administrative offices for local government, the building has become a new focus for the community. Though it is very large and its design vocabulary might be described as regionalist neo-baroque, Böhm's town hall is deftly inserted into a small-scale, medieval urban fabric. Böhm has disguised its large footprint by breaking it down into what appears as a collection of buildings rather than a monolith. He has given the building a palazzo-like facade facing the main street and modest elevations where it joins residential buildings. The building's historicism is only skin deep, however. The interior is completely new and innovative. Its three splendid and monumental civic spaces are patterned after public squares surrounded by shops and offices that wed drama and functionalism. Because a substantial portion of the building is devoted to multiple-use public space, what might have been a 9-to-5 office building instead offers a full range of daytime, evening, and weekend activities to the public.

CHURCH OF THE PILGRIMAGE, NEVIGES, GERMANY. 1968
MEDIUM: CHARCOAL

# MARIO BOTTA

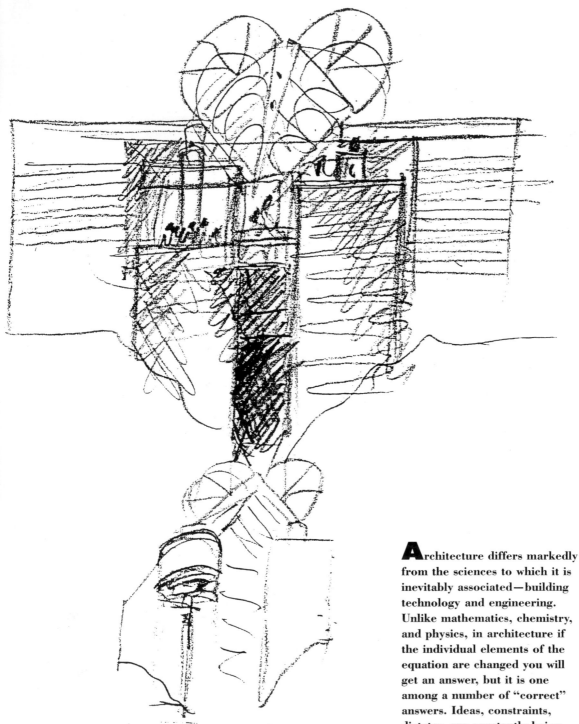

**A**rchitecture differs markedly from the sciences to which it is inevitably associated—building technology and engineering. Unlike mathematics, chemistry, and physics, in architecture if the individual elements of the equation are changed you will get an answer, but it is one among a number of "correct" answers. Ideas, constraints, dictates, are constantly being shifted, changed, and rearranged, and different answers, many of them correct, emerge from the drawing board. It becomes a matter of imagination and creativity on the part of the architect first to envision these various factors, and then to exercise judgment in selecting from the many possibilities. No architect today is more adept at this "posing and selecting" process than Mario Botta.

Botta is one of a handful of post—World War II architects already identified to assume a leading form-giving role in the next several decades of building. He does not fit comfortably into a modernist labeling, but it is easy to see the lasting influences of Kahn, Le Corbusier, and Scarpa on his design philosophy, and it is clear that tenets of modernism have guided the impressive sequence of works he has completed, beginning with the now-famous one-family house in Breganzona, Switzerland near Ticino, in 1971.

HOUSE IN BREGANZONA, TICINO, SWITZERLAND. 1988
MEDIUM: PENCIL ON SKETCHING PAPER

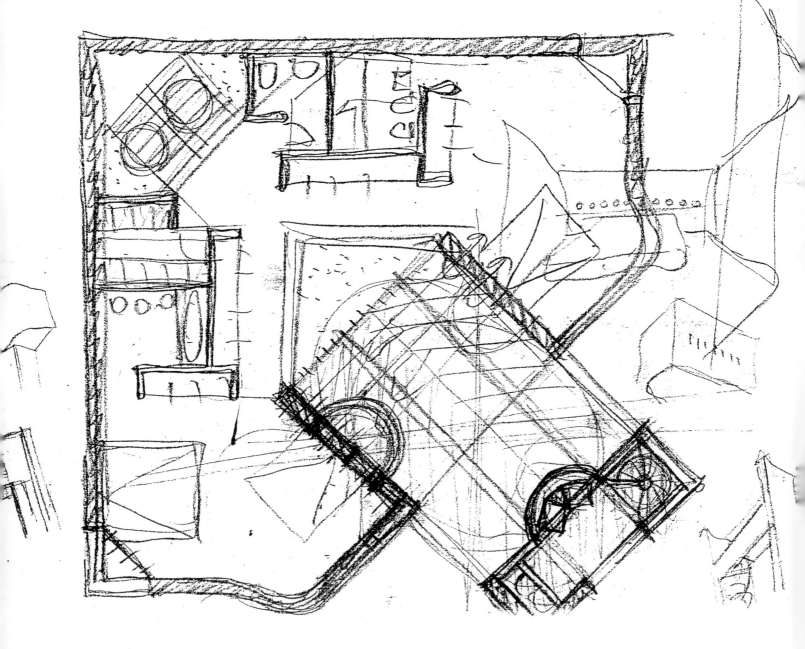

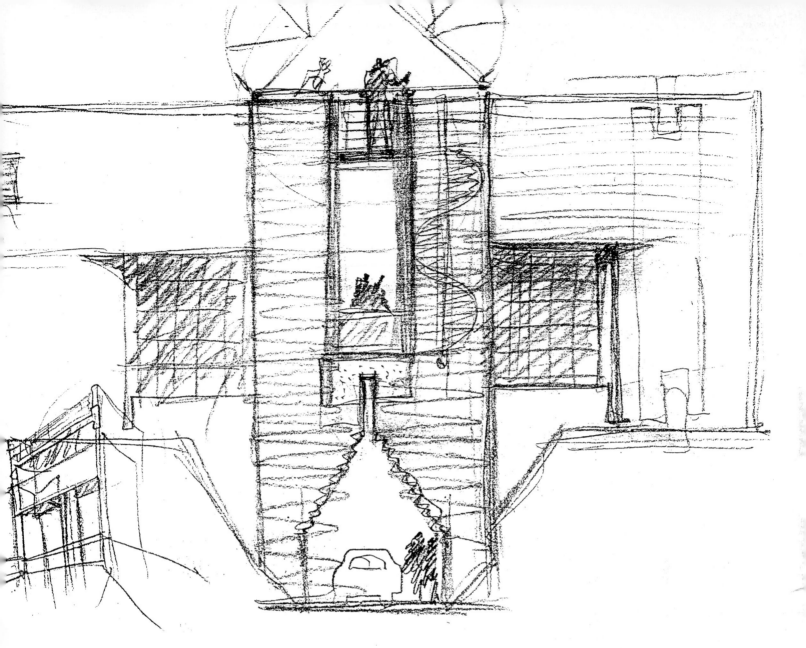

Traditionally architects prefer to have their buildings rather than their words speak for them, but Botta is equally articulate in his designs and written rationale for them. "For an architect to write about architecture is equivalent to superimposing one language upon another language. The course of research and interpretation of an architectural idea is for me much easier and natural when I examine the movement of the pencil on a drawing than when I attempt to express it in words."

Botta comes to drawing quite naturally and easily, having been led to an architectural career by his natural talent in this medium, evident since age fifteen when he left school to become a draftsman in an architectural firm in Lugano. Since that time, with the exception of his sojourns in Milan and Venice to complete his education, Botta has fashioned an internationally well-known practice based on a series of exceptional projects within the vicinity of Lugano. A number of these have been single-family residences, each with strong geometric forms, each with a modeling of light that is a reflection of the lessons he learned well from his three mentors. His buildings are not tied to any single material. Many of them are of poured concrete and concrete block, but more recent projects also show his skill with a brick masonry vocabulary with no noticeable loss of quality or spirit of intentions.

Botta is a prolific virtuoso of drawing as a study technique. "When I draw, I have the sensation that the pencil investigates more pertinently and at a greater depth the message, the ideas and feelings hidden in my work. By proceeding in this manner, I find the most immediate way of expressing tensions and problems."

# JEAN PAUL CARLHIAN

Jean Paul Carlhian is a partner in one of the oldest, most distinguished, architectural firms in the United States—Shepley, Bulfinch, Richardson and Abbott of Boston. The office has a direct lineage back to the famous architect Henry Hobson Richardson who died in 1886.

Over the years the firm has undergone a number of name changes (and intermarriages) but it has remained faithful to its founder's solid principles of an architectural style that brooked no frills, fads, or fussiness. The book ends of buildings that bracket the body of work by this venerable firm might well be the Glessner House in Chicago and the New London Northern Railroad Station at one end and the National Museum of African Art and the Arthur M. Sackler Gallery on the historic Capital Mall in Washington, D.C., at the current end. The latter project was designed by Carlhian, a partner in the firm since 1963.

Jean Paul Carlhian is a cosmopolitan architect, a Parisian by birth, educated at the Ecole des Beaux-Arts and at Harvard University where he taught architectural design under Walter Gropius and Luis Sert. He worked briefly on the United Nations headquarters project for Harrison and Abromovitz before joining Shepley, Bulfinch, Richardson and Abbott. Because of his rigorous training at the Beaux-Arts and his keen interest in the continuity of history, Carlhian has been involved in numerous projects and with organizations that share his preservation interests. Unlike so many architects of the recent decade, his knowledge of the history of architecture is profound and extensive.

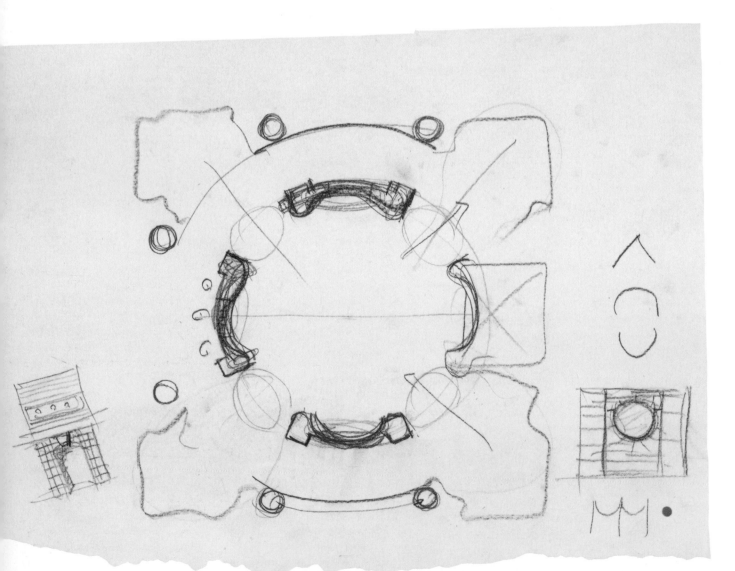

african
vault

Carlhian has served for many years on the design committee of the American Institute of Architects, Washington, D.C., and he is regarded as a highly knowledgeable authority on the capital city. It was no surprise, therefore, that he was chosen to design the South Quadrangle project for the Smithsonian, nor that he would design it in such a site-sensitive manner to enhance, rather than detract from, the grand sweep of the Mall. Carlhian's design for the two museums—the National Museum of African Art and the Arthur M. Sackler Museum (360,000 square footage combined) called for preserving the open space by a brilliant scheme that placed much of the space below ground with small flanking pavilion buildings above as part of a landscaped garden. The three levels of below-grade galleries are ingeniously arranged to receive natural light through stairwells and depressed courtyards. This design, like all of Carlhian's work, displays a steadfast adherence to the tested principles of classical architecture, which when combined with his talent and intellectual curiosity make for buildings that are timeless yet distinctly of their own period.

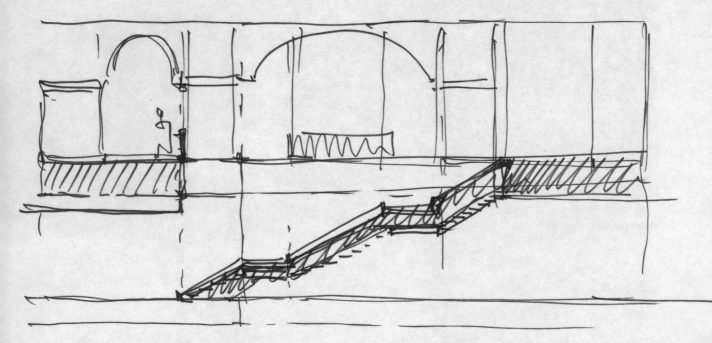

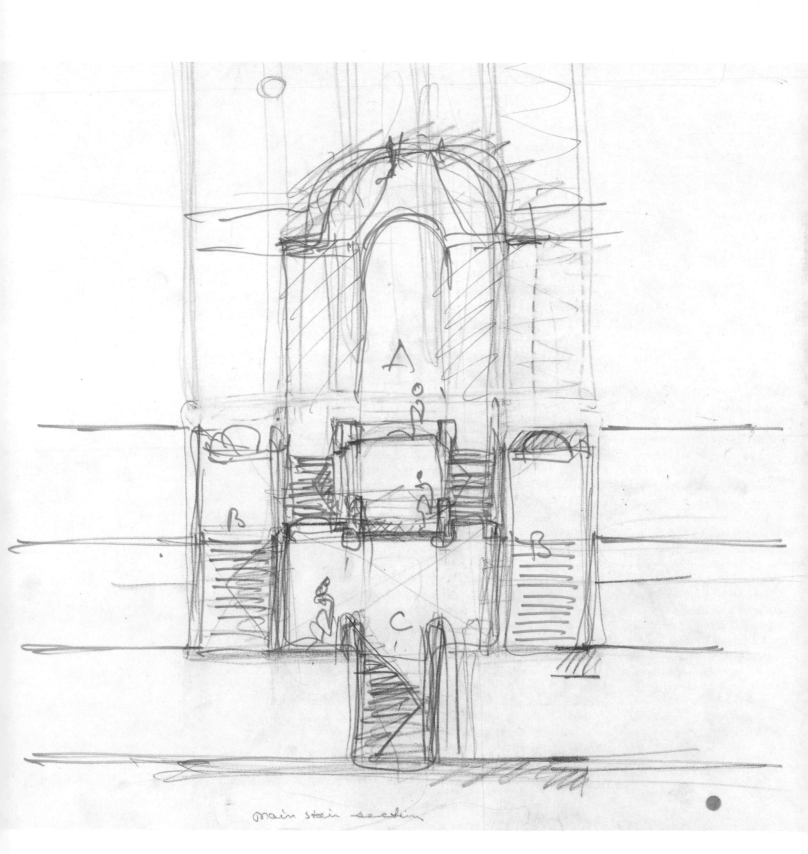

main stair section

# PETER CHERMAYEFF

Cambridge Seven Associates is a rare thing in American architecture, a family affair and a true collaboration. The spiritual progenitor and patriarch was the native-born Russian, Serge Chermayeff, an inspired teacher of a generation of American designers. His sons Peter (an architect) and Ivan (a graphic designer) founded the firm in 1962 together with five additional partners, who were determined not to limit themselves to the design of buildings. In their early days, the Cambridge Seven were filmmakers, graphic designers, and creators of exhibitions. Paradoxically, in recent years the Cambridge Seven have become associated with two particular building types: aquariums and subway stations. They have effectively used both as instruments for urban revitalization.

Their first aquarium was Boston's, then came Baltimore's, and most recently Osaka's in Japan, which is filled with nearly 3 million gallons of water and 16,000 fish, marine mammals, birds, and reptiles. The architects shaped the building of blue-and-red tile and clear glazed volumes with slanting roofs—alluding to the Pacific Ocean's volcanoes—into a microcosm of the Pacific's "ring of fire," the zone of volcanic and tectonic activity outlining the Pacific basin. Visitors circulate through the building via a four-story spiraling ramp around gigantic tanks of sea life.

The Cambridge Seven's renovated and new subway stations in and around Boston marry the firm's far-ranging artistic talent with its increasing flair for urban design. The renovated stations include such whimsical touches as colored mobiles, banners, and castings of workmen's gloves atop escalator rails that appear dropped there at day's end. In the new Forest Hills, New York, station, the architects broke down a huge complex into a cluster of hipped-roof glass structures suggesting an outdoor market. Perched on the highest roof is a radically abstracted clock tower that gives the complex the air of a town center for a principally residential neighborhood made up of three- and four-story walk-ups.

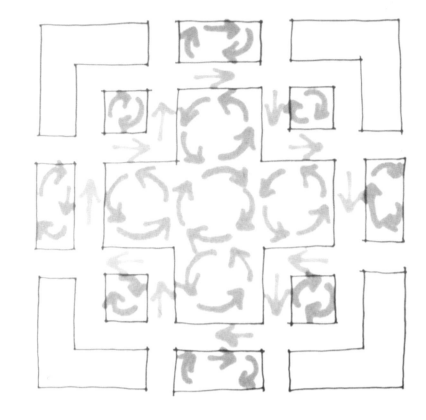

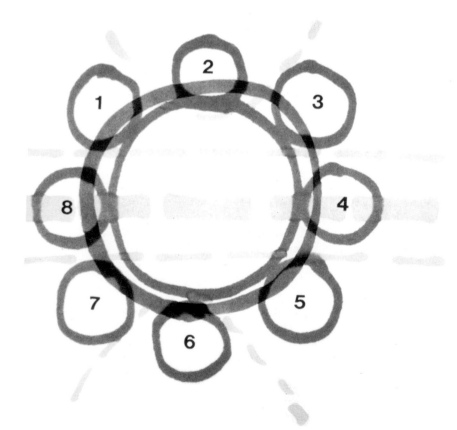

# DAVID CHILDS

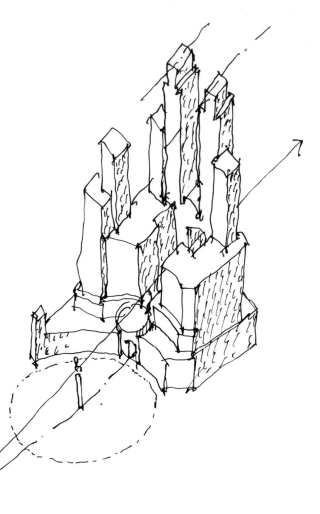

**S**kidmore, Owings & Merrill has dominated post–World War II American architecture because of its size and the quality and consistency of its work. With offices in New York, Chicago, San Francisco, Los Angeles, Washington, D.C., and London, SOM has been called the IBM of architecture because of its preeminent position in the profession and its penchant for serving corporate clients. The firm's considerable planning, environmental, structural, technical, administrative, and other capabilities made it a natural choice for the huge and complex developer projects of the 1980s.

Although Chicago was the founding location of the famous partner-shop, New York has recently become the head office. Its partner-in-charge and chief designer is David Childs. A self-described classicist, Childs joined SOM in 1971 and draws inspiration as readily from Rome as from Manhattan. He studied at Yale at a time when Robert Venturi was a guest professor, and he was heavily influenced by Venturi's anti-modernist theories.

Before moving to SOM's New York office, Childs spent a long apprenticeship in the nation's capital, an architecturally conservative city that strengthened his traditionalist leanings. In Washington, Childs made his mark working with SOM's late founder, Nathaniel Owings, on the Pennsylvania Avenue Development Plan,

Constitution Gardens, and the Mall. He also designed several increasingly historicist office buildings for Washington.

Childs's first design for SOM/ New York was the gigantic World Wide Plaza in midtown Manhattan, which fills the block stretching from 8th to 9th avenues between 49th and 50th streets. World Wide consciously echoes Rockefeller Center, steps back to create a relatively slender tower, and, like the Chrysler Building, is topped by a gleaming crown that acts as logo and symbol from afar. The building is also a good and courteous neighbor, and one of its greatest contributions is to show that even very large, big city projects can revive urban civility rather than extinguish it.

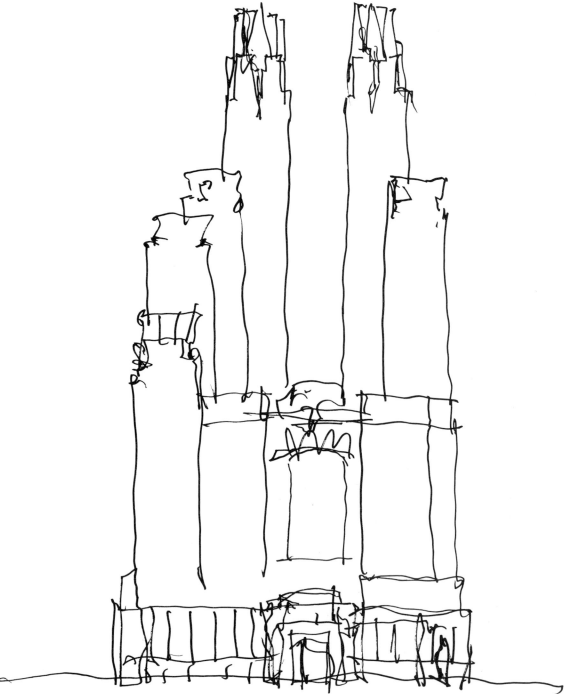

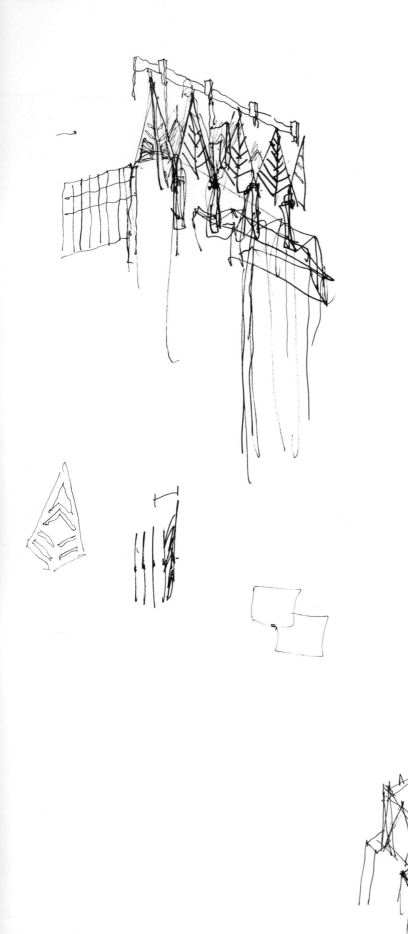

COLUMBUS CENTER, COLUMBUS CIRCLE, NEW YORK CITY. 1989
MEDIUM: COLORED PENCIL ON TRACING PAPER

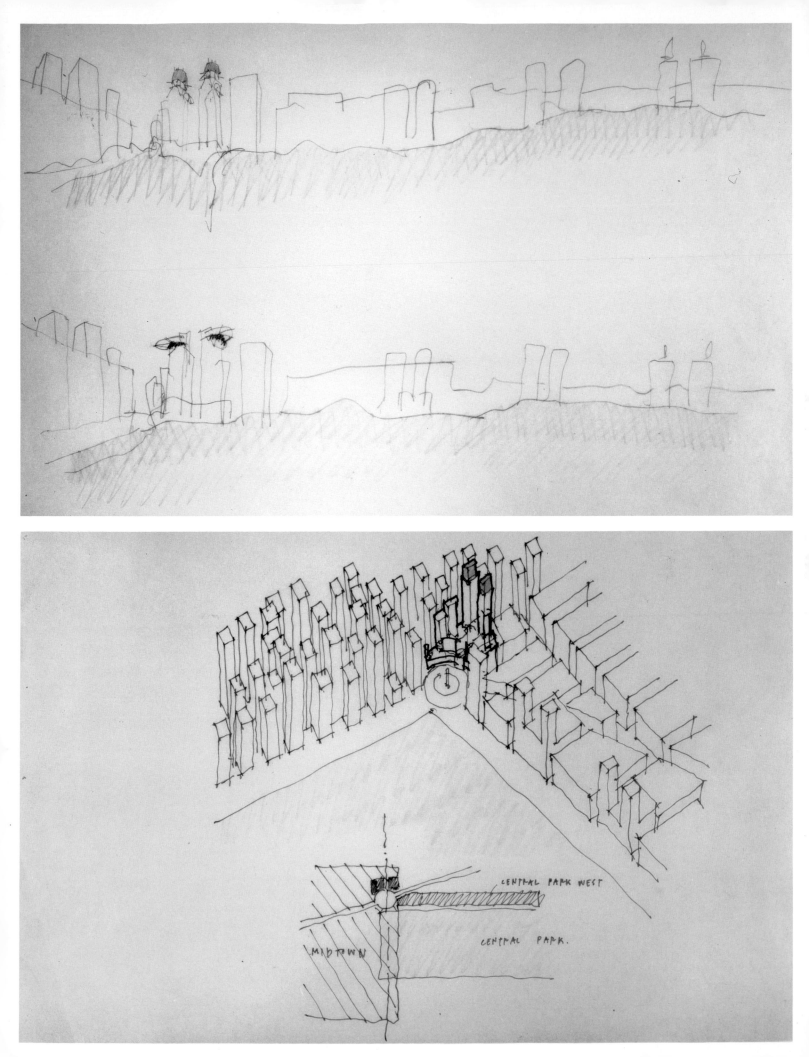

CENTRAL PARK WEST

CENTRAL PARK.

MIDTOWN

HNC
X·67

Church vs Tower

| | |
|---|---|
| Autonomous | Contingent |
| Centered | Decentered |
| Present | Absent |
| Volumetric | Planar |
| Rough | Smooth |
| Ornamented | Unornamented |

**S**ince 1955 the office of I. M. Pei has operated with a design partner who in 1989 achieved name recognition on the masthead when the firm's name was changed to Pei Cobb Freed. That partner, Henry Nichols Cobb, had been known quite well to those in architecture circles prior to that public announcement.

Harry Cobb, as he is known in the profession, commands high esteem from his peers not only for an uninterrupted sequence of buildings that are consistently the best that modern architects can produce, but also because he was the chairman of Harvard's Department of Architecture, from 1980 to 1985. From this highly visible pulpit of the profession Cobb refined the credo that had guided him in producing such outstanding buildings as Place Ville Marie in Montreal, the John Hancock (a plagued but perfectly designed high-rise office tower) in Boston, the Johnson and Johnson Headquarters in New Brunswick, New Jersey, and the First Interstate Bank Tower (Fountain Place) in Dallas.

Although known as a corporate architect, that is, one capable of designing outstanding quarters for prestigious business concerns, Cobb has exhibited a flawless ability to deal with all manner of architectural design problems from the classical addition to a major museum in London to the expansion of a small jewel-like museum in Portland, Maine.

**JOHN HANCOCK TOWER, BOSTON. 1976**
**MEDIUM: PENCIL**

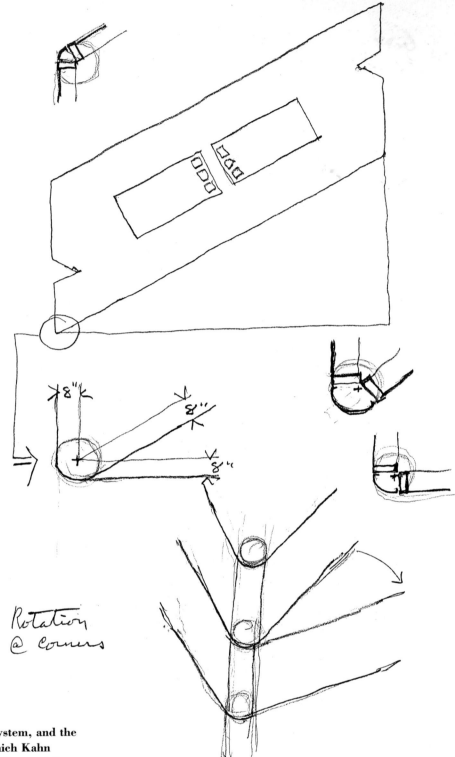

In his charge made in 1980 to the Harvard classes of young architects who would come under his influence and tutelage during the next few years Cobb said, "We must recognize that every design initiative, at whatever scale, is a fragment embedded in a larger context, and that neither the fragment nor the context can be well understood without reference to the other." He also counseled them to make their buildings "coherent" as well as "audacious," citing the tension created by Hagia Sophia with its hybrid structural system, and the Salk Institute in which Kahn brilliantly resolved the need for its specialized scientific community to have both social intercourse and strict privacy. The speech concluded with an admission and credo, common to architects of the caliber of Cobb, who are eloquent both verbally and architecturally. "I am an architect, and however much architects may talk, and some talk a great deal, we speak only through our buildings."

*2000*
*SKYLINE*
*COOP. HIMMELBLAU*
*85*

To come upon the rooftop addition at Falkestrasse 6 in Vienna's First District is a startling experience. There atop a landmark building is a provocative, glass-and-steel-curved object that appears nearly alive—like an exoskeletal fossil. Its designer, Coop Himmelblau of Vienna, borrowed from the structural appearance of an airplane and a bridge, suspended in a state between "explosion and implosion." The bow-shaped cavity that appears to be slipping off the roof was meant to visually form, in the architect's words "a connection between street and roof."

One of the avant-garde architecture firms formed in Vienna in the late 1960s, Coop Himmelblau now consists of the partnership of Wolf D. Prix and Helmut Swiczinsky. Translated to mean "The Blue Sky Cooperative," the motto was "Coop Himmelblau is not a color but an idea—the idea of having architecture through fantasy, as buoyant and variable as clouds."

During the next decade the goal became to dematerialize or "decompose" common architecture structures. And in doing so Coop Himmelblau waged a battle with the prevailing Viennese aesthetic of historicism: "We are sick of seeing Palladian and other historical masks," the group said in 1978. "We don't want to exclude everything from architecture that is disturbing." Instead, Prix and Swiczinsky advocate an architecture "that bleeds, that exhausts, that whirls, and even breaks." Writing in

*Architectural Record* in 1989, critic Karen D. Stein explained, "The architects' vision, still mostly on paper even by the 1980s, required not only a rejection of familiar styles, but also a physical assault on the existing fabric of Vienna."

Coop Himmelblau was preeminent in the growth of the "deconstruction" movement, which aimed at an intentional intellectual fragmenting of the whole in order to put these fragments back together again according to completely new conceptual and operative

standards. In the summer of 1988 Coop Himmelblau gained international attention through the exhibition "Deconstructivist Architecture" at New York's Museum of Modern Art.

Perhaps Coop Himmelblau's search for a humane, radically new vision is most easily seen in Paris's new city center, Melun-Sénart, a plan for a neo-futuristic urban utopia, which won first place in the design competition but which is not yet realized.

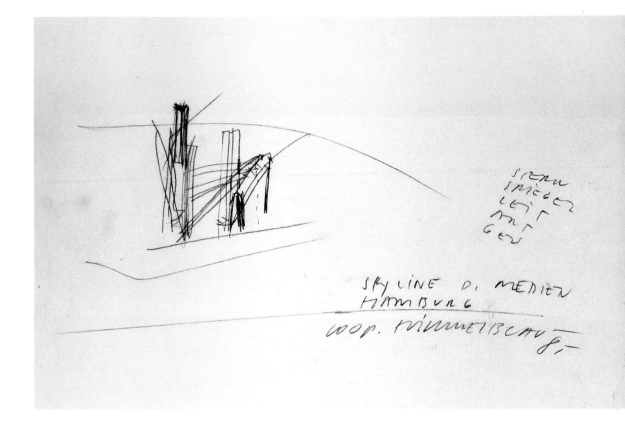

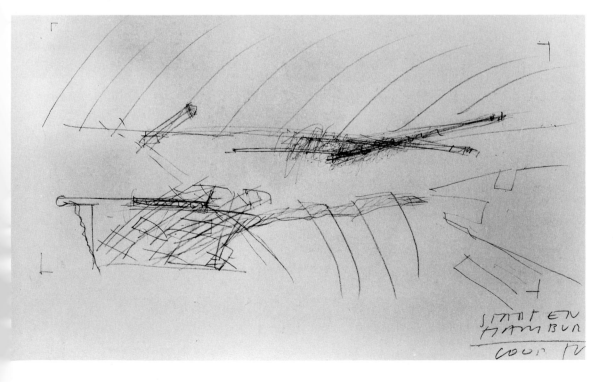

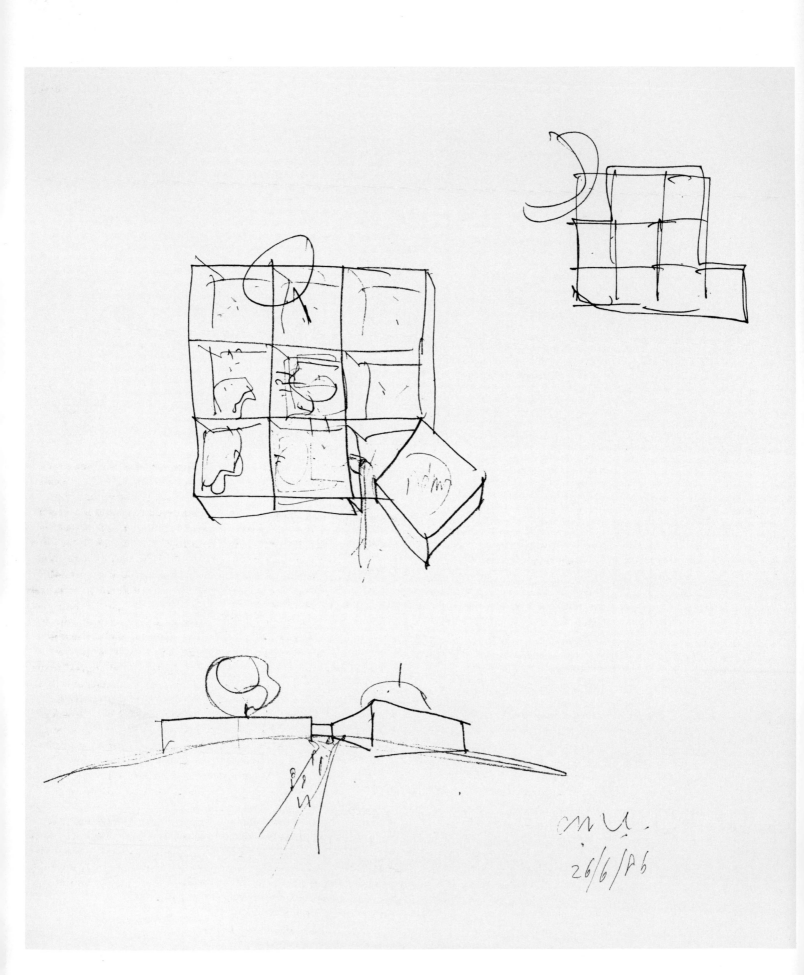

**A**rchitects of the Third World face a different set of conditions for designing humane and aesthetically pleasing environments than do architects of more affluent or developed countries. Sheer numbers of people are an ever-present constraint as is coping with the overwhelming influx of migrants from outlying rural regions to urban centers. While warm climatic conditions are often an ally in solving a design problem (allowing for lighter open-air structures and natural rather than mechanical ventilation), inadequate budgets are *not*, and require great imagination and skill to create durable and beautiful buildings. The challenges are daunting and few architects are able to achieve international recognition where their work is subjected to critical review without allowance for the obstacles and extenuating political and social circumstances under which the designs were created.

One architect, however, has earned the respect and admiration of his peers worldwide for his work in India—Charles Correa. This recognition took the form of the Gold Medal awarded to him by the Union of International Architects in 1990. Correa, who practices in Bombay, was educated first in India and later in the United States at the University of Michigan and Massachusetts Institute of Technology, where he came into contact with Buckminster Fuller and Lawrence Andersen. He then returned to India where his buildings, writings, and teachings have had an enormous impact and influence on post—World War II architecture there. Although trained in the West and frequently a lecturer at many U.S. universities, Correa has never lost his contact with the heart and soul of his native country. His buildings are modern but totally of their place and culture. Correa has led the way out of British colonialism to an indigenous contemporary

Indian architecture, one that never loses sight of the special problems of population and climate that determine its form or of the special opportunities that this ancient land offers. On Third World issues Correa has said, "we live in countries of great cultural heritage, countries that wear their past as easily as a woman drapes her sari. But in understanding and using this past, let us never forget the actual living conditions of many of the peoples of Asia and their desperate struggle to share a better future. Only a decadent architecture looks obsessively backward. . . . At its most vital, architecture is an agent of change: To invent tomorrow— this is its finest function."

Executed for a wide range of clients from the corporate to the homeless, Correa's architecture is one of simplicity and strength, having rich colorful accents and enduring qualities.

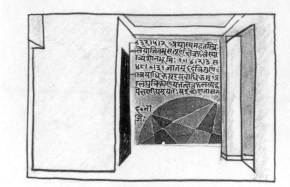

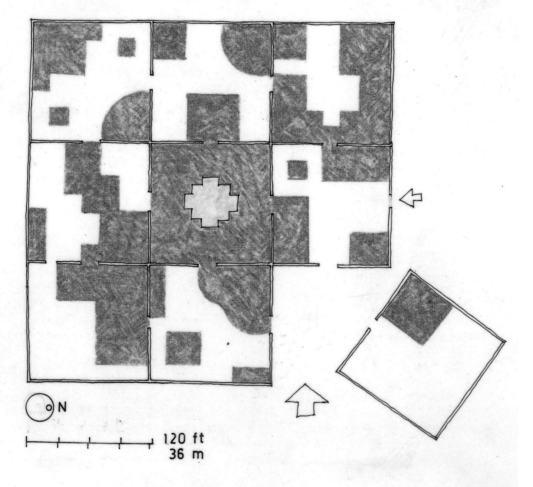

# BALKRISHNA VITHALDAS DOSHI

**I**ndia has always held a special fascination for architects and two of the great masters of modern architecture—Le Corbusier and Louis Kahn—designed major buildings in Chandigarh and Ahmedabad. On these projects they were associated with one of India's most respected architects, B. V. Doshi. Like his countryman Charles Correa, Doshi had to assimilate Western influence into a practice that was still connected to the cultural roots of his native country.

Although educated in India he spent six years in Le Corbusier's office in Paris, and has been visiting professor at principal U.S. universities from 1958 to the present.

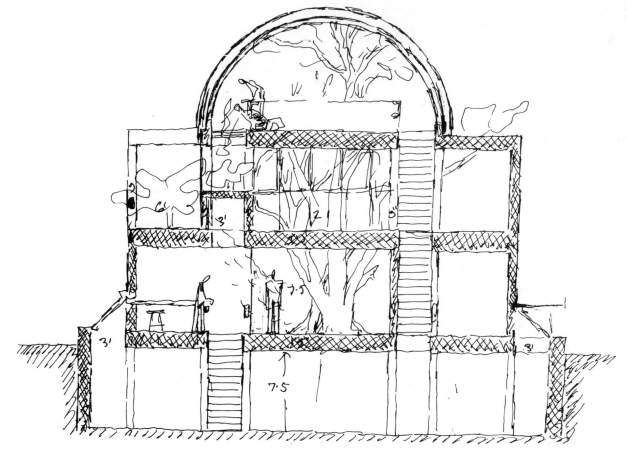

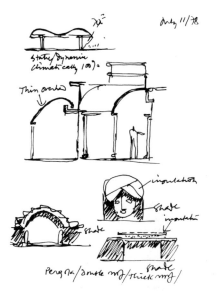

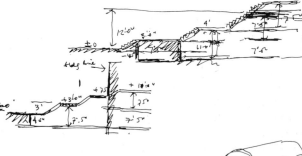

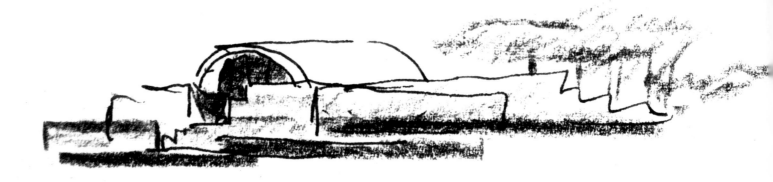

Doshi's approach to architecture is based on a great respect for nature and a deep belief in the need to make the physical setting harmonize with the individual's social and cultural needs. He is a lifelong student of indigenous buildings, observing patterns natural and man-made in what Rudolfsky called "architecture without architects." "I believe that all design should be based on community considerations," Doshi has stated. "It is necessary to consider the family ties and local associations of older buildings, associations that we cannot afford to give up. We should draw the influence that buildings that survive in time have more than material utility.

They indicate meaning in a building, as opposed to the present-day functional structure that has no meaning except in its craving for modernity."

One senses from Doshi's built work and his commitment to the exploration of the meaning and purpose of architecture and from his deep interest in education a hope for a new kind of architecture based on tradition and honesty and truth. Through his eyes architecture is both ancient and modern, and relies on using natural elements in an ingenious way and one that is, above all, humane in every aspect.

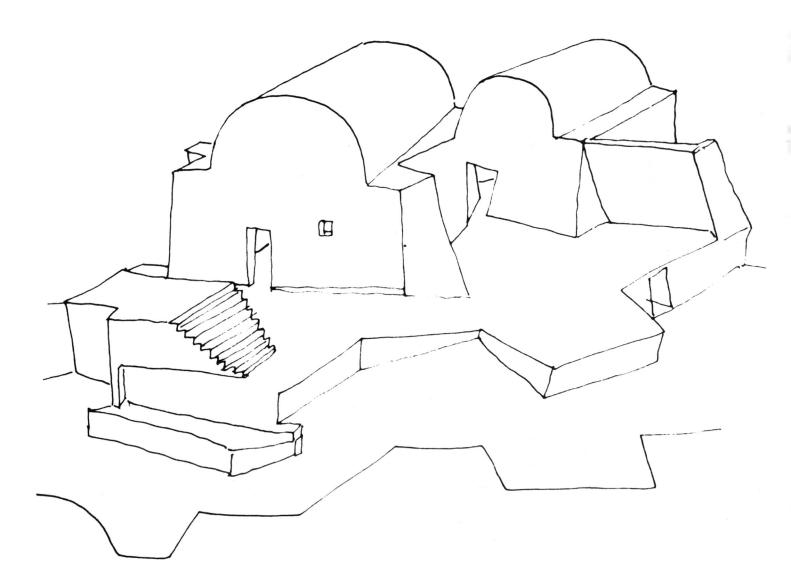

# ANDRES DUANY / ELIZABETH PLATER-ZYBERK

WESTOVER SQUARE HOUSE, FORT WORTH, TEXAS. 1986
MEDIUM: PENCIL ON YELLOW TRACING PAPER

**D**uring the past decade virtually no American city has escaped the sprawling of its suburbs. Anti-sprawl campaigns are growing and architects Andres Duany and Elizabeth Plater-Zyberk have been at the forefront of the battle by carving small towns out of suburban no-man's-lands. Their emphasis is on creating human environments where pedestrians are favored over automobiles and where zoning and building codes bring a certain cohesion to the developments through architectural diversity.

Duany and Plater-Zyberk, the husband and wife principals of an architectural firm bearing their names (and known as DPZ), first gained international recognition in the late 1970s for the plan of Seaside, "the new town, the old ways." On an 80-acre site of prime real estate on the Florida Panhandle, DPZ masterminded a plan for development with zoning laws that create comprehensible streets and squares, a strong focus on the town hall—the ceremonial center of town—and a clear distinction between private and public buildings. There was no single building prototype, which ultimately allowed for an eclectic mélange of many models, ranging from the Charleston side-lot house to the antebellum mansion to the ubiquitous American bungalow. "The strength of the approach lies in its sensitive flexibility and in the architect's realization that the zoning laws should establish positive urban continuity," wrote critic Charles Jencks.

Since then DPZ has been involved in the design and replanning of 30 new towns and suburbs, ranging in size from 60 to 3,500 acres. In building these new communities, the architects say there are two essential ingredients: design and policy.

On the policy side, existing methods of planning and the rules that govern them can actually contribute to the problem. Common among their plans is the dictum of one car per family, with emphasis put on walking to shops, school, day-care centers, and playgrounds. Central focus is placed on civic space—town squares, public buildings, schoolyards, shops.

Andres Duany and Elizabeth Plater-Zyberk, along with their colleagues at DPZ, are committed to creating a new vision for the American suburb. As Duany told *Architecture*, unless the current system of developing the suburbs of American cities is radically changed, "All the energy that we put into all this growth is going to be the heritage of misery. If we're not careful, we are going to be remembered as the generation that destroyed America."

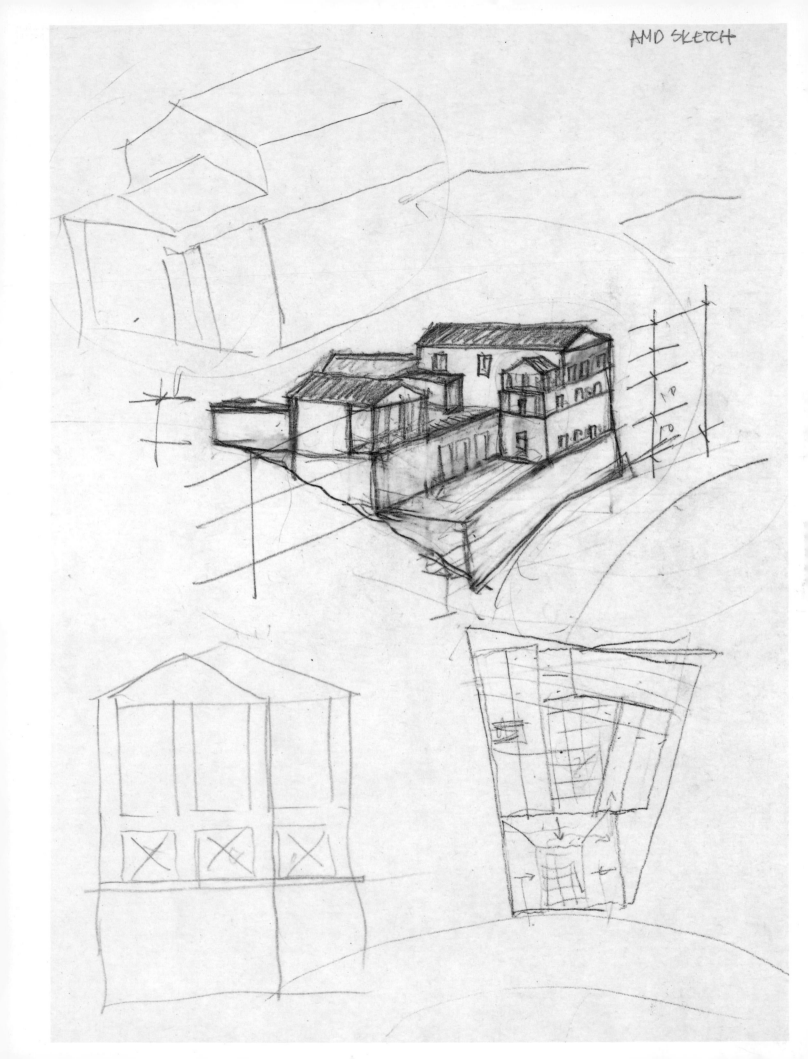

AMD SKETCH

# PETER EISENMAN

For the determinants of their building forms some architects look to the site, to the clients' program of needs, or to the clients themselves. Others look to the past for historical and evolutionary clues to gauge their work. Peter Eisenman, on the other hand, has maintained a consistent development of his design beliefs by exploring the outer fringes of esoteric rationale for his architecture. He believes that before there were columns that came to represent classical buildings there were ideas which needed form to express authority and purpose.

Listening to Eisenman explain an Eisenman building leaves the impression of a brilliant person describing a kaleidoscopic view of the built world which changes with each turn of the instrument. Peter Eisenman has fashioned one of the more central and independent roles in modern architectural theory and practice. He has been a theorist, an academician, a critic, an author, and most recently, a practicing architect. Among his numerous educational accomplishments can be listed his professorships at Harvard, Princeton, and Cooper Union, as well as his founding and

nurturing the highly regarded Institute for Architecture and Urban Studies. The latter was a post-graduate atelier for "adult" students of architecture who wanted to explore architecture problems outside the framework of both university and practice—a kind of "hospital" where an aspiring architect could serve his "residency."

In addition, and in the tradition of European architects of an earlier generation, Eisenman founded a journal, *Oppositions*, published from 1973 to 1982. *Oppositions* provided a

propagandist outlet for his theories and appealed to others who related to them.

A member of the well-known New York Five—the others being Graves, Stern, Hejduk, and Meier—Eisenman became neither a neo-modernist nor a Post-modernist. Eisenman's buildings are complex, multilayered, overlapping, fragmented, and difficult to understand or assess, but always intriguing and never ordinary. The Wexner Fine Arts Center at Ohio State University in Columbus aptly illustrates all these characteristics.

22 MAR 83
OSU

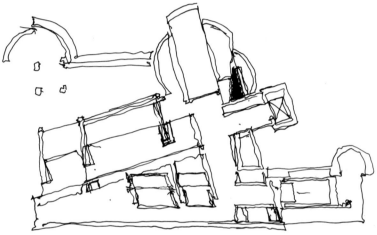

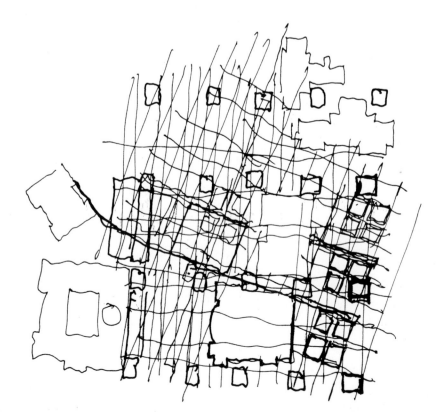

PLANTL WLENA
MASSIVE RTZ

VAC AS
OBJECT
CONTAINER
GROUND

26 FEB 83

# ARTHUR ERICKSON

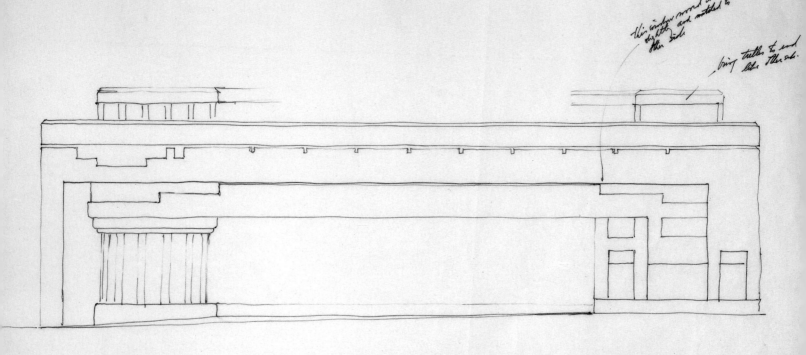

Over the years Canadian architect Arthur Erickson has created an extremely personal expression of architecture. It is one that borrows its pragmatism from the tenets of modern architecture, but which steps outside those rules. For Erickson, "the best design of the continent has from the beginning been utilitarian, with a beauty that comes from a purity of line and form and an honest respect for materials."

The site of a project and its context in a broader view determines the form of the building in Erickson's work. The Canadian Chancery in Washington, D.C., for example, completed in 1988, takes cues from its surroundings: the U.S. Capitol, I. M. Pei's East Wing of the National Gallery, and the National Gallery of Art. The robust stone massing of those buildings is echoed in the Chancery. And, too, classical elements are borrowed: gigantic columns, grand staircase, and cornice.

In the Chancery's expansive courtyard, Erickson's interest in the natural environment is apparent. A tiered wall of the embassy is planted with cascading greenery, connecting the Chancery visually with the adjoining park. A pool of water rushes out of the buildings toward the stone wave with monumental sculpture. A 2-story-high "Rotunda of the Provinces" symbolizes Canadian unity. The Canadian Chancery is meant to be "a panorama that may extend all the way to the horizon."

"My preference," wrote Erickson, "is for horizontal line and for simple forms and materials that are uncomplicated, if not austere. At the same time there is a yearning for the dramatic." This technique gained Erickson international recognition in the early 1960s. Then Erickson (and Geoffrey Massey) extended a linear building across two high points of a low mountain at Simon Fraser University in Burnaby, British Columbia. That building, as many others of Erickson's designs, addressed the "sensibilities of those who live in them and use them, who look out, more often, than in," in the words of Washington, D.C., architect Peter Blake.

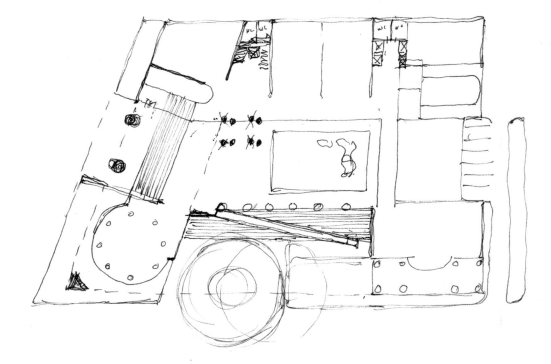

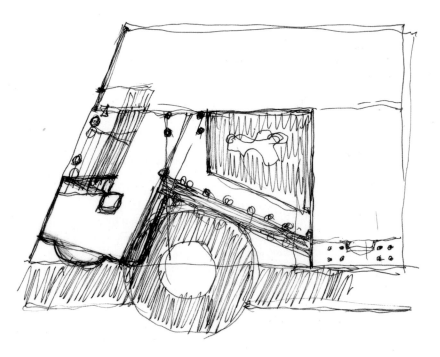

# NORMAN FOSTER

Architects, right or wrong, come to be associated with one or two of their buildings. Their entire body of work is not readily grasped by a public that takes note of such matters. For Pei it is the East Wing of the National Gallery of Art and the Louvre Pyramid; for Johnson it is the Glass House and the AT&T Building; for Richard Rogers it is the Centre Pompidou in Paris and the Lloyds of London skyscraper.

The building most readily identified with Norman Foster and which sums up a consistent production of well-designed projects over a distinguished thirty-year career is the Hong Kong and Shanghai Banking Corporation headquarters in Hong Kong. Seven years in the making, this steel colossus of a skyscraper stands out uniquely among a dense collection of lesser high rises along the Hong Kong water port, one of the several wonders of the modern world of architecture. It is unquestionably the most important tall building to be built in the last decade and perhaps in this century.

Foster, who is often linked with Richard Rogers as being the "high-tech" twins of England, was in fact a partner with Rogers at Team 4 in the mid-sixties. Foster's work is characterized by a steadfast adherence to an architectural aesthetic that utilizes the most advanced technologies of structure and materials currently available. His is not an architecture of the past. In this attitude he is not dissimilar from Buckminster Fuller, who contended that architecture should go on a diet . . . that lighter buildings were better buildings. Foster's architecture is about steel, aluminum, and glass, not bricks and stones. It is an architecture that is of its time the same way that an airplane is. His exquisite new air terminal at Stanstead outside London underscores this fact.

At the Willis Faber building in Ipswich, England, Foster displayed an early talent for exhausting the possibilities of a single material, in this case, glass. The building is in essence a line drawn around a floor plan that becomes a sheer glass enclosure, seemingly without any connecting devices, a curving wall that reflects its neighboring provincial streetscape. Inside, Foster's interest in the social functioning of his buildings is apparent by the choice of unenclosed escalators rather than elevators, arranged like a waterfall of steps from the bottom to the top thus giving employees maximum openness and the greatest opportunity for social interaction.

This startling building was followed by a series of highly imaginative solutions to design problems, each different but each clearly reliant on a technological, not a nostalgic, solution. The Sainsbury Centre for the Visual Arts consists of elegant buildings that resemble an airplane hangar; a warehouse for Renault has bright yellow masts and a circus-like structural attitude; a brilliant winning entry in the competition for a Media League in Nîmes, France, juxtaposes Foster's high-tech entry with the ancient Maison Carrée. In this latter building Foster again demonstrates that his palette of technically advanced methods is in no way limiting.

But it remained for the Hong Kong and Shanghai building to team Foster with a client that would allow him to give full range to those creative powers. The custom-designed building was made possible only by allowing Foster to design every detail, to build mock-ups at all scales, and to employ industrial design techniques in developing products for this specific building and its needs. The building's structure is its most striking feature, looking like a giant erector set that is "self-building" along with permanent window-washing cranes on top. From its carved see-through glass floor banking lobby to its state-of-the-art computer tracking sun scoops, the Hong Kong and Shanghai Bank is a technological tour de force by an architect who continues to search for a true twentieth-century architecture, one who contends that, "high technology is not an end in itself, but rather a means to social goals and wider possibilities."

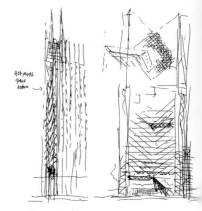

SECOND VERSION - INCLINED SUSPENSION STRUCTURE

TRANSITION TO FINAL DESIGN - SETBACKS WITHIN TOW

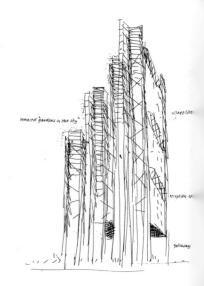

RECURRING THEMES - RICH MIX OF SPACES & ACTIVITIES W

**HONG KONG AND SHANGHAI BANKING CORPORATION
HEADQUARTERS, HONG KONG. 1985
MEDIUM: PEN AND INK**

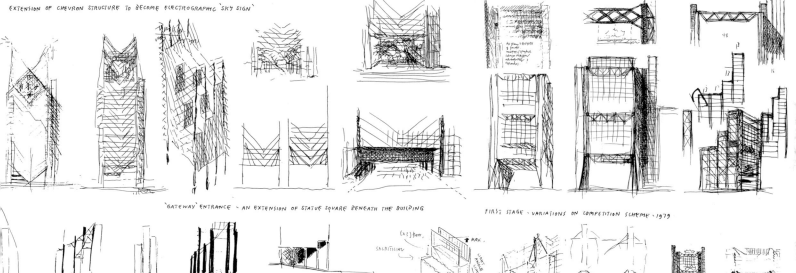

EXTENSION OF CHEVRON STRUCTURE TO BECOME ELECTROGRAPHIC 'SKY SIGN'

'GATEWAY' ENTRANCE · AN EXTENSION OF STATUE SQUARE BENEATH THE BUILDING

FIRST STAGE · VARIATIONS ON COMPETITION SCHEME · 1979

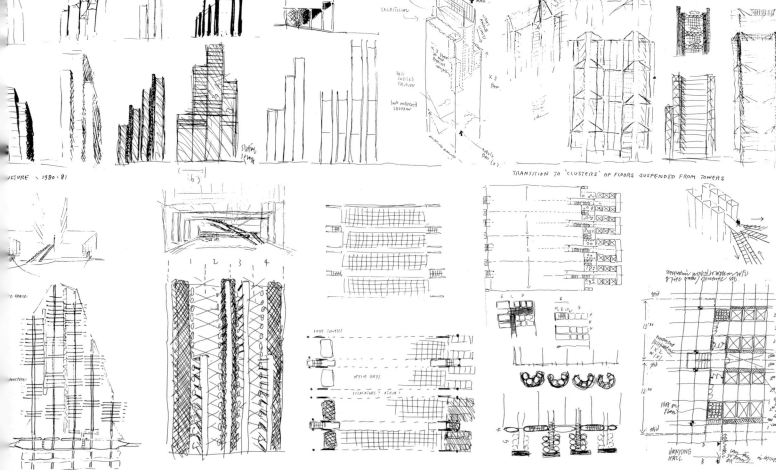

TRANSITION TO 'CLUSTERS' OF FLOORS SUSPENDED FROM TOWERS

OF STRUCTURE & TOWERS FOR VERTICAL MOVEMENT & SERVICES

PLANNING STUDIES

# ULRICH FRANZEN

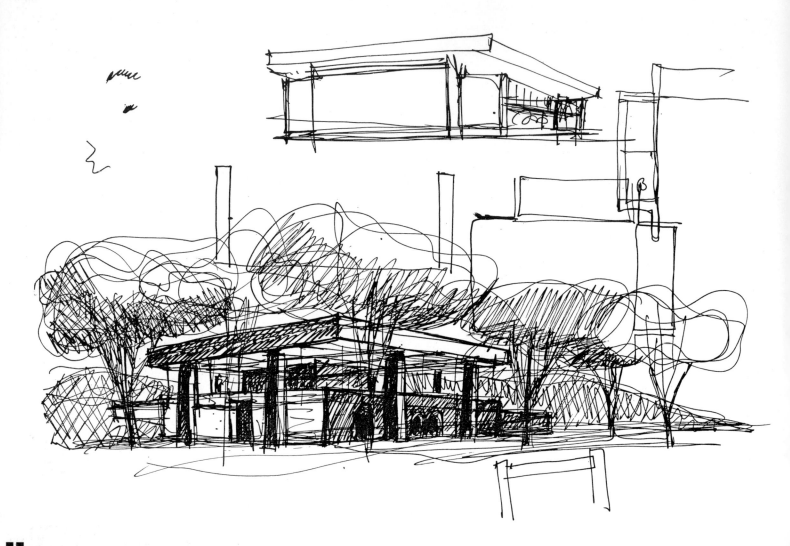

Ulrich Franzen received his schooling in modernism from Marcel Breuer and Walter Gropius at Harvard in the 1940s; this tutelage is evident in the forms and composition of Franzen's Alley Theater in Houston (1968) as well as in his more recent work at Hunter College in New York. Although his projects are now large in scale, his letter below attests that his residential commissions still play an important role in honing his design and analytical skills.

Dear Bill:

Your interesting idea for a book is a most welcome one. Architecture has become so verbal and so intellectualized that the real beginning of good work is not understood by [an] interested public and even certain architects.

Sketches that flow from head and heart to the hand that guides the pencil or pen are indeed the "genesis" (to borrow your phrase).

I imagine there are many ways an architect sketches. I have used sketchbooks as a means of recording my thoughts and intuitive responses to the questions of form and essence when starting a project. My sketches are not intended as "presentations" or "renderings" to bowl over a client but are a means of guiding the design process.

I am sending you reproductions of sketches arranged in an approximate chronological order showing the evolution of a house design. My design sketching often becomes an unintended rumination of all sorts of things and often they seem to become ambitious beyond budget and program. Sooner or later, however, they settle down and the final result is in part a distillation of the sketches and reality.

You may ask why a house? Houses, and I have built some 60 or so, are the laboratory of my architecture. The one I have sent you deals with "structure" and "the constructed elements of building" standing on the land, all parts of my approach.

Whether dealing with a residence or an urban university, Franzen's work has always been characterized by its logical response to a set of conditions and programmatic demands. Like an author who revises texts in a steady evolutionary process until the final manuscript is set, Franzen approaches architecture as a sequence of steps, each one an improvement on its predecessor.

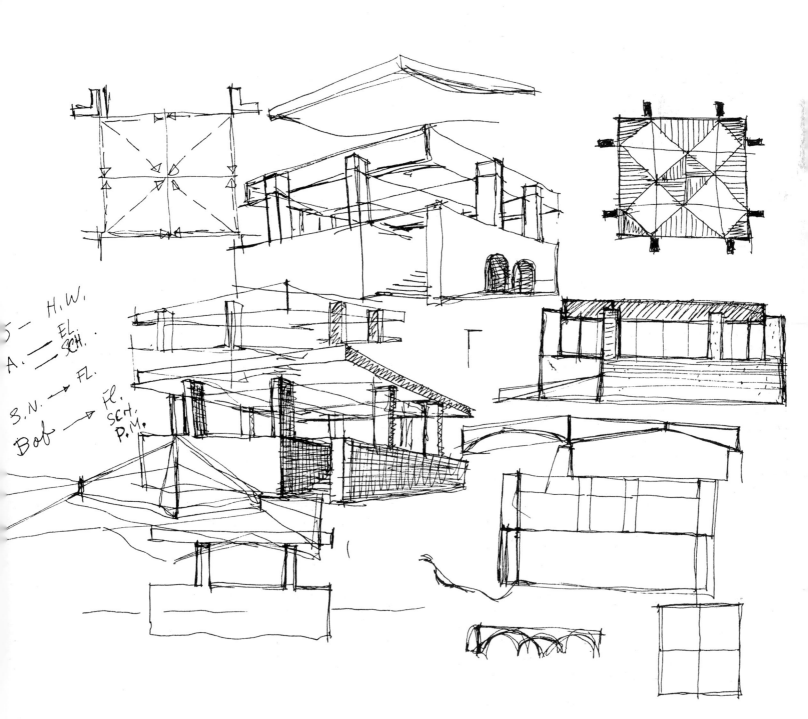

# JAMES INGO FREED

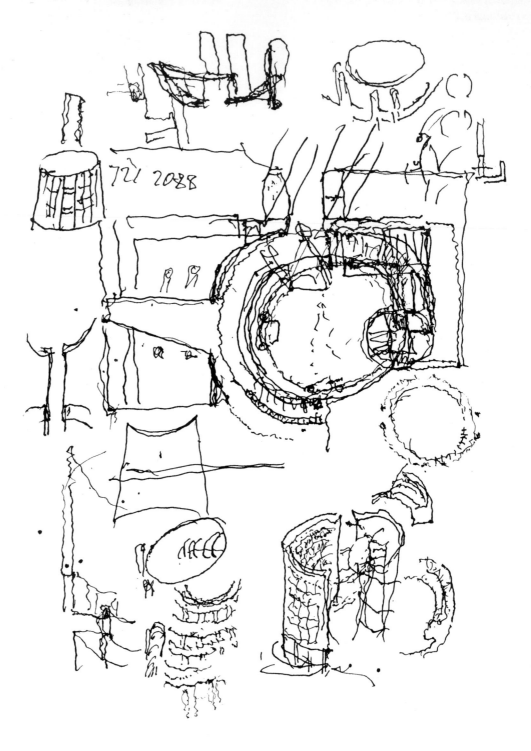

The firm which until recently was I. M. Pei and Partners was renamed Pei Cobb Freed, thereby giving equal billing to two partners who were already well known in the profession for their considerable design talents. It is not unique, but it is unusual to have an architectural firm in which all the name partners are designers of stature. The more normal arrangement represents one designer, one business person, and someone well versed in construction and management.

James Freed joined Pei's office in 1956, where he designed a number of meritorious buildings. In the years 1975 to 1978 he assumed the leadership of the architecture program at his alma mater, the Illinois Institute of Technology in Chicago, while maintaining his practice at the firm.

More than almost any other major architect practicing today, Freed is comfortable with the scale of the twentieth-century city. He seems to relish opportunities to reclaim and transform large metropolitan sections through his buildings. His highly modernistic and technologically sophisticated Jacob K. Javits Convention Center in New York seems to sum up what the international and modern styles were about.

Freed has shown with this vast, black prismatic building (followed in rapid succession by two commissions in San Francisco and two in Washington, D.C.) that he has an extraordinary grasp of urban architecture and its contexts. In an era in which considerable lip service has been paid to achieving compatibility and harmony between the new and the old, Freed has been able to design monumental buildings that truly have this delicate balance without sacrificing contemporaneity.

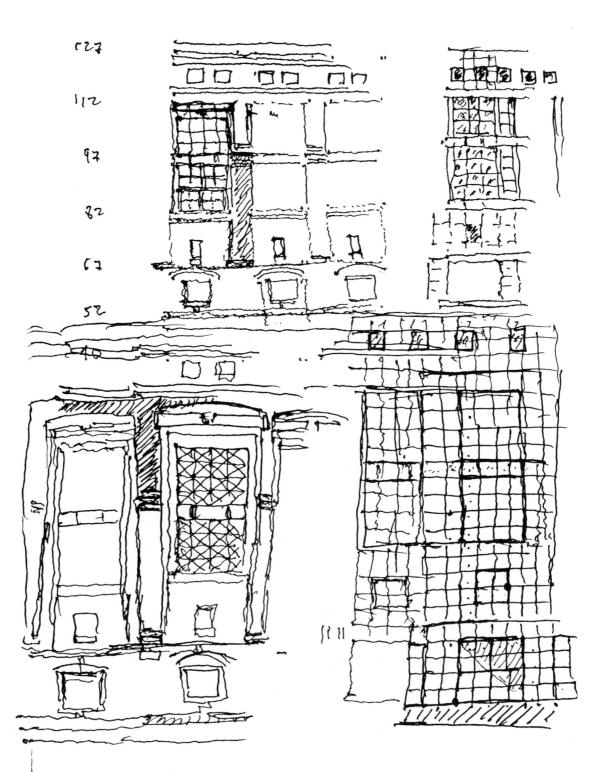

# FRANK GEHRY

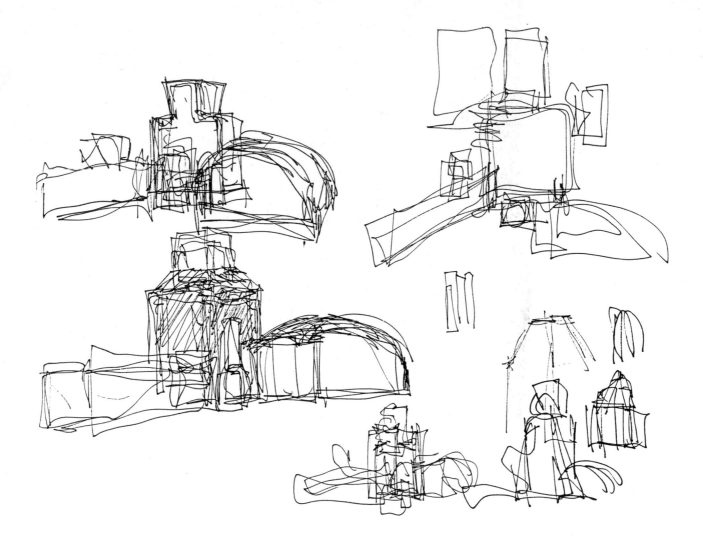

**F**rank Gehry is Canadian born (Toronto), but he took root in the sunny soil of Southern California and has become its most famous architectural export. His office is located in Santa Monica, a section of Los Angeles not far from the studio of the famous Eames design team whom Gehry greatly admired and after whom he has fashioned a career that also includes architecture and furniture design. His string of iconoclastic structures recently earned him the Pritzker Architecture Prize as the latest approbation of his rise to the upper echelon of internationally known architects.

Gehry, like many architects, took a number of years to find his "voice," to feel comfortable with the aesthetic he brought to the solution of architectural problems. His apprenticeship was served in offices like those run by Victor Guren, whose penchant was planning, not design flair.

Earlier buildings for corporate clients totally belied the architect-cum-artist who would emerge first with his own outrageous house with its now-familiar Santa Monica explosion of shapes and forms. The house which shocked neighbors and passersby introduced lowly materials such as chain-link fencing, corrugated metal siding, and unfinished wood surfaces into this staid residential district. By way of further "insult" to the uninitiated, Gehry pulled away sections of the original house and rearranged them in an artfully haphazard way like some mischievous giant.

The recurring word in any conversation with Frank Gehry on the subject of architecture is sculpture. In many respects he is as much a sculptor as an architect, a three-dimensional collage artist who sculpts spaces and encases them more often than not in plywood and metal surfaces. He readily concedes this predilection for the visual arts and its influence on his work. A frequent collaborator with Claes Oldenburg and other visual artists, Gehry, more than any other current architect, eschews historicism as a source and proceeds directly from the artistic. Nowhere is this inclination more evident than in his winning entry for the $100 million Disney Symphony Hall in Los Angeles.

# ROMALDO GIURGOLA

People outside the architectural profession might think that Giurgola's first name is Mitchell rather than Aldo, since the firm has practiced for many years as Mitchell/Giurgola. Formed in 1958 as a partnership with principal offices in New York City and Philadelphia, Aldo Giurgola, the "design" partner, headed the New York branch along with his duties as chairman, Department of Architecture at Columbia University; Ehrman B. "Mitch" Mitchell, Jr., ran the office in Philadelphia. Mitchell was the

partner who provided the management skills to support and augment the artistic design strengths which Giurgola brought to the firm, a distribution of duties not an uncommon arrangement in the profession. In 1980 a "marriage of convenience" was effected when a separate firm name was created—Mitchell, Giurgola & Thorp—to accommodate Richard Thorp, an Australian. The reason? In order to be eligible to enter the 1980 international competition for the gigantic project of designing the new Parliament House in Canberra, one of the partners

had to be Australian. Thorp, a newly hired junior architect of the firm, thought they could win; he was right. As a result, the firm's name and their body of work was irrevocably reshaped.

The competition for the commission to design the new $800 million Parliament House in Australia was entered by 329 architects from around the world. The winning entry from the newly formed office of Mitchell, Giurgola & Thorp is centered on a rounded hill, a site that has been designated and

waiting for a building since the 1912 city plan was approved. Giurgola's scheme pares away two sides of the hill and molds it into something of a stately formal "mountain" of government culminated by a monumental flag pole 265 feet above the building. Of their entry the architects wrote, "The primary task in the design has been the search for a relationship of balance and reciprocity between the built and the natural, between the imposition of government and the natural state from which government evolves."

Giurgola's intense search for content in this complex of buildings as in all his projects stems from a classical European education (he is a graduate of the University of Rome) and the strong influence on his architectural thinking by the late Louis Kahn, Philadelphia architect and teacher. Giurgola is one of the most thoughtful, sincere, and humble architects practicing at the highest level of his profession. And while the Parliament House represents a certain kind of high-water mark for his career, it is only one among a host of buildings that range in the early years from superb residences, such as the one for the Daytons in Wayzata, Minnesota, to the numerous crisp and elegant corporate headquarters for IBM and Volvo and other major manufacturers.

Giurgola's drawings and early conceptual sketches, like the completed buildings, display a sureness of stroke and line that reveals the artist's eye and hand, coupled with a pragmatist's will. "My 40 years of work," he once wrote, "has taken me from the dogmatism of the Modern Movement through exposure to the rhetoric of Fascism; from the lyricism of Le Corbusier to the reductions of Mies and from the ironic perversity of Post-Modernism to infatuation with technological products." And while he acknowledges a strong sense of debt to Asplund, Aalto, Kahn, and Utzon, it is obvious that the major influences on Giurgola go back further to classical Rome and the anonymous builders of Italy.

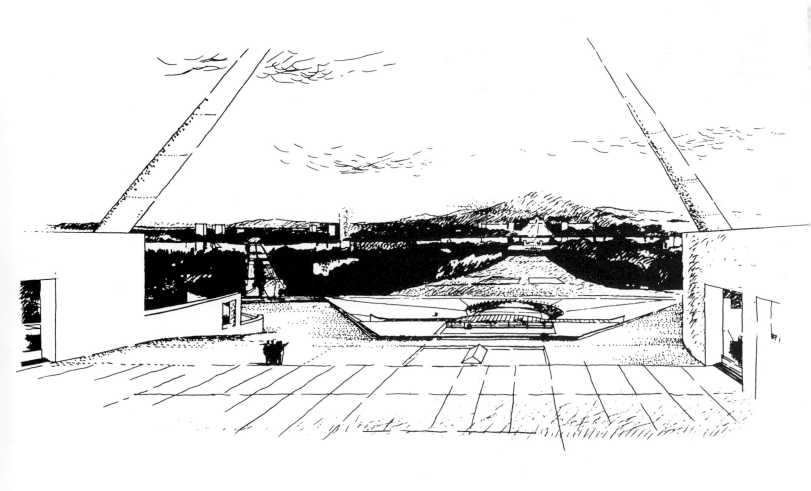

# CHARLES GRAVES

Charles Graves is an architect who, like Alden Dow in Michigan and Fay Jones in Arkansas, has become identified with a state, in this case Kentucky. After studying with Kahn at Pennsylvania, he formed the school of architecture at the University of Kentucky in 1958, becoming one of the youngest deans in the country. He continues to serve the school as Dean Emeritus and as a member of the faculty. His influence in the state through generations of graduates, and through his active involvement in projects of historic importance (the renovation of Shaker Village outside Lexington, the Henry Clay statue) to contemporary consultations on the Cincinnati master plan, has been significant for Kentucky and the Southeastern United States. This guidance and counsel to students, faculty corporations, and governments has been a valuable contribution to the profession.

Like Charles Moore, a frequent collaborator, and many other architects, Graves has spent the majority of his career in architectural education and in tending to matters of the profession. He became the first dean of the University of Kentucky when it had an enrollment of 4,000 students. Today that number is up to 26,000 and during the period of striking growth in numbers of students, the school of architecture has grown in stature and international reputation. The latter is due to having one of the first architecture programs abroad, located in Venice.

Graves has produced a number of buildings of note in various associations and practices over the years. Each of his projects are intelligent, clear statements, strong in their use of modernist forms and materials.

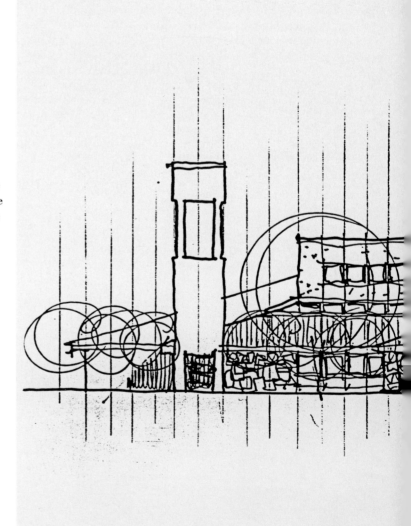

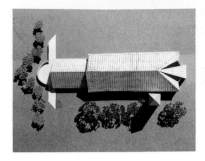

NORTHSIDE BAPTIST CHAPEL, ELIZABETHTOWN, KENTUCKY. 1990
MEDIUM: PENCIL

**NORTHSIDE BAPTIST CHAPEL,
ELIZABETHTOWN, KENTUCKY. 1990
MEDIUM: PENCIL**

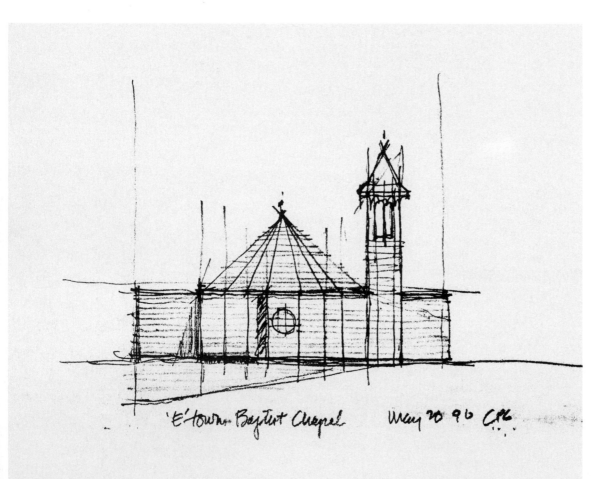

'E'town Baptist Chapel     May 20 90 CPG

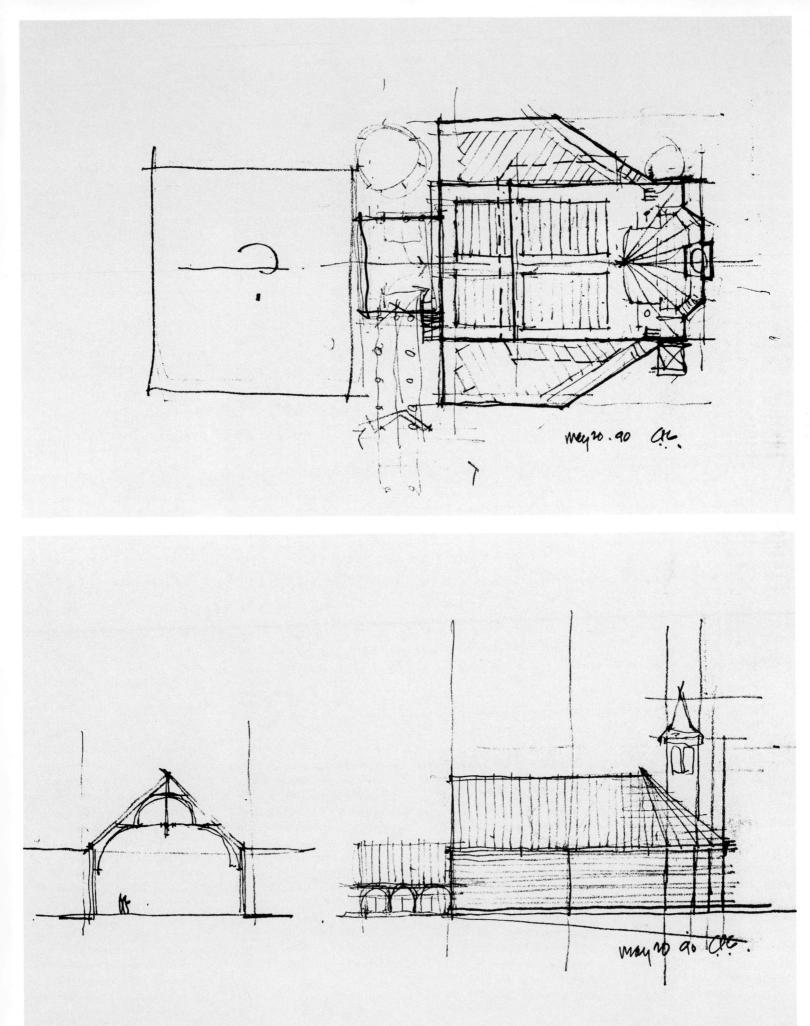

# MICHAEL GRAVES

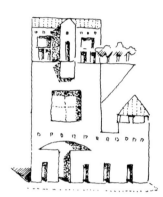

**M**ore than any other contemporary architect, Michael Graves's architecture proceeds from a passion and facility for drawing. Graves, another member of the famous New York Five (Eisenman, Gwathmey, Hejduk, and Meier), became well known within the profession as a result of the publication *Five Architects* (Museum of Modern Art, 1970). The book singled out the work of five relatively unknown young architects whose efforts were more theoretical than tangible. Graves was a

professor at Princeton at the time, where he has spent almost the entirety of his professional life.

While many architects are proficient at drawing and painting, as a consequence of a college curriculum that emphasizes the importance of the fine arts in the education of an architect, Graves can lay legitimate claim to the title of artist as well as architect. His drawings, watercolors, and paintings were the subject of a one-man show in 1979 at the

Max Protetch Gallery in New York. Since that time his art has been exhibited in numerous galleries and museums throughout the world, and is owned by private collectors and major institutions. Evidence of his keen interest in drawing can also be seen in his published articles, such as "The Necessity of Drawing: Tangible Speculation," (1977) and later "Le Corbusier's Drawn References," an essay about sketches by the master French

architect. This interest in the artistic aspects of architecture was well served by Graves's selection as a Rome Prize Fellow in 1960, which afforded him the opportunity to study for two years at the American Academy in Rome. In the academic sanctuary created by one of America's noted nineteenth-century architects, Charles McKim, Graves came into contact with a community of classical scholars and was exposed to the historical riches that Rome provides for all serious students of architecture.

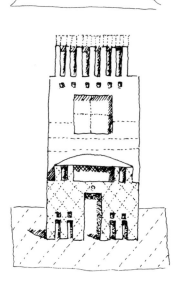

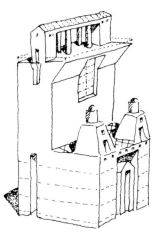

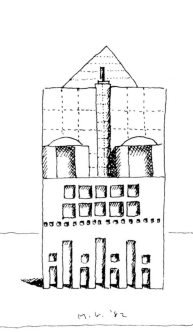

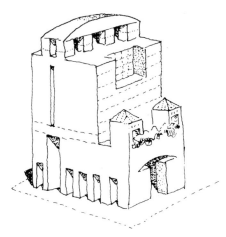

Graves prefers to describe his colorful designs that are replete with historically evocative forms as Figurative Architecture, referring to his firm belief that the scale of architecture should always be determined by the measure of man. In Graves's view, modern architecture lost its way (and its audience) when it ignored this relationship and created buildings of scaleless window walls and blank divisionless facades.

It is too great a simplification to say that Robert Venturi's writings spawned the Post-modern movement in architecture, which dominated the field in the late 1970s and early 80s, or that Graves's buildings became the trademark most associated with it. Battle lines were drawn within the ranks of critics, the public, and peers over Graves's first major public commission, the controversial office building for the federal government in Portland, Oregon. The debate that raged around this building, which had come to stand for Post-modern architecture, continued with the Humana Corporation office tower in downtown Louisville, Kentucky, in 1985 and was rekindled with heated debate surrounding the triply revised schemes for the addition to the Breuer-designed Whitney Museum in New York City.

This notoriety has resulted in additional commissions for Graves, not just restricted to architecture. For a decade he designed showrooms for the SunarHauserman furniture company which proved to be more irresistible as designs than the chairs and sofas for which they provided a backdrop. Graves's interiors employed the same muted palette of arresting pastel colors as his architecture and became little "architectures" within the larger context. From interiors it was only a small step to *objets* within the interior framework, and Graves's designs for dinnerware, coffeepots, jewelry, wristwatches, rugs, tables, and chairs were added to his repertoire and in turn added to his status as a design celebrity.

Michael Graves has brought a colorful and indelible mark on the face of twentieth-century architecture and design.

**HUMANA BUILDING,**
**LOUISVILLE, KENTUCKY. 1982**
**MEDIUM: PENCIL, COLORED PENCIL**

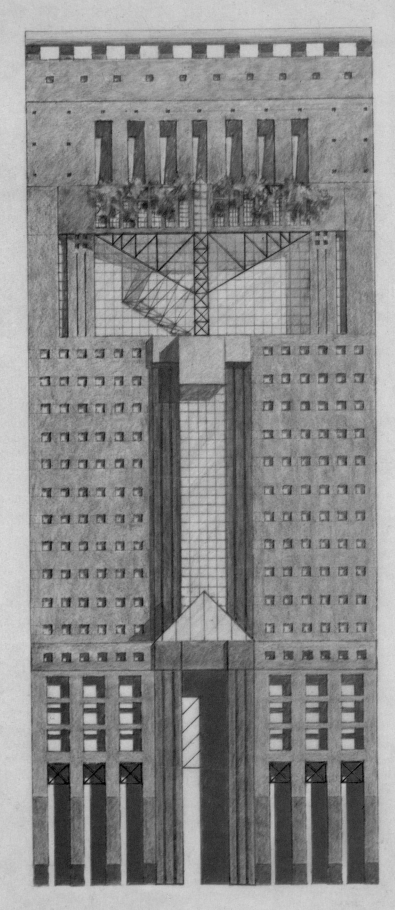

south facade
Humana
Graves
1 9 8 3

# ALLAN GREENBERG

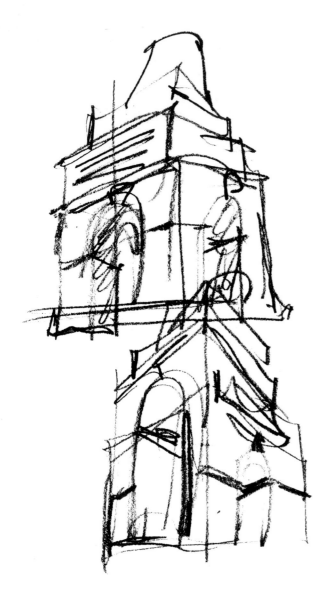

One of the abiding issues each architect practicing in the latter half of this century has had to come to grips with is the question of history and its appropriate influence on their design philosophy. Some, like the pure modernists, have chosen to ignore its effect on their work or at least to minimize it. Others, the mainstream Post-modernists, have elected to incorporate various elements of the classical and traditional or to recall these motifs in some contemporary and sometimes caricatured fashion.

Allan Greenberg stands somewhat alone as a twentieth-century architect, who is actively practicing and teaching at Yale and Pennsylvania universities, who embraces the classical tradition of architecture without apology, who has elected a path that is neither modern, Post-modern, nor any hybrid version between, but instead is a relatively pure extension of the architecture of Jefferson's time, what he calls new classical. Greenberg finds the classical language of architecture, developed as it was over centuries of use and refinement, challenging and completely adequate to solve the building needs of contemporary society.

Born in South Africa (he became a United States citizen in 1973), Greenberg is credited with reviving and revisiting the work of the prominent English architect Sir Edwin Lutyens (1869—1944), whose residential designs were like Greenberg's, an individualized classical style drawing heavily on the Renaissance period.

5

# CHARLES GWATHMEY

**T**he consequences of our world population doubling now at ever-increasing exponential rates is reflected in architecture by more and more commissions dealing not with first-time buildings but rather with additions to those buildings. Bulfinch, an American architect of the early nineteenth century, discouraged his sons from becoming architects because he felt he had done all the important buildings there were to do. He could not imagine the world today where the tearing down and building up of cities takes place at a noticeable rate in a single generation. This additive architecture is nowhere more evident in recent years than in the expansion of museums in the United States where the National Gallery in Washington, D.C., the Metropolitan Museum, the Whitney, and the Guggenheim, all in New York City and the Kimbell in Fort Worth, commissioned architects to design major additions to existing buildings. In each of these instances the original building had been the work of the best architect of the day and in each case the architect chosen for the expansion was also an architect of repute. All of these projects, though to a lesser degree the National Gallery, created a furor of public discussion and controversy.

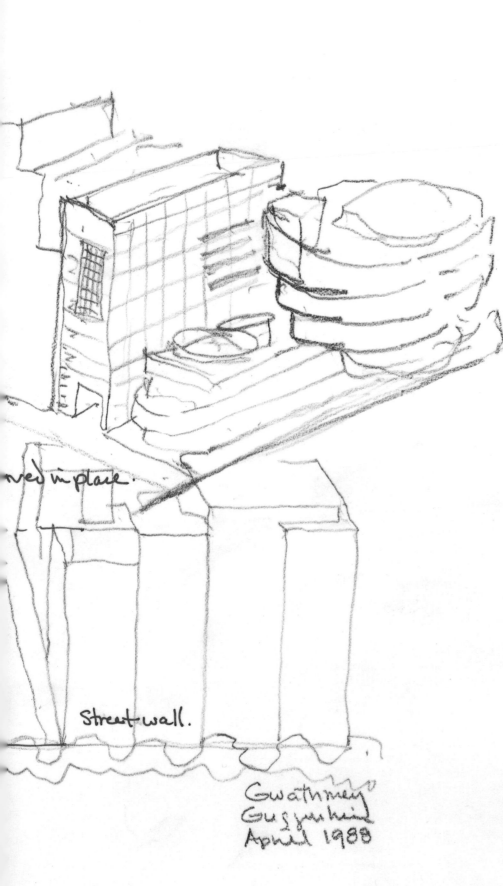

ved in place.

Street wall.

Gwathmey
Guggenheim
April 1988

Charles Gwathmey, of the firm Gwathmey Siegel & Associates, was the design architect whose lot it was to add to Frank Lloyd Wright's familiar drumlike building on Fifth Avenue, the Solomon R. Guggenheim Museum. Like his colleague Michael Graves at the Whitney, Gwathmey encountered a storm of criticism from the public and fellow professionals for his proposed modernistic cantilevered box, which reflected his belief that "form is generated by site, orientation, climate, program and technological references." In this instance public opinion became a very real constraint and part of the context as well. In the end the Gwathmey design, in a modified version, prevailed, adding further distinction to a career that has included many outstanding residences such as Toad Hall in East Hampton for François and Susan de Menil, his own home in nearby Amagansett, office buildings, college and university structures, and a number of interior design projects.

Although Gwathmey studied with Venturi and Kahn and worked for Edward Larrabee Barnes for three years, the biggest influence on his design philosophy is obviously Le Corbusier. The late C. Ray Smith described Gwathmey's work as the sophisticated vocabulary of the International Style as developed by Le Corbusier but in "a distinctly American way."

# ZAHA HADID

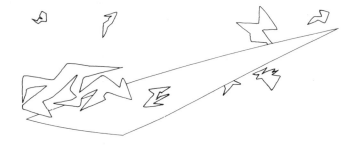

There is a new architectural expression that deals with motion rather than the conventional language of static elements. It manifests itself in the work of firms like Coop Himmelblau and Mack Scogin, in projects such as Tschumi's Parc de la Villette in Paris and in the visionary drawings of Lebbeus Woods and Daniel Libeskind. Another member of this group of practitioners who draw their inspiration from the Russian Constructivists and from an age of speed, electronics, and dynamic forms is Zaha Hadid. Ms. Hadid is a young London-based architect of Iraqian birth, whose fledgling practice is already global with projects in Tokyo, Berlin, and Hong Kong.

Ms. Hadid creates extraordinary designs for buildings that strive for a sense of weightlessness, and she describes them through dense and elaborate multilayered sketches. These drawings are unlike conventional architectural renditions and yet, like her buildings, are filled with the suggestion of movement. "They are sequential," Hadid says, "they move along. You really need to do a movie or a cartoon to show all these things in motion."

Hadid rebels at the idea that architect's drawings should only be able to show plans, sections, and elevations. "We, the architects, invented the codes of presentation, so why can't we change them?" She bridles at any suggestion that her nearly abstract delineations are merely illustrations. Hadid's projects, mostly on the drawing boards at this point, show great promise for an architecture that defies the accepted ideas about vertical and horizontal planes, and about weight and permanence. Her vision offers a fresh and exciting possibility for the future of architecture in the twenty-first century.

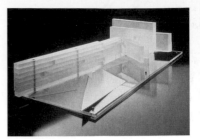

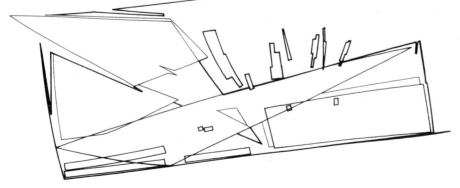

# HUGH HARDY

**A**rchitects are prone to explain their work in terms that tend to elevate a profession concerned with making spaces out of building materials into a lofty religion, one with its own special and mystical language. Within the last decade as architects have become more and more media conscious, this phenomenon of "speaking in tongues" to explain architecture has become endemic to the profession. One architect who is certainly equipped to engage in such semantic exercises through his sheer intelligence, education, and caliber of built work is Hugh Hardy, and yet he chooses not to do so. Hardy feels that this "use of an impenetrable prose style borrowed from literary criticism gives the layman scant access to the world of architectural discussion." It is his contention that buildings should not be "literary symbols." They should be experienced, not decoded, by a high priesthood.

As an architect, Hardy has been influenced as much by the theater (he apprenticed for four years with the famous scene designer Jo Mielziner) as by his architectural training. He has conscientiously avoided creating a "style" of architecture that could be identified with the firm of Hardy Holzman Pfeiffer Associates. "Too many architects have become trapped in their own rhetoric," he has said, but he will admit to a working credo for the firm that has as its goal "the resolution of opposites."

Hardy further explains the work of the threesome—each of the partners designs as well as shares in the management and marketing aspects of the firm—by saying that from the year they began practice in 1962 they "set out to prove that architecture can be made of anything." To observers of their architecture of that early period it also seemed that this brash new firm was intent not only on widening the range of legitimate possibilities for materials not normal to current projects, but also in altering the accepted geometry of the box and rectangle. Hardy Holzman Pfeiffer's plans were noted for strong and unexpected diagonal planes (usually 45°)

destroying the conventionality of any space, which when combined with a somewhat zany juxtaposition of patterns and colors and unusual materials gave their projects an exciting and rebellious flavor. Limited budgets also played a part in another feature of Hardy's early work, the exposure of mechanical ductwork and structure, giving the buildings, not surprising considering Hardy's background, a definite theatrical quality.

Side by side with the influence of the theater and Hardy's penchant for an architecture that strives for democratic inclusiveness in materials, form, and philosophy is a long-standing interest in additive architecture. Believing as he does that no building in our contemporary society is ever really finished, Hardy has made a specialty of adding onto existing historical buildings, and in renovating interiors of old buildings to serve new purposes, usually cultural ones.

It is hard now for architects and fans of architecture to imagine a time when the appreciation of old buildings was not a unanimous national sentiment. Hardy Holzman Pfeiffer Associates were forerunners in the recycling of buildings beginning in 1974 with their study for converting abandoned railroad stations to arts centers. This was soon followed by an equally keen interest in old movie houses, fire stations, and other substantial but unappreciated buildings from the past. Addressing one of the principal tenets of the firm, Hardy has said that "Old and new are of equal importance. There is no present without the past and putting new life in old structures is as valid as the creation of new buildings. The present includes the past. The future is more of the present, not Utopia."

Hardy has put this belief into practice with a long list of landmark renovations—the Cooper-Hewitt Museum, the Plaza Hotel, both in New York, the St. Louis Art Museum, the Toledo Museum of Art, and many others.

No firm has more crucially influenced the recent architecture of Washington, D.C., than Hartman-Cox Architects. George Hartman and Warren Cox have, in turn, built on the predominantly neoclassical and beaux-arts monumental core of the capital. Theirs is not a stylish or trendy architecture. "They do not show off; instead, they demonstrate a finely tuned sense of the relationship between continuity and creation," in the words of Roger Kennedy of the Smithsonian Institution. The equally talented partners, whose style is virtually indistinguishable, are switch hitters who vary the style to fit the situation. To quote Cox, "The farther this stuff goes toward self-expression and artiness, the worse it gets. We don't see [John Russell] Pope and [Paul] Cret being deliberately 'creative.' They were deliberately problem-solving professionals."

Until 1980, their designs— consisting of houses, religious and educational buildings, and office buildings—remained modern in feeling and style, though they echoed nearby architectural elements before it became popular to do so. Beginning in the 1980s, Hartman-Cox's designs became increasingly regionalist and revivalist. They were rehabilitating and adding to old Washington buildings, "and we ended up *just liking the old ones better.* They're richer, handsomer, more functional," said Cox. Their little Immanuel Presbyterian church resembles a northern Virginia farmhouse, their office building on Washington's Connecticut Avenue resonates with nearby art deco buildings, and their additions to the Folger Library and the Sumner School are barely recognizable as new. Conversely, their *new* buildings for Pennsylvania Avenue and nearby streets have become increasingly conservative and have embedded in them facades from older, small buildings.

Hartman-Cox's recent commissions have included contextual additions to the University of Virginia campus and the Chrysler Museum in Norfolk, and a mostly new, neoclassical corporate headquarters building in San Antonio. Their interiors are consistently splendid, especially in their use of diffused, soft natural light. Accused of being reactionary, Cox parries, "I'd rather be in the mainstream of Latrobe, Burnham, Cret, and those guys than with a bunch of people doing spec buildings in the suburbs."

MARKET SQUARE, WASHINGTON, D.C. 1991
MEDIUM: WATERCOLOR AND INK, OPPOSITE
MEDIUM: PENCIL AND WASH, BELOW

# JOHN HEJDUK

John Hejduk asserts that he heard a Frank Lloyd Wright lecture in the Great Hall at Cooper Union in New York City when he was an undergraduate and that the event was an epiphany. He changed to an architecture major, graduated from there and Harvard, and later returned to his alma mater, Cooper Union, as dean of the School of Architecture.

Cooper Union is an unusual, small college located in the Bohemian reaches of the lower East Village of New York City. It is the last tuition-free college in the country and is extremely competitive without being elite. It offers degrees in only three areas: art, architecture, and engineering. Unlike most universities, where the architecture program must struggle for priority with other disciplines, at Cooper Union it is the reason for the college.

Hejduk has not strayed far from this three-building urban campus, one building of which, a bulky fortress-like brownstone built by the founder in 1859, was extensively remodeled by Hejduk in 1974. He taught for a few years in the mid-fifties at the University of Texas where he did his first series of seven Texas houses as a design exercise.

Much of Hejduk has been unrealized in actual buildings but his ideas have been influential through his teaching, copious articles written about him and his work, and his own books. He is highly regarded in the United States and abroad as a teacher of great persuasion and passion and as a theoretician. Although still better known abroad than in the United States, Hejduk came to the attention of the profession most visibly with his inclusion in the book *Five Architects*, published in 1975. Along with

DRAWINGS FROM THE VLADIVOSTOK PROJECT, 1988
MEDIUM: WATERCOLOR AND GOUACHE

Peter Eisenman (who is now a professor at Cooper Union), Michael Graves, Richard Meier, and Charles Gwathmey, he became identified as a member of the fabled New York Five. Unlike the others who have each developed extensive practices and a body of built work, Hejduk is only now beginning to test his in built form. His earlier designs were influenced by Juan Gris and artists, but now writers and poets are his focus. Hejduk contends that great authors can "create" settings through word association and that the architect should be able to profit from these word images in creating physical corollaries.

Hejduk has a doggedness in his pursuit of an idea, from which he eventually wrests meat, bone, and marrow. His latest works are highly original, object-laden scenarios for real and imagined clients. He is a highly provocative and extremely talented individual.

# HERMAN HERTZBERGER

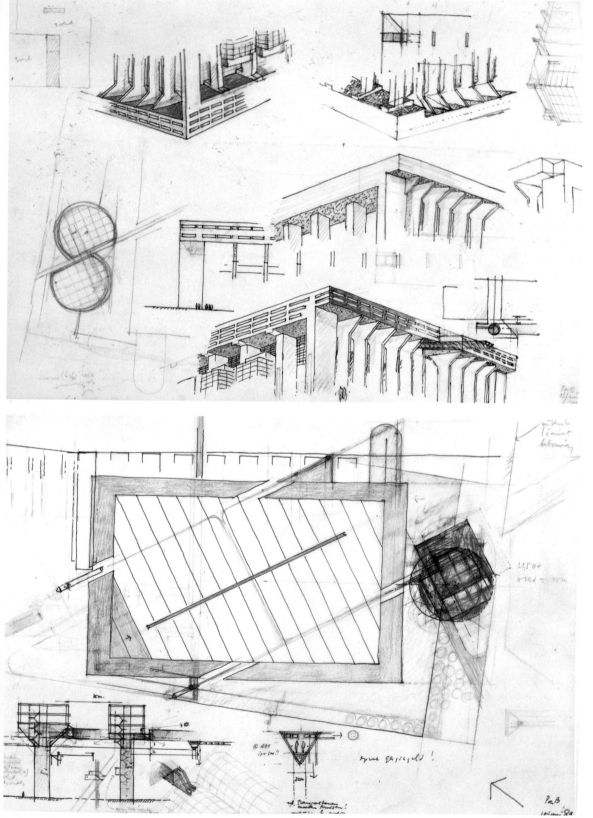

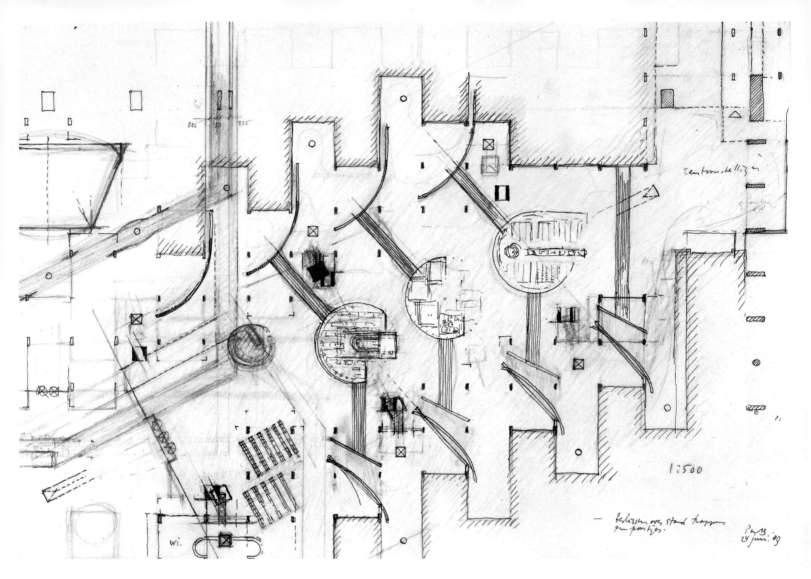

**BIBLIOTHÈQUE DE FRANCE COMPETITION, PARIS. 1989**
**MEDIUM: PEN AND INK, COLORED PENCIL**

Architecture exists at many different levels of experience and many levels of understanding. To the average layman who thinks of it at all, architecture is simply a matter of enclosure against the elements, its sole purpose being to serve a set of intended functions. To those who are architects, however, and those who spend their lives thinking about the larger, more complex meanings of buildings and their effect on their inhabitants, architecture is a gloriously complex art form; it is fraught with a multitude of interpretations of meaning, symbolism, and cultural manifestations.

The Dutch architect Herman Hertzberger views his buildings not so much as a means of serving functions or providing spaces for activities as he does a stage in which the participants are actors. Hertzberger tries to design spaces that permit the optimum number of ways in which the user can interact with the spaces.

Everything we make must be the catalyst to stimulate the individual to play the roles through which his identity will be enlarged. The aim of architecture is then: to reach the situation where everyone's identity is optimal, and because user and thing manifest each other, affirm each other, make each other more itself, the problem is to find the right conditioning for each thing.

Hertzberger has been influenced in his design philosophy by the teachings and examples of an earlier, internationally respected architect and countryman, Aldo van Eyck. Van Eyck was a prominent member of Team 10, a group of architects who made important contributions to the theory of architecture in the 1950s. In turn, Hertzberger has inspired a generation of architects with his humanistic approach to the art of architecture and his keen interest in the much-neglected field of housing.

His thoughtful, intelligent, and sensitive attitude toward the making of buildings is present even in the first early sketches for a commission. The drawings have a lyrical quality and strength that already hold the promise of a building which will enlarge, and be enlarged by, its occupants.

# STEVEN HOLL

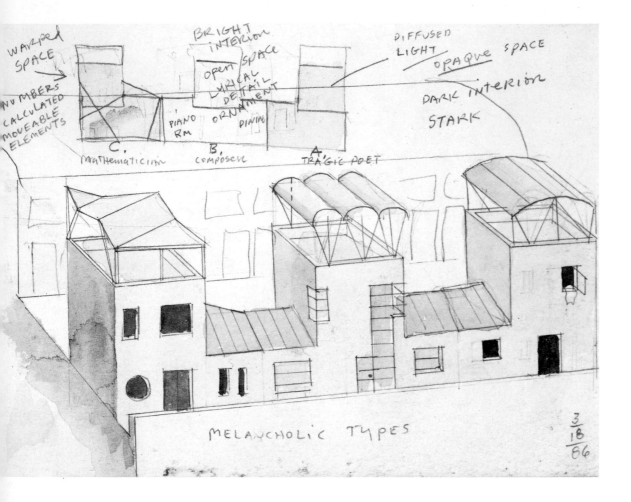

The maturation of architectural talent, like fine wine, takes many years. In Steven Holl's case, it is approximately twenty. He graduated cum laude from the University of Washington in 1971 and in 1989 the Museum of Modern Art exhibited his work at the same time that *Time* magazine featured him as a rising star among the younger generation of architects.

Holl's style of architecture, which has been described accurately by the respected editor of *Progressive Architecture* magazine, John Dixon, as one of "unadorned clarity," draws from modernist tenets but does so within a personal framework of careful proportions and planar compositions. His architecture, like many of his generation, is quietly rebellious against the slickness of modernist materials and finishes and is arresting in its honesty and its sophistication. He enjoys the juxtaposition of elegant finished surfaces with coarse unworked materials and is predisposed toward a straightforward palette of stone, glass, concrete, and stucco. Within this ascetic range of old-fashioned construction choices, Holl is extremely inventive;

none of his projects to date demonstrate this more than his somewhat controversial Dreamland Heights building in Seaside, Florida, which the architect continues to call by its more accurate working title, the Hybrid Building. In a planned model community of strict design code restrictions calling for period roofs, windows, and other historical allegories, Holl has managed to subvert the rules in a creative manner to produce a starkly modern 4-story mixed-use, retail-office-residential complex.

In each of Holl's designs there is the presence of the poet and the artist. At Seaside it manifests itself in his division of apartment dwellers into those who revel in sunsets and parties and those less sociable—"one for a poet, one for a musician, and one for a mathematician."

His early sketches, somewhat reminiscent of Aldo Rossi in their directness and honesty, capture the eccentric and arresting quality of the finished building and are encoded with the architect's instructions to himself regarding lighting, materials, and space.

# HANS HOLLEIN

In 1985 Austrian architect Hans Hollein was awarded the Pritzker Prize. Unlike earlier recipients of the award—Luis Barragán, Philip Johnson, I. M. Pei, Kevin Roche, James Stirling, and Richard Meier—Hollein had completed only one major building at that time, the 1982 Municipal Museum in Mönchengladbach, Germany. (The Frankfurt Museum of Modern Art was then under construction.) Instead, his genius was evidenced in small, exquisitely executed commissions and in his writings and teachings. Of Hollein, author Brendan Gill wrote, "He is that comparatively rare thing in contemporary architecture, an artist-architect, combining great technical prowess with a gift for astonishing the eye. His buildings, like his drawings, have a playful seductiveness. One is happy in their presence."

Born in 1930 in Vienna, Austria, Hollein was educated there in the traditions of native Viennese Otto Wagner, Josef Hoffmann, and Josef Frank. He ultimately developed a "very personal brand of postmodernism consistently marked by a fascination with ritual, fantasy, and light; by a fusion of images from times past, present, and imagined; by combinations of sumptuous natural materials with lowly synthetics; and by elevation of the flawless detail to monumental importance," in the words of architecture critic Andrea Oppenheimer Dean.

Hollein's first public appearance came in 1963 in an exhibition with Walter Pichler which consisted of two models of utopian towns. Gigantic in scale and scope, these projects decried functionalism, the ruling aesthetic of the day, and claimed the right with this exhibition to reconsider architecture as an art. Pichler and Hollein predicted what horrors might happen if functionalism were to continue to dominate architecture.

The early works of Hollein are small gems. Among them are the Retti Candleshop of 1965, the Richard Feigen Gallery in New York City, Strada Novissima for the 1980 Venice Biennale, two jewelry stores in Vienna, and the Austrian Travel Bureau in Vienna, whose gleaming palm-tree columns are widely known and copied.

A man of intellect and artistic vision, Hollein has recently proposed an audacious subterranean design for a branch of the Solomon R. Guggenheim Museum in New York for his native Salzburg. With its hybrid manmade and natural forms of sheer clifflike rooms and with spectacular light shafts, Hollein has once again demonstrated his penchant for the elegant and the dramatic.

SALZBURG-GUGGENHEIM MUSEUM PROJECT, AUSTRIA. 1989

MEDIUM: PENCIL AND WATERCOLOR

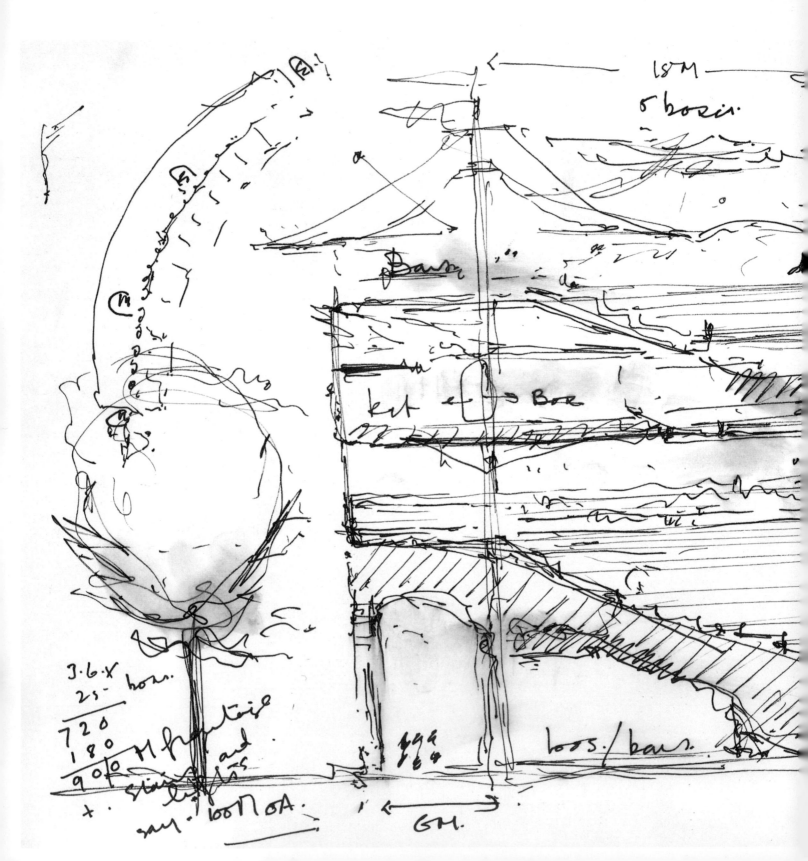

light through
der the canopy.

daylight between
upper + lower stand

M.H. 10.2.85

An architect's design direction can be influenced by the faculty of the particular school he or she attends, or by the affiliation with a certain architectural firm during the early formative years of employment after graduation. Conversely, it can be argued that the choice of college or firm shows a predilection for that influence in the first place. In considering Michael Hopkins, it is easy to see the direct and indirect influences on his work that stemmed from his having worked in the firm of Norman Foster.

Richard Rogers and Norman Foster are well known as the principal advocates and practitioners of a style of architectural design that harks back to the pioneering lead of Mies van der Rohe, a philosophy which places its faith in the manifest destiny of technology as it is represented in architectural form. Popularly referred to as high-tech architecture and exemplified most memorably by Piano and Rogers's Centre Pompidou in Paris and Foster's bank in Hong Kong, this branch of contemporary design has found few ardent champions since the execution of a series of early post–World War II lean, steel, skeletal buildings in Southern California. Structural determination of form, and especially of steel and glass buildings, disappeared with the waves of rediscovery of the past and the subsequent influences of Post-modernism in the 1970s.

One of the notable holdouts from the earlier era of structural determinism of form is the young architect Michael Hopkins, whose designs enclose space in a means faithful to contemporary technology. Hopkins's architecture is more puritan in its use of industrial components than that of Rogers or Foster, but it employs the same attention to detail that characterized Mies van der Rohe's buildings. The resulting aesthetic from such a rigorous attitude toward precise proportions and flawless construction is a welcome antidote in a society where shoddy workmanship and cheap materials are more and more the normative.

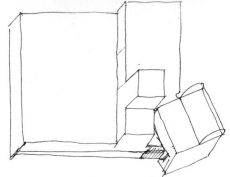

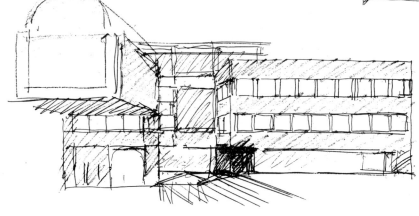

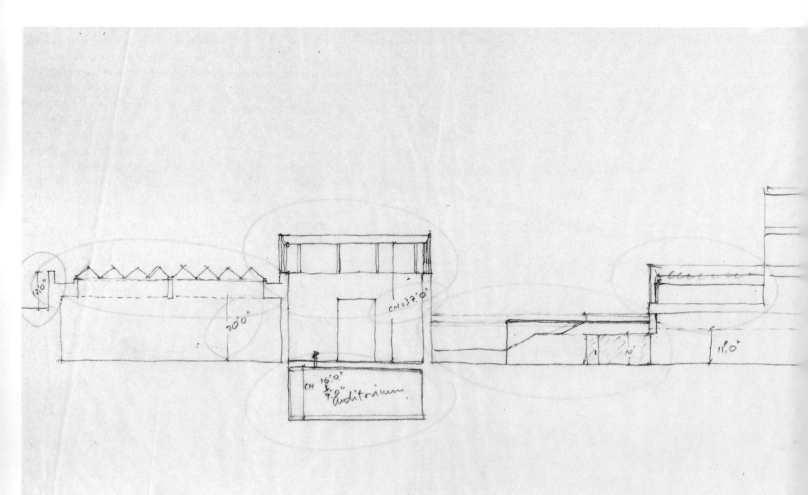

**MUSEUM OF CONTEMPORARY ART, LOS ANGELES. 1981**
**MEDIUM: PENCIL, PEN AND INK**

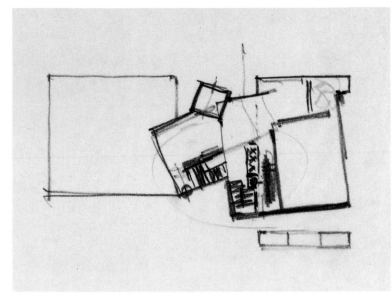

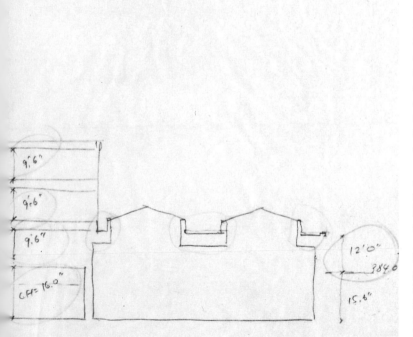

In the United States, at least, the lyrics, "If you can make it here [New York], then you can make it anywhere" are regarded as being a fairly accurate statement about the performing arts. It is not entirely parochial or chauvinistic to say, similarly, that in the world of architecture making it in America gives a designer international status.

Arata Isozaki achieved that milestone when he designed the highly acclaimed Palladium discotheque in New York City in 1985—an amalgam of flashing lights, high-rise television sets, grids that rotated and gyrated kinetically, and theater-set interiors for this venerable renovated movie house. If the Palladium captured the public's eye, the new Museum of Contemporary Art (MOCA) in Los Angeles of 1986 confirmed Isozaki's superior design skills. Situated among towering nondescript, glassy modern office buildings, the ruby red museum is a small, sophisticated, meticulously crafted jewel. Its neatly arranged architectural forms—a red sandstone brick barrel vault, pyramidal skylights, curved walls—are only the tip of the iceberg, the rest of which is below grade. Inside, a sunken court leads beyond the lobby to an abundance of north-facing galleries, which are illuminated by pyramidal skylights of various sizes; to the south is the barrel vault-topped library and more galleries. While the museum's exterior is a rich palette of materials and forms comprising an urban tour de force, its interiors are minimalist, rigorously geometric compositions of white walls, pure proportions, and neutral space.

Isozaki is a member of that small club of contemporary Japanese architects who have obtained widespread international fame for their inventiveness, boldness of form and color, and scrupulously careful detailing.

# HUGH NEWELL JACOBSEN

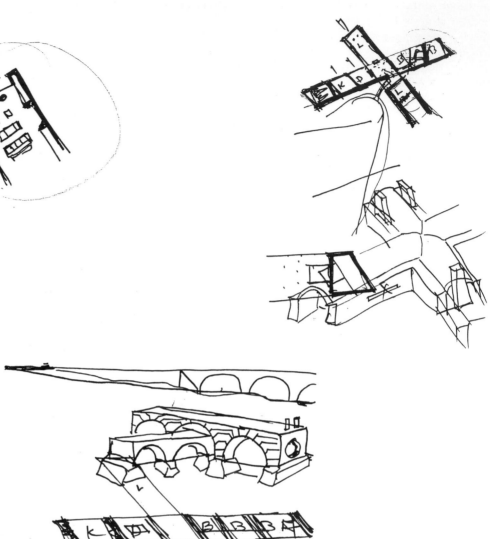

For most architects, the house is the beginning point of their practice, then they gradually move on to larger and larger, and more expensive projects. Eventually the successful architect can no longer afford to design the single-family residence because for the same amount of attention he can design a high-rise office building for a considerably larger fee.

This is not the case with Hugh Jacobsen, whose name has become synonymous with beautifully designed houses as the mainstay of a practice that is hardly of the second tier. Since beginning his practice in 1959, after an amazingly short apprenticeship in the two offices of Philip Johnson and Keys Lethbridge and Condon in Washington, D.C., Jacobsen set out to fashion a career, as one critic put it, as a "gentleman architect" in the nation's capital.

Jacobsen has designed larger buildings in the last decade such as the University of Michigan Alumni Center and executed a number of significant restoration projects, including the Renwick Gallery and the Arts and Industries building in Washington, D.C., but he is still most closely associated with an unbroken string of skillfully designed and executed residential commissions.

If architects had specialties as do medical doctors, Hugh Jacobsen's would be residential. Where most architects treat houses as lesser design problems or as abstract exercises for their larger oeuvres, for Jacobsen the house is a complex and fulfilling set of conditions for which he must find the solution. Where other architects lament the necessity for dealing with difficult and demanding clients and their idiosyncrasies, Jacobsen seems to relish this immediate contact with the primary user, unlike situations where the user is never dealt with in the course of the design for so many other types of buildings.

It is also a matter of vocabulary and scale. Jacobsen has developed such a sophisticated sense of the appropriate scale of one part to the other in his residential designs, and become so skilled at employing his arsenal of forms—the gable, pyramid, chimneys, and other residentially scaled elements—that even his larger works carry this play of scale and form.

No single house of Jacobsen's design can be said to be typical or predictive of the next since he is a master at devising unusual, yet appropriate, schemes for each client and site situation. The Welles house in Ohio, with its unorthodox X-shaped plan and distinct view, contains the unmistakable earmarks of a Jacobsen house. The most dramatic feature of the site, and no doubt the single most influential organizing element of the plan, is a Roman-looking thick masonry railroad bridge in picturesque ruin dating from the early part of the century. It looks for all the world like a Piranesi drawing come to life and the architect has framed this unforgettable tableau of bridge and river perfectly in various rooms of the house. The dramatic impact of this unusual feature is further heightened by the adroit way in which the building is tucked away, out of sight from the road that passes through this bucolic horse country of central Ohio. Once revealed as the entry drops down from an upper plateau, the white house with its tall sentinel-like towers makes a perfect contrasting modern sculpture to complement the older fragment of the railroad bridge.

**WELLES RESIDENCE, BOWLING GREEN, OHIO. 1984**
**MEDIUM: INK ON PAPER**

# HELMUT JAHN

**UNITED AIRLINES TERMINAL, O'HARE AIRPORT, CHICAGO. 1987
MEDIUM: INK AND COLORED WASH**

**A**rchitecture stopped being a tweedy, pipe-smoking profession some time ago, but it remained for Helmut Jahn to challenge even the memory of that image. Jahn's flamboyant dress and chiseled face won him a place on the cover of *Gentlemen's Quarterly* in the mid-1980s beside the caption, "like his designs: to kill." Although his flashy attire and life-style irk some colleagues, Jahn has proved that there is a great deal more to him than eccentric taste in clothes.

Jahn came to the United States from Germany in 1966 to study at the Illinois Institute of Technology, the architecture school founded by the great International Style master Mies van der Rohe. In 1967, at the age of twenty-seven, Jahn joined the firm of C. F. Murphy Associates, noted for its commercial projects. Fourteen years later the practice changed its name to Murphy/Jahn. Jahn has made a dazzling rise to the top of his profession with skyscrapers located in cities all over the world. In Philadelphia, his 67-story Liberty Place was the first building to exceed the height of the historic William Penn statue atop City Hall. It has changed the city's skyline. Jahn's 59-story Messe tower in Frankfurt, to be completed in 1991, will be the tallest building in Europe.

Jahn's development as a designer paralleled that of the International Style in the 1970s and 80s, as it was increasingly enriched and adapted to better suit the existing context, history, and social needs of a building. While the bulk of Jahn's work is commercial office towers, his principal acclaim in recent years has come from transportation-oriented buildings. His CTA O'Hare Rapid Transit Station and United Airlines Terminal, both of 1984 in Chicago, show Jahn's sure hand with his chosen vocabulary. It is at once high tech and art deco. The United Terminal, which combines German efficiency with American pizzazz, is the first facility since Dulles Airport in Washington, D.C., to capture the spirit and adventure of flying.

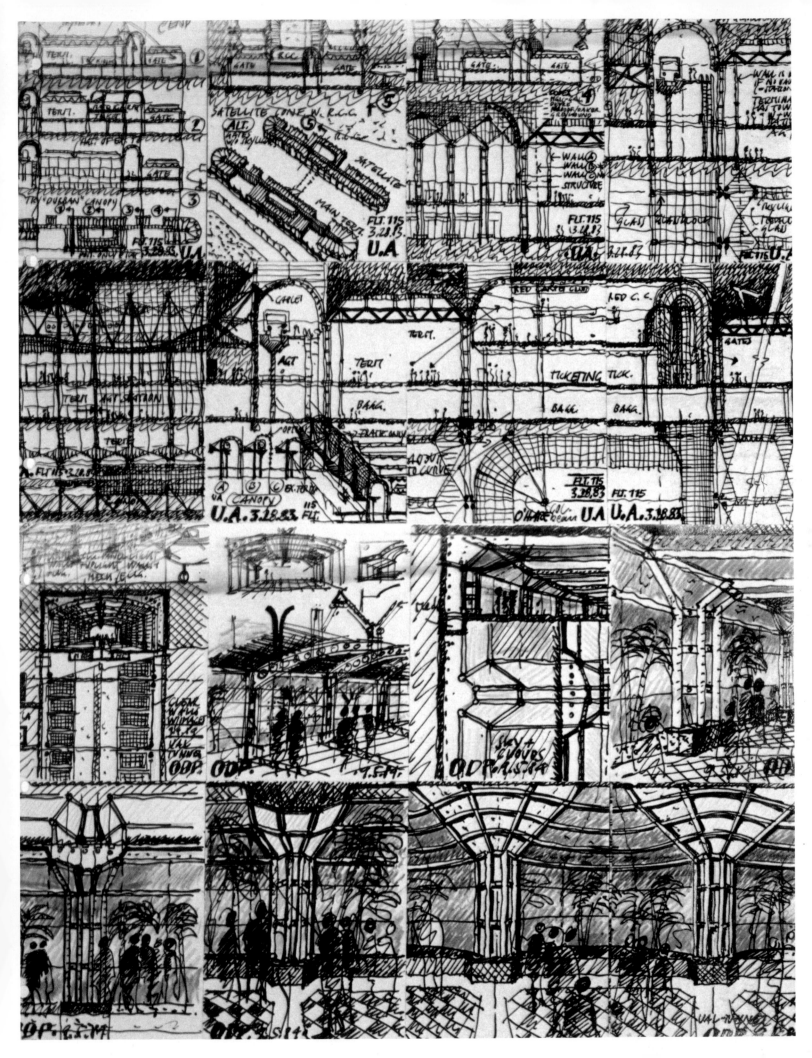

# CARLOS JIMENEZ

**HOUSE ALONG RIO GRANDE, DEL RIO, TEXAS. 1988
MEDIUM: PEN, INK, AND PASTEL**

The young architect Carlos Jimenez, like many other architects before him, has used himself as client and patron to gain initial recognition. Jimenez, a native of Costa Rica, having gained his initial professional education in the United States at the University of Tennessee, settled in Houston where he received his degree and found an artistic and cultural climate suited to his particular talent and temperament. Two works, his own house and studio compound, and a fine-art printing plant on a skinny lot, established Jimenez's position among the promising new wave of younger architects. Both projects show strong influences of the great Mexican architect Luis Barragán, Aldo Rossi, and Gunnar Asplund. Bold colors and the confident handling of natural light are trademarks of his work, coupled with an unusual sensitivity for the manipulation of interior and exterior space.

There is a clarity to Jimenez's architecture that is refreshing in its simplicity and directness. There are no historical allusions or fashionable "tricks," just the straightforward solution to the client's "brief" and to the dictates of site and climate.

# JOHN JOHANSEN

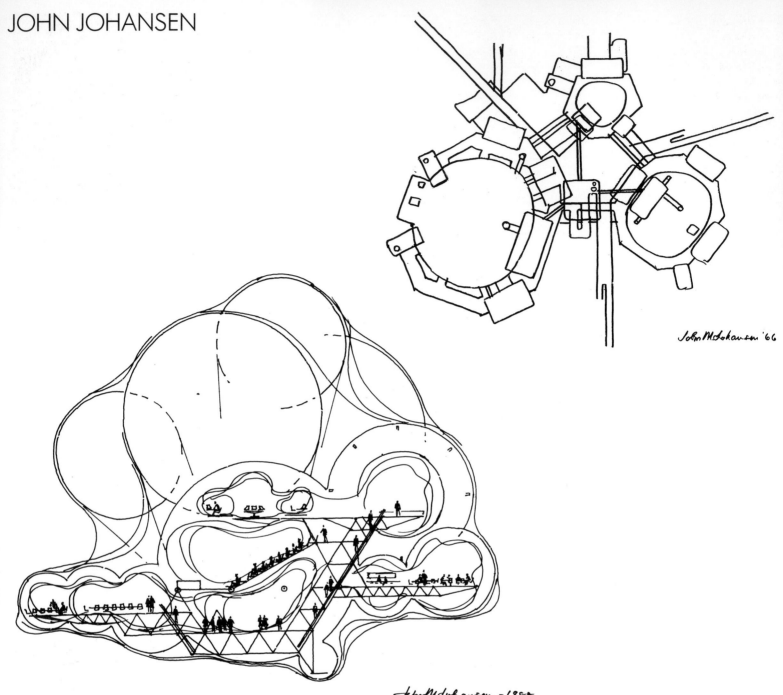

*John M Johansen '66*

*John M Johansen – 1988*

Architects, as a breed, take pride in their profession and its long history which stretches back to the pyramids of ancient Egypt and beyond. Such a lineage can be reassuring and it can also be inhibiting, calling as it does for a certain homage to, and respect for, the past. As a consequence, there are architects for whom the future does not exist as a mysterious and intriguing world they cannot know. It is rather a place that is arrived at by taking daily steps in that direction one at a time.

John Johansen is not cut from this timid, self-assured cloth. For his entire career he has maintained an unwavering faith in an architecture that would truly reflect the scientific and technological advances of our era. Here is an architect entirely comfortable with a future that to his fellow architects seems more Buck Rogers and science fiction than like Vitruvius or Jefferson in nature. Like a determined and accomplished surfer, Johansen has maintained his balance on the "cutting edge" of futuristic thinking about architecture during his whole career. In the fifties Johansen startled the profession with his "bubble houses," which suggested cities unlike anything seen before—cities where rocket ships and plastic capsule trains whirred by, propelled by some yet-to-be discovered energy source. Students were excited by these visions; practitioners were skeptical.

In 1965, Johansen received a commission to design the Mummers Theater in Oklahoma City. He was blessed with a client who had a strong will and the courage to build what the architect drew. Oklahoma, by virtue of having Bruce Goff in residence at the university, had seen other buildings on the prairie that were pioneering in spirit and somewhat shocking in situ. Even so, the Theater Center put this southwestern laissez-faire attitude of acceptance to a stern test. The building, like Corbusier's Villa Savoye, another design that sought to look modern rather than actually be modern, made a total break with existing architectural form and tradition for theater design. To many critics it appeared to have been modeled after giant oil refineries and grain silos rather than anything having to do with the dramatic arts.

Johansen remains an unreconstructed champion of the future and continues to espouse a philosophy of an architecture that is "moving from the industrial age where mechanics are predominant, to an information age characterized by electronics." He envisions an architecture of the future that is "organic" in a way not foreseen by Frank Lloyd Wright—one with kinetic parts and electronic intelligence.

**OKLAHOMA THEATER CENTER, OKLAHOMA CITY. 1970**
**MEDIUM: FELT PEN**

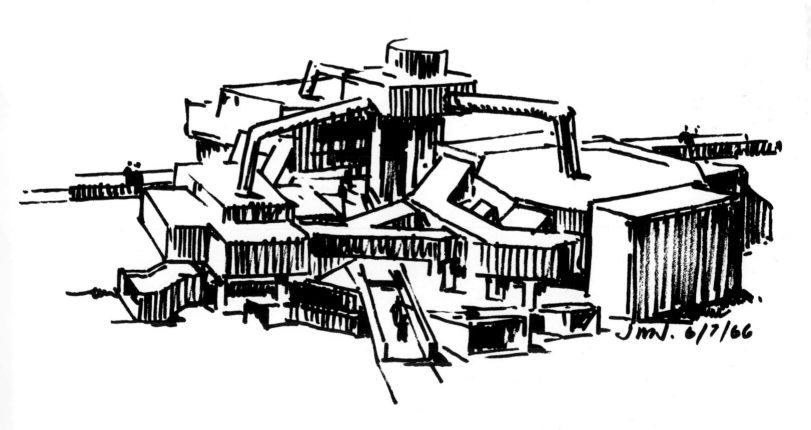

# PHILIP JOHNSON

An apt protégé of Mies van der Rohe, Philip Johnson is an architect to the manner born. Architectural historian Vincent Scully, Jr., said that Johnson has "the most ruthlessly aristocratic, highly studied taste of anyone practicing in America today." His sophisticated, pristine buildings tend to bear out that assessment.

Philip Johnson occupies a unique position in the field of modern architecture. Until the late age of thirty-six he had not designed a single building, but by the age of eighty he had become one of the most well-known and prolific architects of this century. It is not uncommon for architects to produce their most important works in their later years since a certain maturation is necessary to assimilate all the knowledge required for designing complex and important buildings.

Johnson greatly admired Mies van der Rohe, with whom he collaborated on what many call the finest high-rise building in the United States, the Seagram Building in New York City. Like all of Mies's skyscrapers, it has the look of fine jewelry, its proportions as carefully studied as those of Greek temples. No compromising setbacks along the building's height mar its bronze rectilinear purity. Instead, a generous forecourt plaza sets it apart from the busy traffic and enhances its "sculpture-on-a-pedestal" quality.

Johnson began as an architectural historian and was the first director of the Department of Architecture at the Museum of Modern Art. His association with Mies gave him instant credibility as an architect. This was followed in 1949 by the design of his own residence, the famous Glass House, his master's thesis project come to realization. There are a few buildings of each era that sum up much of what there is to say of the aesthetics of a style, and often they are residences in which the use requirements are simple enough to allow clarity of ideas without the confusion of functional requirements. The Eames House in Los Angeles was such a building, encapsulating the possibilities for a new kind of architecture wholly constructed from readily available twentieth-century manufactured components. The Farnsworth House (1959) by Johnson's mentor, Mies van der Rohe, is another example, and Johnson's Glass House belongs in this trilogy of important architectural statements at mid-century.

What could not have been predicted from the earliest of Johnson's architectural designs and his collaboration on the Seagram Building, was that by the end of his career he would be regarded by the public as having totally revised those earlier modernist views. Johnson was author of one of the "shrines" of the International School of Architecture (a term he coined with an exhibition at MOMA), and his Glass House stood for an entire epoch of technology and industrial art. The other bookend of this unusual career path, and the building that creates a total polarity of contrast with the Glass House, is the AT&T Building in New York City. The building proved to be one of the most controversial designs of this century. It's now-famous "Chippendale" top was a lightning rod that caused a storm of debate and division among architectural critics, students, and practitioners. It was seen by some as a travesty against the principles of modern architecture and by others as a welcome return to classical ornament and the graciousness of bygone periods. Johnson, with his phalanx of loyal apostles in close ranks behind him, assumed the position of self-appointed spokesman for architecture in the United States. Like Knute Rockne's wedge, he rolled across the media landscape unopposed. The press, with few detractors, lionized his projects and made him an instant celebrity in an art form that had not known such notoriety since Stanford White was shot by the outraged husband of his mistress in Madison Square Garden in 1906. Lesser architects hope to be in *Time* magazine, but only Philip Johnson has been on its cover.

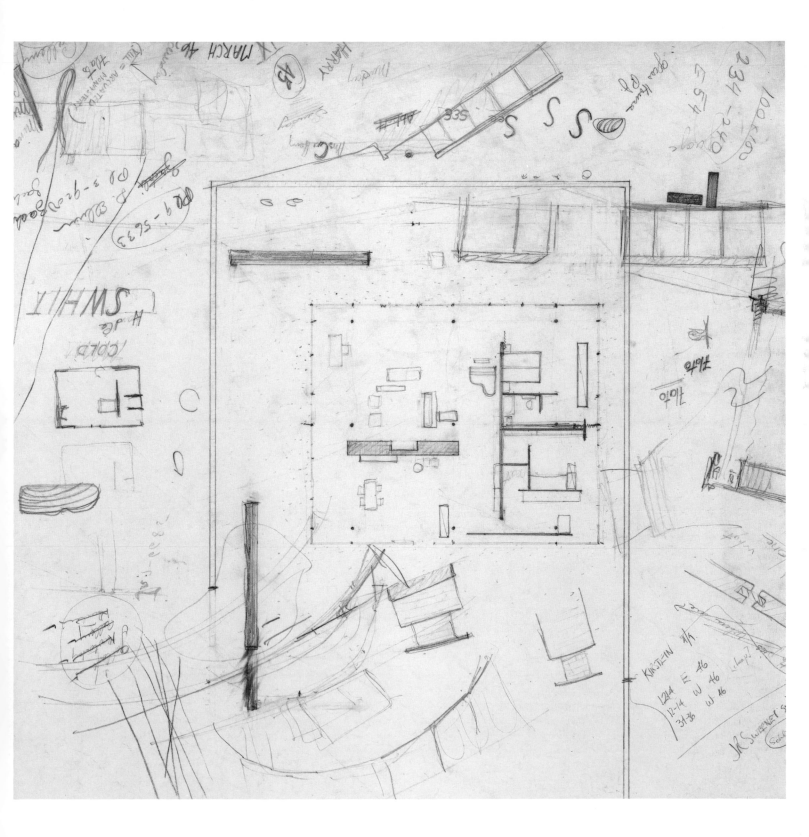

# E. FAY JONES

MILDRED B. COOPER MEMORIAL CHAPEL,
BELLA VISTA, ARKANSAS. 1988
MEDIUM: PENCIL ON TRACING PAPER

COOPER CHAPEL

SECTION

**F**rank Lloyd Wright's prolific outpouring of masterful work over an unusually long and active career made him both the best-known twentieth-century American architect and the one most difficult to follow. Wright's lack of eminent followers was not for lack of expounding his philosophy—he published several books and lectured frequently. Nor was it for lack of training potential successors—he raised apprenticeship to near-religious heights at Taliesin East and Taliesin West. Still, none of his acolytes, with the possible exception of Paolo Soleri and Bruce Goff, who both pursued eccentric offshoots of Wright's style, made an original mark in the architectural world.

Now comes an exception. He is E. Fay Jones, a modest architect who has worked quietly in the relative isolation of the Ozark Mountains. From his native city of Fayetteville in Arkansas, he has created buildings that a young Wright might have proudly designed. Jones has ignored architectural movements and fashions as he has continued to perfect a basic Wrightian vocabulary of indigenous and natural forms and materials tailored to Jones's own individuality.

Part of that individuality has been to put into built form preferences that other architects consign to sketches. Many designers would love to leave a structural framework before cladding it with the "flesh" of enclosing materials, but Jones has actually done so. His two most renowned buildings—Thorncrown Chapel in Eureka Springs and the Mildred B. Cooper Memorial Chapel in Bella Vista, both in Arkansas—appear as transcendental sketches. Both are graceful, wooden, outdoor structures about which Jones has said, "I did a small house 20 years before the chapels, just a little thing, but when I showed it to people in the framing stages, they always said, 'this reminds me of a chapel.' I thought at the time it was the proportions and the openness that created the response, and I vowed to do a chapel some day and try to recapture that feeling of minimal enclosure."

For these works of enduring spiritual quality, Jones was awarded the AIA Gold Medal in 1990, the highest honor given by the American Institute of Architects.

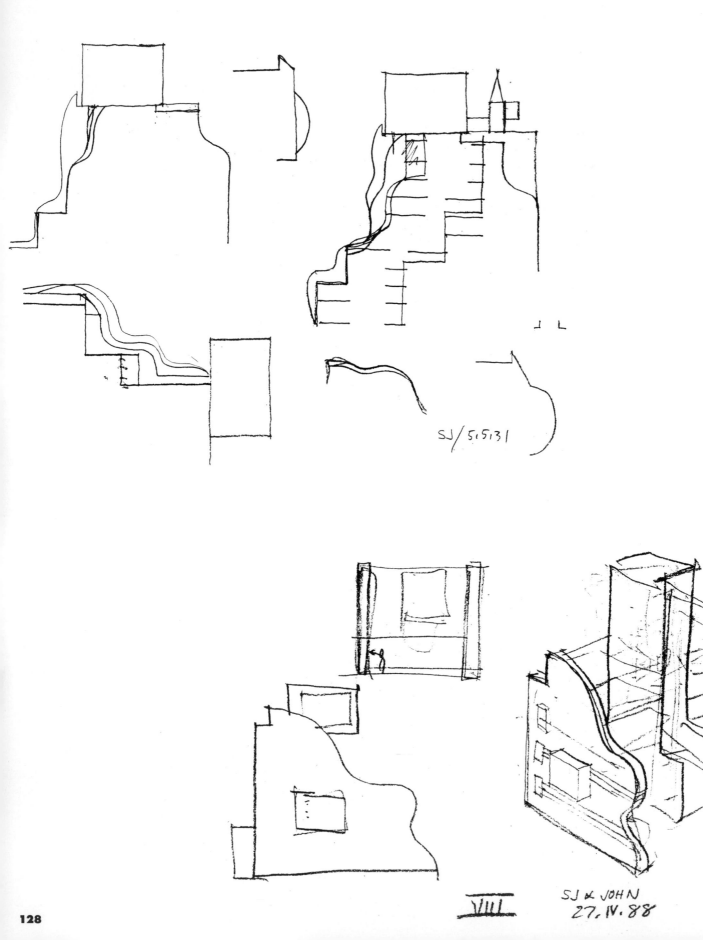

SJ/5.5.31

VIII    SJ & JOHN
27. IV. 88

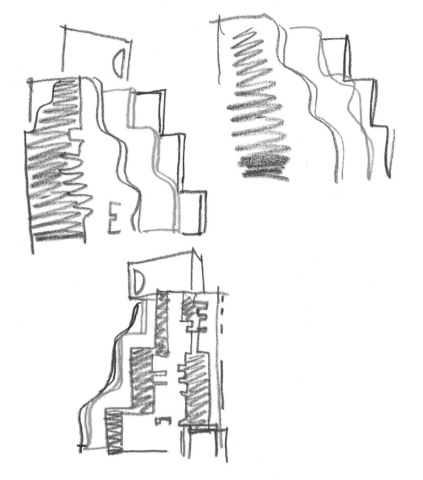

SJ/4.33

**A**t least one architect in the world is not distressed either by his perceived demise of high-tech architecture or the waning influence of Post-modern dogma. Sumet Jumsai, a Thai architect educated at Cambridge and listed as one of the "fifty outstanding architects in the world" in an article written by Ivica Mladjenovic, Belgrade, in 1984, believes that Post-modernism has "become a refuge for many who cannot design . . . and whose pursuits reflect an intellectual bankruptcy." He is equally harsh in his assessment of architecture that makes "technology a thing

of beauty," contending that it "cannot have its life extended beyond Centre Pompidou." According to Jumsai, the future lies in the direction of a design breakthrough which he describes as "robot architecture" and "cubist architecture." The former concept is represented in his 20-story Bank of Asia building in Bangkok. Jumsai intended the bank to be a hybrid realization of the gradual symbiosis between man and machine depicted literally in this building's form.

Jumsai's manner of working is somewhat unorthodox in that his early studies for a building often as not take the form of a painting; the various design elements of the building are represented in a painterly composition. Thus, a robotlike painting preceded the robot bank building, and a Cubist-inspired painting that had overtones of Braque and Picasso was the basis for early studies of the building for the Nation Publishing Group Company in Bangkok. The design for the Nation Building, which resulted from this artistic stimulus, and

from an attempt to depict in architectural terms the literal imagery of a newsman on a stool slouched over his computer, is as original as it is controversial. In the architect's words he was trying "to be free from 'architecture,' from the current intellectual cul-de-sac."

Jumsai is regarded as one of the leading intellectuals among architects in Southeast Asia and his startling designs are the ongoing subject of intense critical debate.

# GERHARD KALLMANN / MICHAEL MCKINNELL

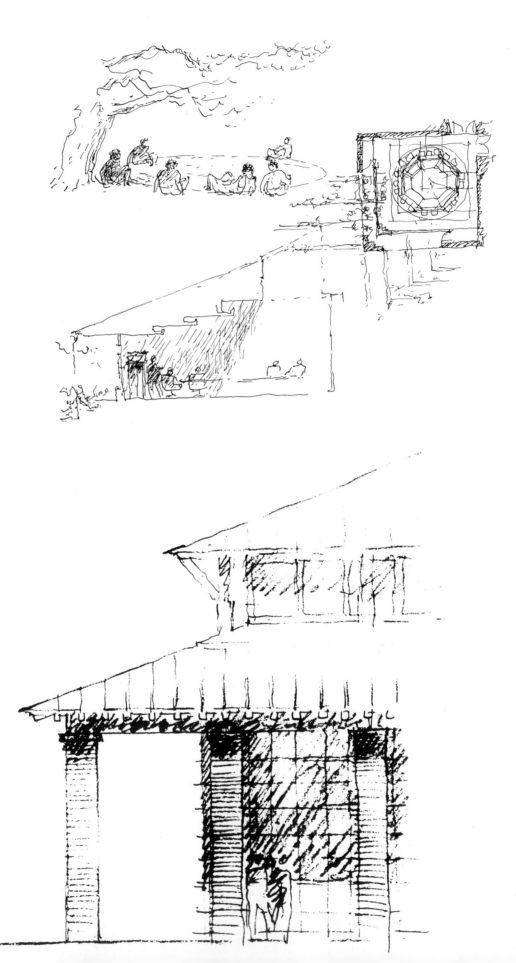

**G**erhard Kallmann, with his longtime partner Michael McKinnell, burst onto the American architectural scene in 1962 when they won the Boston City Hall competition. The winning entry, a brooding hulk of a raw concrete building rising out of a sienna brick plaza, quickly became a central building in the mainstream of the Brutalism Movement that swept the world in the 1960s. Kallmann, today a professor at Harvard, was born in Berlin and had fled Nazi Germany for England. There he attended the Architectural Association, made his way to the United States and thence to Harvard in 1949. Like Louis Kahn, he had come to prominence in the profession somewhat late, but the City Hall project launched him on a career that showed steady growth in maturity and accomplishment.

If earlier works had been influenced by admiration for Kahn and Le Corbusier, these later chapters show a sympathy for the warmth of materials and planar forms of Frank Lloyd Wright. The American Academy of Arts and Sciences, Cambridge, Massachusetts, completed in 1981, with its copper roof striking long horizontal lines above glass clerestories, seems more American and somehow less European than other Kallmann/McKinnell buildings, most notably the Becton Dickinson & Company Corporate Headquarters in Franklin Lakes, New Jersey.

The American Academy of Arts and Sciences building is located on the former site of the grand antebellum estate of Eliot Norton, a homestead of an earlier, genteel time. Kallmann and McKinnell have done justice to that civilized precedent by building a haven for scholars with serene views of landscaped "walls" surrounding and protecting the tranquility within the sanctuary. A unifying and organizing central atrium, a characteristic of the Kallmann, McKinnell and Wood office, is surrounded by reading and conference rooms and gives access to an upper story of offices and a library. Tucked away in one wing is a somewhat sybaritic couch-furnished amphitheater for a constituency that "does not like to be lectured at."

The university buildings at Saint Louis University show Kallmann's evolution from Brutalism to a careful articulation of forms, materials, and proportions that are masterful in execution and refreshingly devoid of posturing. "The modernity of our buildings is essential," Kallmann explains, "but it is always necessary to look back for instruction from the past. We are neither historical nor trendy, but try instead to design buildings of quality, suited to the site and appropriate to the purpose."

No architect could aspire to more.

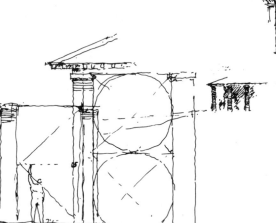

Rustic Temple fabrique / Brongniart 1783

131

# RAM KARMI / ADA KARMI-MELAMEDE

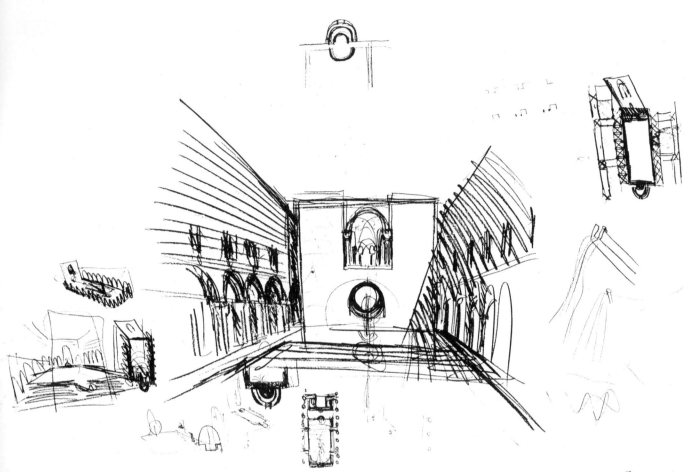

Rami—Pencil

**R**am Karmi and his younger sister, Ada, have been practicing as Karmi Associates in Tel Aviv since 1962, following the death of their famous architect father, Dov Karmi. Dov Karmi is acknowledged as one of the early design pioneers in Israel and a leader of the modern movement there. In 1972 Ada opened the New York branch office of the firm, when she was teaching at Columbia University. In 1983, after winning the major international design competition for the new Supreme Court Building of Israel—a gift to the country from the Rothschild

Foundation—she returned to work with her brother on this important commission in Jerusalem.

The design competition to select the architect and the building design for the Supreme Court was a multilayered process open to all Israeli architects in the first stage, and an invited group of outstanding international architects in the second stage. Cesar Pelli, Charles Moore, the philosopher Sir Isaiah Berlin, Colin Amery, Daniel Havkin, David Reznik, Chief Justice Meir Shamgar, and Lord Jacob Rothschild were among the

members of a jury chaired by Bill Lacy. The Karmis' design was selected in a stiff competition from a handful of the best architects in the world, which included Meier, Legorreta, Safdie, and Freed. Their winning solution to the prominently sited and symbolically charged building was a low-lying structure that blended with the landscape and recalled the strength and character of "wall architecture" in the city and region.

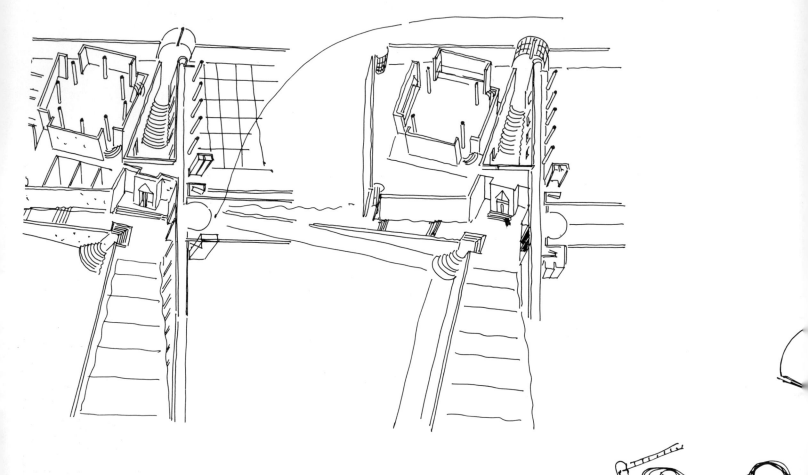

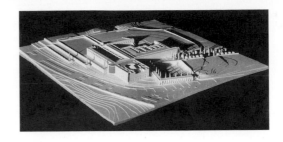

# JOSEPH PAUL KLEIHUES

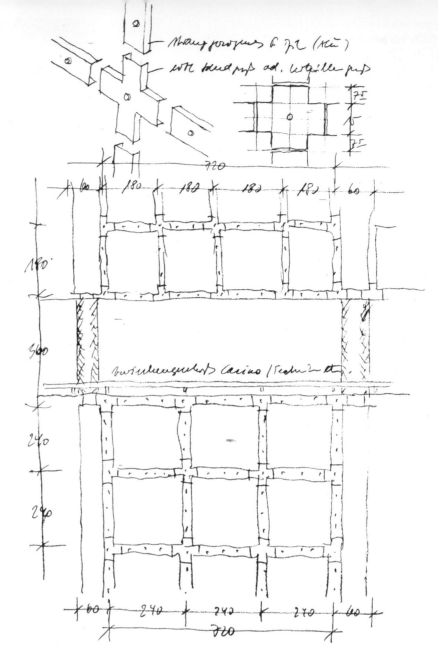

There is no building, with perhaps the exception of laboratories, whose proper function is more critical than a hospital. Its efficient operation is essential and the specifications which architects are presented with are extremely complex and do not encourage any considerations for aesthetic criteria. It is a cliché, but too often true, that hospitals are designed for the doctors and staff and not for patients and their families. This is happily not the case, however, of the new Neukölln hospital in Berlin by Joseph Kleihues. The building took twelve years to plan and build, and required over 3,000

drawings. It is an imposing low-lying structure on the landscape stretching more than 300 meters in length and only 6 stories high. It has a strong industrial appearance created by the straightforward exterior wall treatment of white aluminum panels attached to the building by a gridwork of black plates with visible screws. The overall effect is a cheerful and sanitary look, not unlike a great ocean liner. The porthole windows at the circulation corridors enhance that nautical feeling.

The architect had three stated goals: "First, we wanted to build a modern building. Its technical equipment, the construction details and its architectonic appearance should point to the

future. Secondly, we wanted to build an efficient building. The functional macro and micro organizations and their sound execution should guarantee the best care for the patients, and this for a long time. Third, we wanted to build a humane building." On the latter point the architects succeeded in designing an open and friendly hospital unlike any today. The plan, which resembles an elongated racetrack, is open in the center thus creating a soaring space not unlike the nave of a Gothic church except that the roof is all glass panels and giant contemporary murals cover the walls. Unlike most hospital waiting rooms, the one at

Neukölln is a joyous, uplifting space where one enjoys being. In spite of the success of Neukölln, Kleihues is not a hospital architect nor is he easily categorized. He is a teacher, a prolific author and publisher, and a master exhibition planner. With seemingly endless energy and enthusiasm, Kleihues has played a significant role in Berlin's exemplary redevelopment of recent years.

Vittorio Lampugnani says that Kleihues's architecture "develops in the mind and not on the paper [that] the first lightly drawn sketch already contains everything that will be later defined in the final construction drawing."

**NEUKÖLLN HOSPITAL, BERLIN, GERMANY. 1986**

**MEDIUM: PENCIL ON PARCHMENT, OPPOSITE AND BELOW**

**MEDIUM: INK ON PARCHMENT, RIGHT**

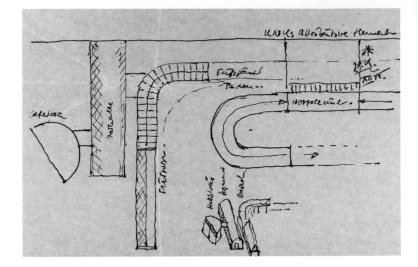

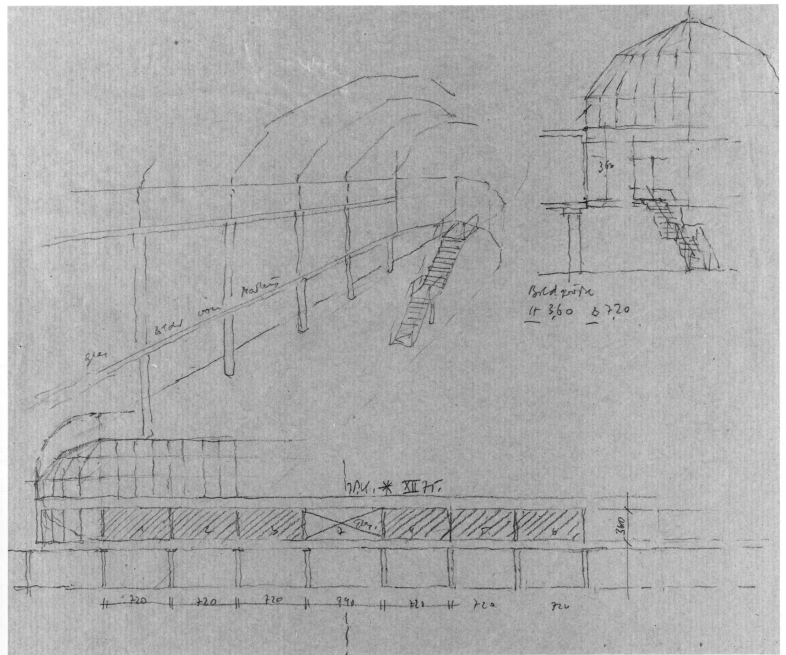

# REM KOOLHAAS

**A**s an architect/philosopher/ artist, Dutchman Rem Koolhaas has expanded and continues to expand our perceptions of cities and civilization. Most provocative is Delirious New York, the late-1970s examination of Manhattan by Koolhaas and his colleagues at their Office for Metropolitan Architecture. (OMA was founded in 1975 by Koolhaas, Elia Zenghelis, Zoe Zenghelis, and Madelon Vriesendorp.)

Born in Rotterdam in 1944, Koolhaas worked first as a journalist and film-script writer. He attended the Architectural Association in London from 1968 to 1972. From there he extended his education in the United States to Cornell University in Ithaca and the Institute for Architecture and Urban Studies in New York City. He began to see the metropolis as a constantly self-generating, anachronistic system of signs and symbols. Delirious New York, he maintains, was a "search in the influence of the metropolitan masses and culture on architecture and urbanism."

Returning to Europe at the end of the 1970s, Koolhaas found architects "completely obsessed with the historic centers of Europe," much to the detriment of modern architecture. "Their activity," he said, "threatened to completely deny, ignore—and ultimately repress—crucial aspects of the modern world such as scale, numbers, technology, programs, needs, that were at complete variance with their ideal of a 'rediscovered' history. This created a colossal reservoir of denial that sought an outlet in the periphery of the cities or that was pathetically masked to conform to the new dogmas and led to a mounting confusion between 'real' and fabricated history."

His own designs, such as the addition to the Netherlands Parliament (1979), the Boompjes apartment building in Rotterdam (1981), the City Hall for The Hague (1986), and housing at Kochstrasse and Friedrichstrasse in Berlin (1980), are self-proclaimed "polemical demonstrations." In Koolhaas's words, they show that "aspects of modernism—both American and European—can be made to co-exist with the historical core, and that only a new urbanism that abandons pretensions of harmony and overall coherence, can turn the tensions and contradictions—that tear the historical city apart—into a new quality. The projects celebrate the end of sentimentality."

BIBLIOTHEQUE DE FRANCE COMPETITION, PARIS. 1989
MEDIUM: PEN AND INK

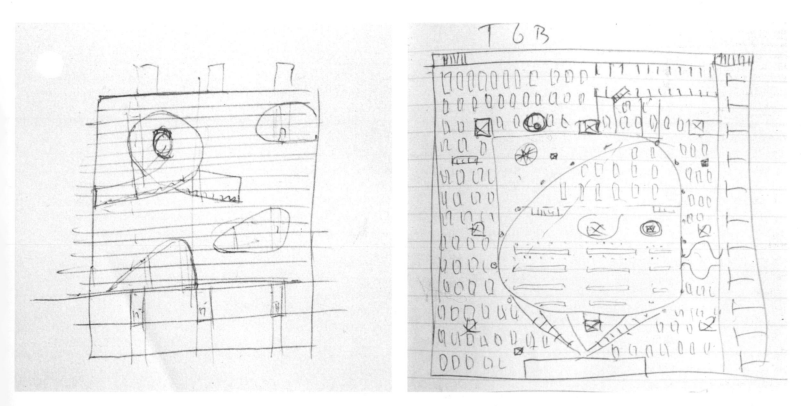

# KISHO KUROKAWA

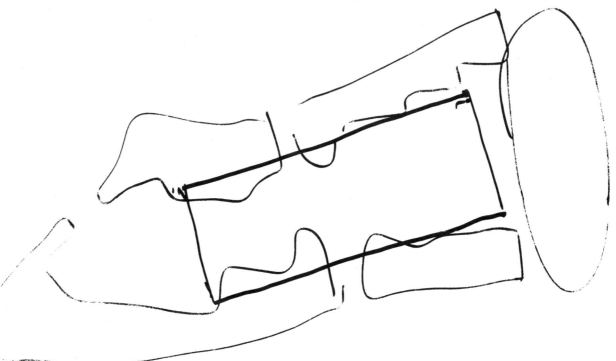

**T**he Japanese equivalent, perhaps, of the New York Five might well have been a group of architects known as Metabolists who surrounded Kenzo Tange as their leader in the early sixties. They derived their name from the fact that their designs grew organically or metabolically from the architectural and urban planning problems to be solved. Their proposals were large-scale highly imaginative schemes to accommodate the post–World War II urban and national dilemma that beset Japan. The group consisted of Tange, Maki, and Kurokawa, among others, and like the New York Five, the paths of these architects merged together around a philosophy that seemed agreeable at the time but which diverged sharply over the years. Each, while acknowledging that earlier youthful fling at solving large problems with inventive schemes, has settled into an architectural practice that reflects his own individual approach.

Kurokawa was once known primarily for a small avant-garde building in the heart of the Ginza district that was the equivalent of the Monsanto Plastic House at Disneyland. It predicted an industrial designed world with a habitat for that future. A transit hotel with ocular windows and rooms that resembled an elegant ocean-liner stateroom, it was a state-of-the-art technological proclamation.

Since that time Kurokawa, one of the most ambitious and prolific architects of our time, has fashioned a career of extraordinary dimensions. Since graduating from Kyoto University in 1957, he has received numerous awards and commissions for major buildings in Japan and throughout the world. He has also published a number of books, and in Bulgaria in 1989 he was awarded the Grand Prix Gold Medal (sponsored by the Union of International Architects) for his Hiroshima City Museum of Contemporary Art.

Kurokawa is an architect who, unlike Mies van der Rohe, is not content to let his buildings speak for themselves and has written extensively on the principles which underscore his design philosophy. His primary tenet is that modern architecture in this century has been dominated by Western thought and reason. Kurokawa contends that the modern architecture movement "sought an internationalism, a universalism that transcended its own personalities and regional characteristics." The next generation, according to him, will witness the following:

Symbolism will replace Analysis,
Deconstruction will replace
 Structuring,
Quotation will replace introduction,
Intermediation will replace
 synthesis,
Transformation will replace
 adaptation,
Sophistication will replace
 clarification,
and Connotation will replace
 denotation.

Kurokawa believes that modern architecture is the child of the industrial age and that Postmodern architecture, an architecture of the information age, will be characterized by variety and multiplicity, and will seek to instill and evoke new meanings in architecture. His thesis for a new architecture that follows the modern period is specific. Although he states that his design philosophy is grounded in the Edo Period (17th–19th centuries), one would be hard pressed to confirm that by viewing his streamlined, futuristic buildings—the most recent example being the art museum in Hiroshima City. The museum is a gleaming jewel, with its metal-clad roofs of shimmering aluminum set in a linear arrangement along a wooded ridge of Hijuyama Cultural Park.

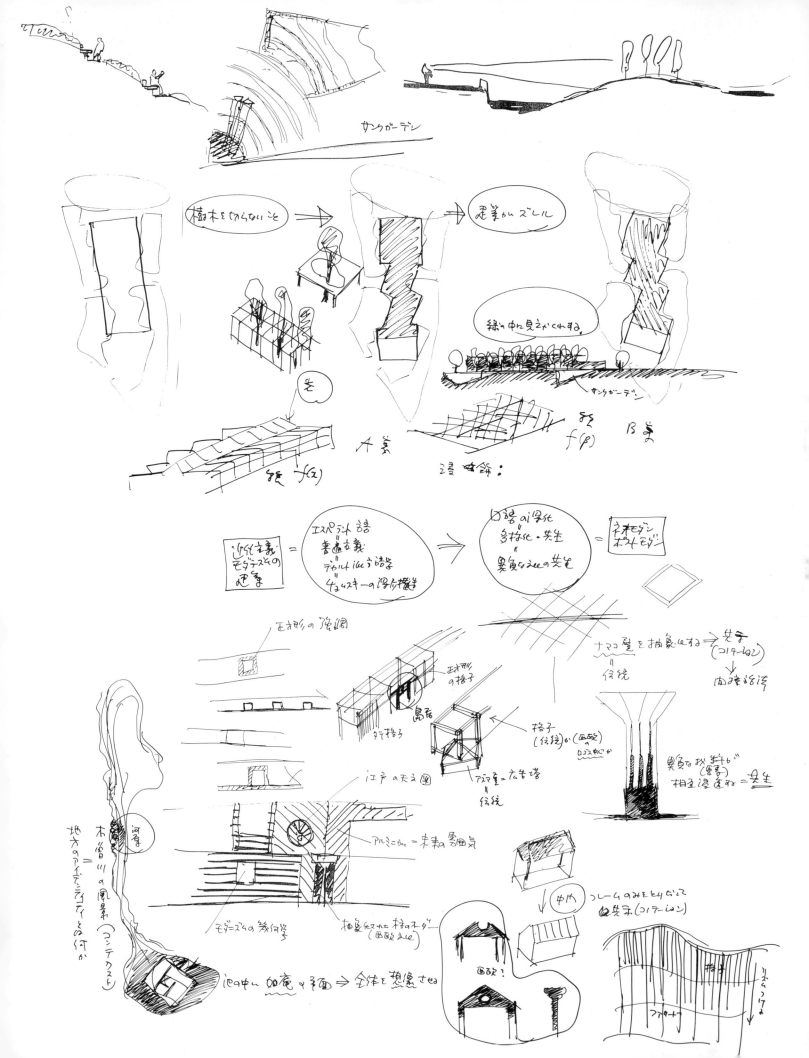

# RICARDO LEGORRETA

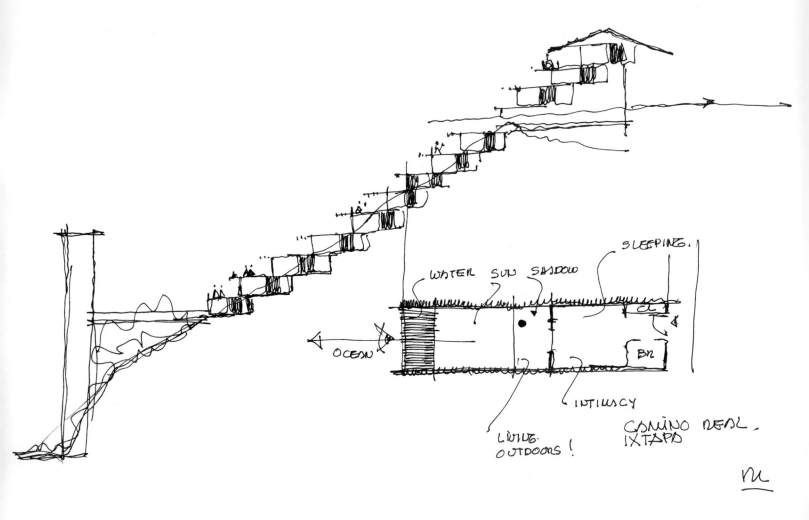

At one time, Luis Barragán stood for Mexican architecture. Since his death in 1988 that position has been increasingly assumed by one of his most devoted admirers, Ricardo Legorreta. Legorreta's work falls within the proud Mexican heritage of open spatial forms, bold colors, and striking silhouettes. Like Barragán, Legorreta is also skillful at making buildings relate to the elemental nature of things. Water, sun, light, and the texture of earth are important ingredients in his architecture. One never feels far from nature in a Legorreta building.

What first brought Legorreta to the attention of the international architectural press were his excellent designs for Camino Real hotels in Mexico—at Cancun, Mexico City, and Ixtapa. In these buildings he firmly established Mexican architecture, according to Anthony Antoniades, as an "architecture of walls" and himself as an architect able to incorporate native Mexican values and forms without demeaning them by imitation.

In his subsequent hotels and recent U.S. projects, Legorreta showed, among other things, his ability to comfortably accommodate and incorporate landscape and sculpture. At IBM in Southlake, Texas, a new satellite suburb of Dallas, Legorreta used bright, exterior colors to give a distinctive, psychedelic presence on the rural horizon. Unlike the typical suburban scattering of discrete buildings on individual sites, IBM follows an urbane, integrated plan. Legorreta also designed the bridges and underpasses leading to the building, as well as a dramatic outdoor plaza. The building itself is a low multijointed entity with oversized stucco walls, small mullionless windows, and interior courtyards. Even the parking—arranged in covered outdoor spaces and garages massed to create public spaces—has character.

CAMINO REAL HOTEL, IXTAPA, MEXICO. 1981
MEDIUM: PEN, PENCIL, COLORED MARKERS

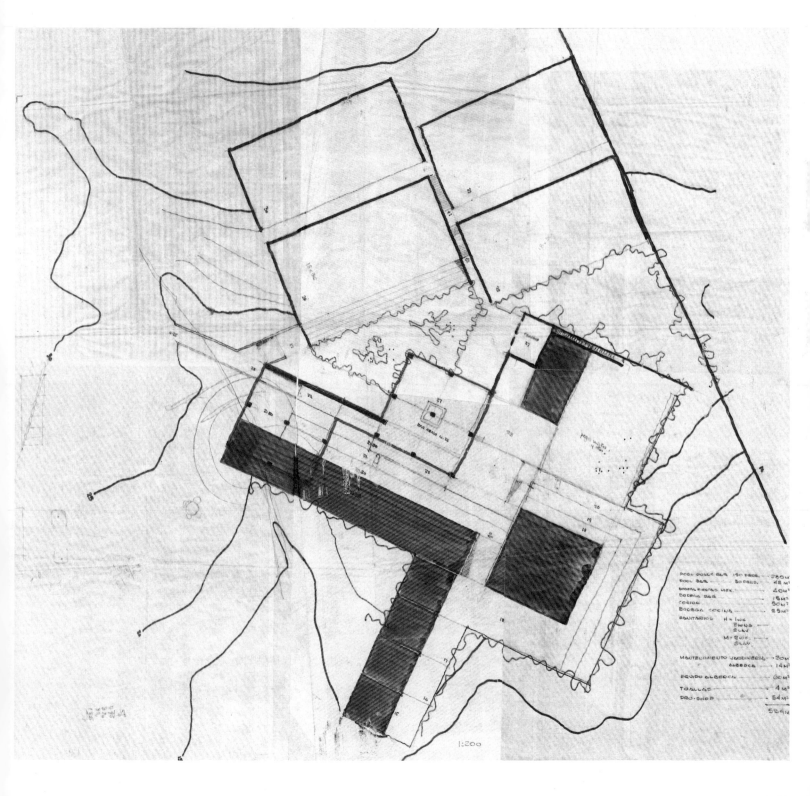

143

# DANIEL LIBESKIND

CITY EDGE PROJECT, BERLIN, GERMANY
SCHEDULED FOR COMPLETION 1992
MEDIUM: INK AND PENCIL ON PAPER

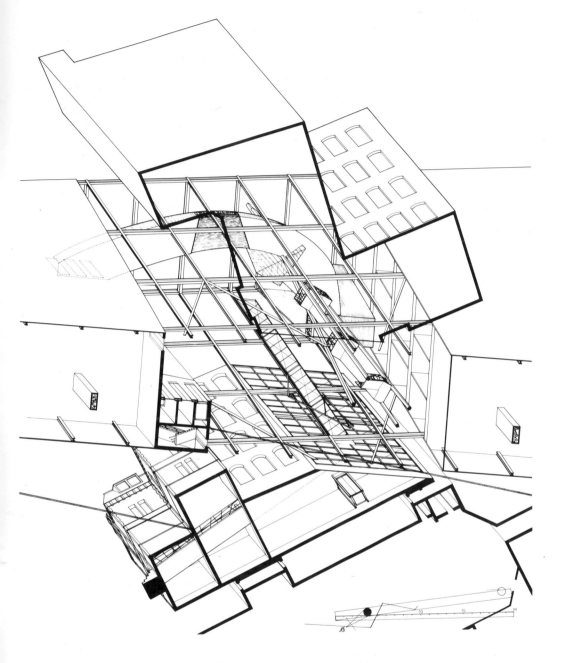

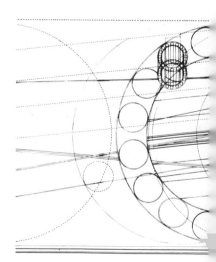

**D**aniel Libeskind is, like his drawings, complex, intriguing, and something of a conundrum. To gaze into one of Libeskind's drawings is to peer into the labyrinth of the human intellect and its ability for artful expression. Vézelay describes Libeskind's drawings as being "beyond the reality of Cubism, constructivism or collage, close to the horizon where most of the non-figurative movements of this century fought their last battles and where our imagination is permanently challenged by the inner possibilities of abstraction." Pallasmaa likens his compositions to an "architectural Milky Way" and his former teacher and long-time associate John Hejduk sees "a dance of cacophonic geometries" and "a profound new vision."

The architect who evokes such poetic and enthusiastic descriptions of his work is one of the younger generation of architects who achieved early recognition as head of the architecture department at Cranbrook Academy of Art, who served as visiting professor at many of the major universities around the world, and who, although having no body of built work, has been widely published and critically acclaimed in professional journals. Libeskind, like other precursors of architectural styles such as Louis Kahn and Le Corbusier, has captured in his drawings the possibilities for an architecture that will now move from the theoretical and visionary to the real during the decade of the nineties. Current commissions in Berlin, Osaka, and Groningen will take his intriguing two-dimensional ideas into a built reality.

In his own words, Daniel Libeskind "attempts to deal with architecture in an analytic, interpretive, symbolic, and non-representational manner." He does not follow the easy path of cyclical fashions in the field, each one replacing the other, only to be later replaced. His keen interest in music and mathematics is reflected in his search through architectural drawings and philosophy for a new approach that lies beyond the present boundaries of tradition and convention.

The exquisite chaos of Libeskind's early drawings, like the conceptual sketches of other architects, are the forerunners in visual thinking of the architecture that will follow.

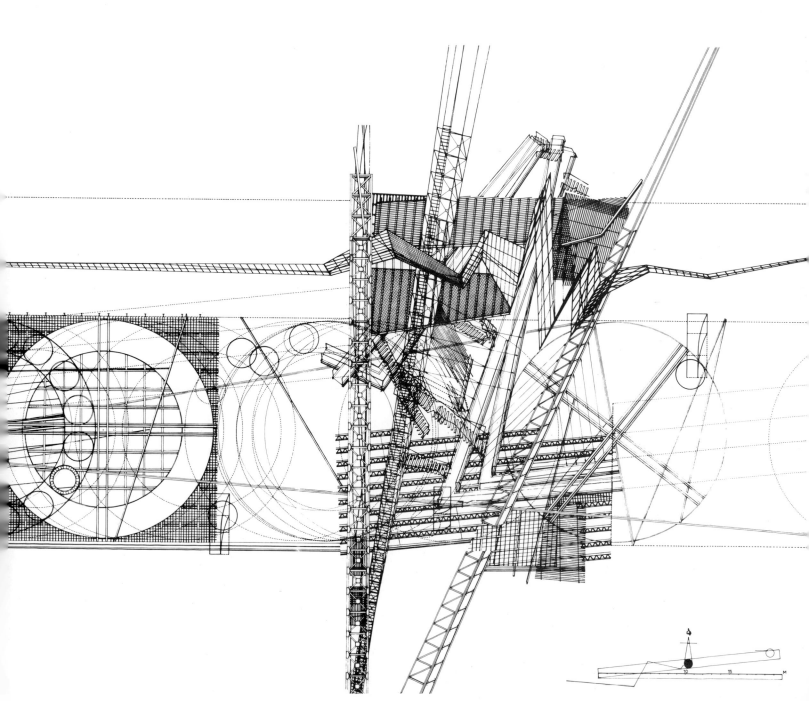

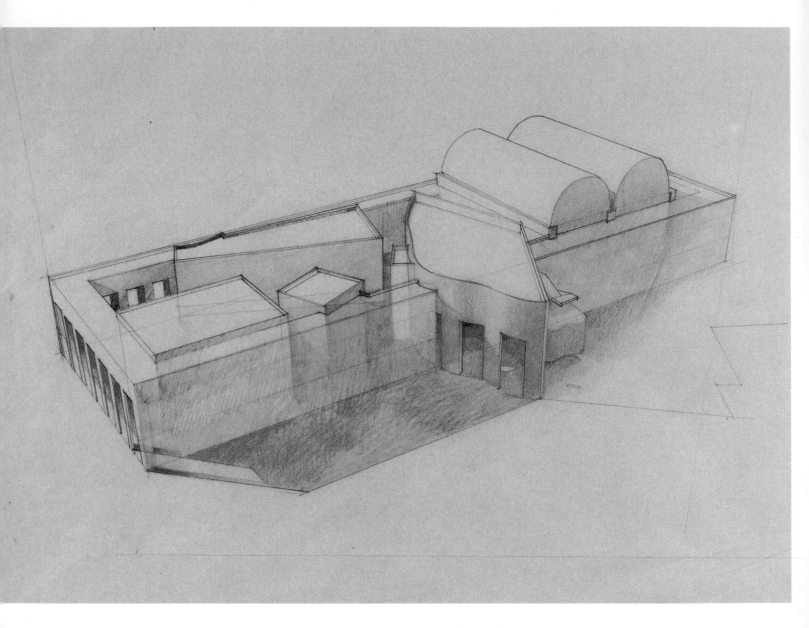

**A**rchitects in some respects are like conductors of symphony orchestras. To be successful in achieving their goal they must be concerned about the performances of a variety of persons on their staff. The "name" partner (and usually only the one who does the actual "designing" of the building if there is more than one partner in the firm) receives most of the public and peer recognition. But there are draftsmen, delineators, code and specification experts, production detail staff, and an array of consultants on mechanical, structural, and electrical matters. In large-scale or special projects, this phalanx behind "the architect" for the project increases further to include acousticians, lighting engineers, transportation and civil engineers, city planners, landscape and interiors experts. The realization of architecture of quality is a complex business and art.

One architect who has gained a reputation for his work with and belief in the team approach for the design of projects is William Lim. Singapore-born, educated at the Architectural Association in London and at Harvard, Lim believes firmly that "the idea of the so-called master architect is dead." Instead he has fashioned a successful practice that relies on group dynamics and participation in which team members (usually four to eight) design a project through an interactive criticism process. Under Lim's system all members of the design team are equal, and all bear the responsibility and the credit for the solution to design problems, which more often than not are concerned with housing environments and other socially relevant projects. Lim is a personally committed outspoken advocate for improving the urban environment of the Third World, and his buildings reflect that concern.

**TAMPINES COMMUNITY CENTER, SINGAPORE, 1989**
**MEDIUM: COLORED PENCIL ON PAPER**
**DRAWINGS BY LIM CHENG KOOI**

# MARK MACK

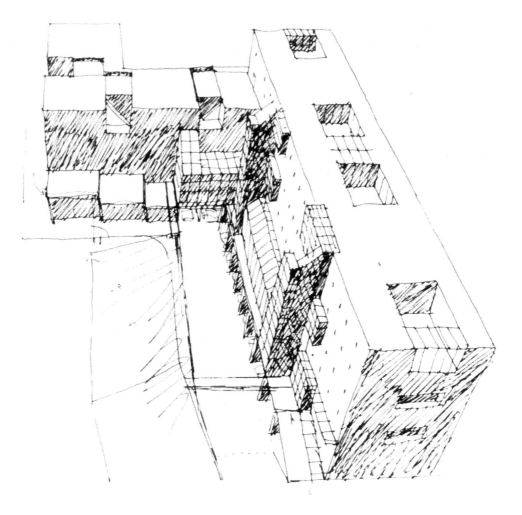

Over the years California has been a major breeding ground for avant-garde architecture in the United States. Among the recently emerging talent is the Austrian-born and -educated architect Mark Mack, whose work is distinguished by its clarity of form, simplicity of construction, and appreciation of tradition, climate, and materials. Aspects of Mack's early work have been described as "investigations into primitivism." As his architecture has matured, it has gained recognition as being "simple in plan and straightforward in form" and "an honest expression of structure and construction that emphasizes the inherent integrity of real materials."

Often residential architecture allows for a true expression of one's style. While the design for the Gebhart house perched on a hill above Sausalito, California, aimed to fulfill the owner's request for something "constructivist and monumental but at a modest scale," it also allowed Mack an opportunity to experiment with rugged forms in the landscape, one of the basic tenets of his work. As explained by Karen D. Stein in *Architectural Record* (1988),

"Mack modified a standard gabled roof by scalloping one corrugated metal edge. He then purposely exaggerated the thickness of the resulting curved street facade by splaying all openings. Smoked-glass panes within Mack's grid of windows further screen the interior." To take advantage of magnificent views of Sausalito and the Golden Gate Bridge, Mack placed the living and dining rooms and kitchen on the upper level. Overall, the house appears as an intricate geometry of intersecting roof planes.

In another more recent project, this one in Fukuoka, Japan, Mack demonstrates his ability to transpose his knowledge of single-family residential requirements into multiple-unit housing. Mack was invited, along with six other architects of international reputation, to design a project for this new development in the Kashii District. In arriving at the interlocking design Mack studied ways to create private and public zones with rising flats, duplexes, and a courtyard house. The final solution is both ingenious and entirely livable with its small sunny plaza, intimate spaces, and honest use of materials.

**KASHI DISTRICT HOUSING, FUKUOKA, JAPAN. 1989**
**MEDIUM: PEN AND INK**

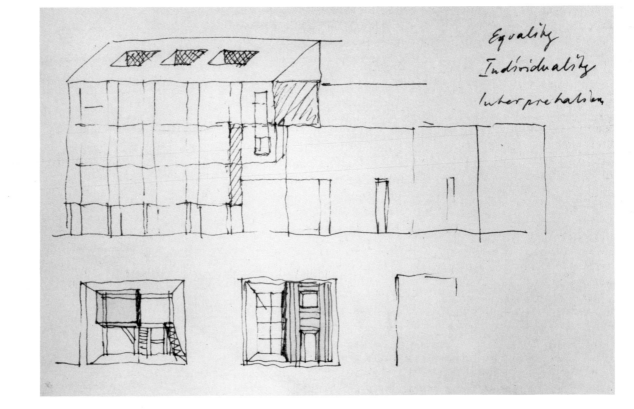

Equality
Individuality
Interpretation

# FUMIHIKO MAKI

Of the group of Japanese architects who rose to international prominence after World War II, Fumihiko Maki is the most Westernized. Although he began his education at the University of Tokyo in the design studio of Kenzo Tange, the acknowledged modern master of early post-war Japanese architecture, Maki earned a master's degree in architecture from Harvard. He subsequently spent several years in the United States teaching and designing, and his first completed building is on the Washington University campus in St. Louis.

Maki's architecture is urbane, sophisticated, and precise. His preference in materials has tended in later works toward metal, glass, and concrete composed and detailed with extraordinary skill. Maki has been an empiricist and gradualist, "wary of the one-shot solution," as Tokyo architecture critic Hiroshi Watanabe wrote.

Maki was a founding member, in 1960, of the Metabolists, an association of visionary planners who captured the design world's attention with imaginative, large-scale urban designs based on natural organic growth. Despite this interest in huge structures, his buildings are not "megastructures," a word Maki invented and introduced into our lexicon. His gigantic Nippon Convention Center in Tokyo, for instance, shows how a huge building can possess qualities missing in the vast megastructures of the modernist years. The center's organization is modeled on the prototypical Japanese community nestled among hills and was intended to set the tone and direction for future urban growth in the area. Its vast volume and distinctive silhouette becomes a man-made mountain range in an otherwise flat, waterfront topography. The facility is organized along a central spine nearly one-third of a mile long and its vast exhibition hall is covered with a curved roof. But these elements are designed as background forms for a diversity of human-scaled components.

**FUJISAWA MUNICIPAL GYMNASIUM, FUJISAWA, JAPAN. 1984**
**MEDIUM: INK ON TRACING PAPER**

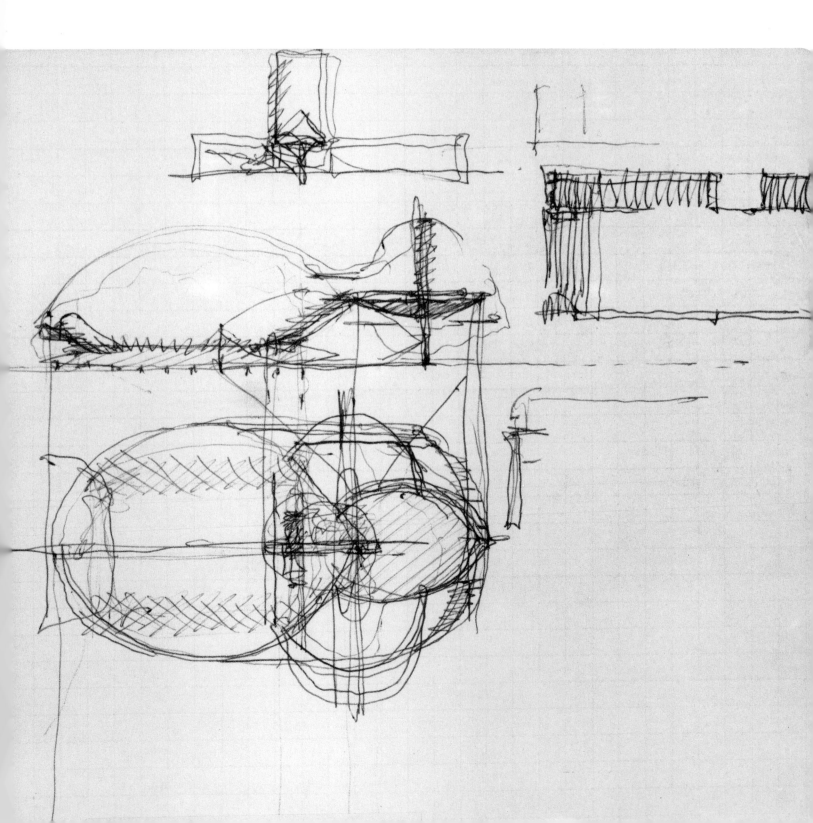

# IMRE MAKOVECZ

Imre Makovecz spearheaded the rise of a singularly fertile regional approach to architecture in Pecs, Hungary. Expressing national roots and consisting of buildings with local flavor, Makovecz's architecture was a reaction to the anonymous, bland modernism of Hungary's government-run, post—World War II architectural bureaus, which disregarded local context and nearly destroyed the historic Hungarian village and town. It is Makovecz's conviction that "architecture that is not born out of local inspiration may be outstanding in volume and space, may be elegant, may be good art, may be anything, but it cannot be a vital influence in our cultural life." In addition to showing the influence of local forms, scale, and materials, Makovecz's churches and civic buildings show the influence of Hungarian folk art, of Makovecz's fascination for the philosophy of Rudolph Steiner's anthroposophy, and of such "organic" architects as Gaudí, Aalto, Wright, Goff, Herbert Greene, and the Dutch and German expressionists.

In his search for organic solutions, Makovecz progressed from the use of interior concrete columns that become wood members branching out and growing into space like live trees to the use of actual trees as supports. An example is his farm restaurant in Visegrad of 1980, designed as an ages-old Hungarian farm organized around a central court. With its tentlike structures resembling huddled, helmeted heads of ancient warriors surrounding a central open space, the restaurant shows Makovecz's interest in simple, almost archetypal shapes in wood construction.

Since designing a large community center for the city of Sarospatak in the early 1980s, Makovecz has been commissioned by numerous Hungarian towns to both re-create and add to traditional buildings. His work has also spawned a Pecs school of architecture which includes such increasingly renowned designers as Josef Kerenyi, Sandor Devenyi, Arpad Weiler, and Peter Varnagy. Their work is characterized by a synthesis of forms from the past to create "a thoughtful translation that appears vigorously new while it fits effortlessly into the existing fabric of this old city," writes John Macsai, a Hungarian architect and critic who now works and lives in Chicago.

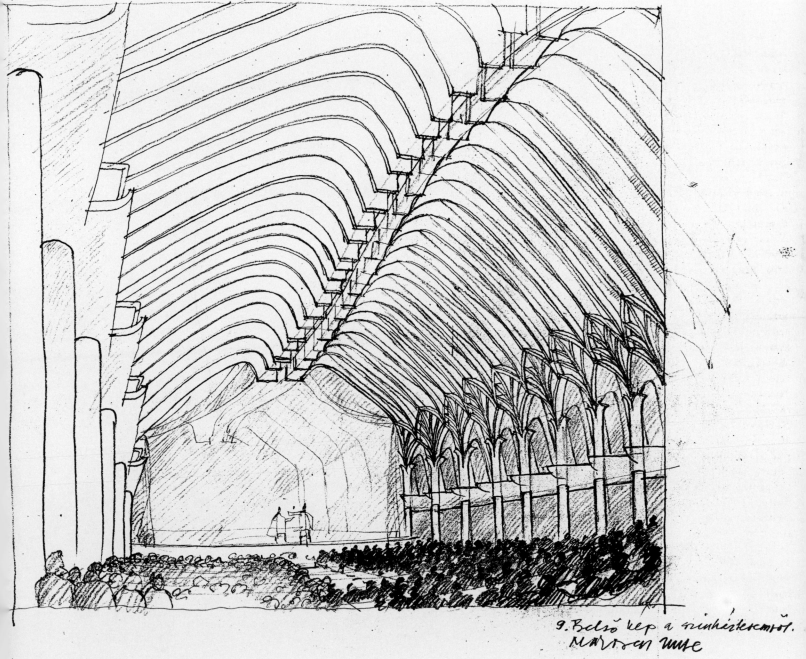

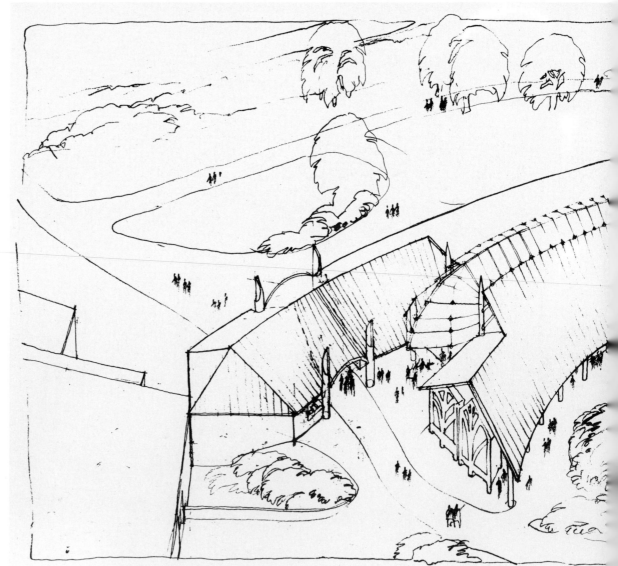

ROMAN CATHOLIC CHURCH, HUNGARY. 1989
MEDIUM: PENCIL

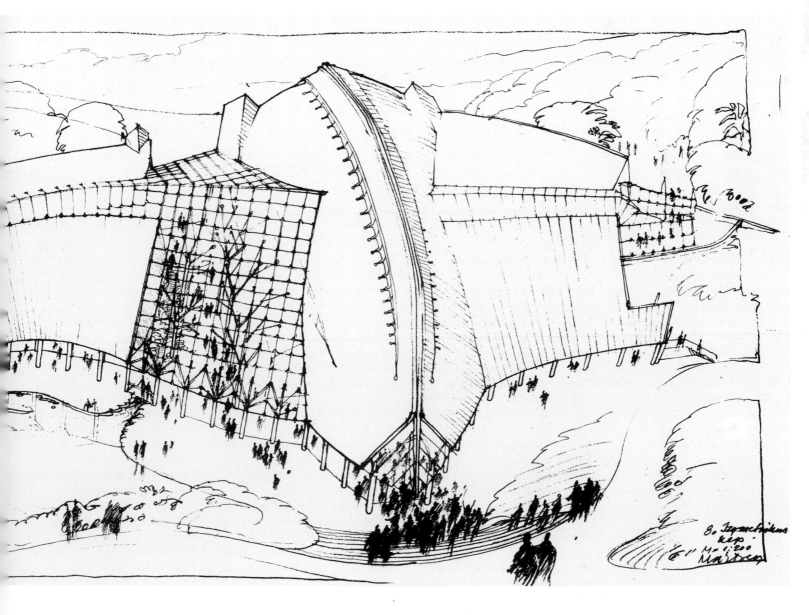

# RICHARD MEIER

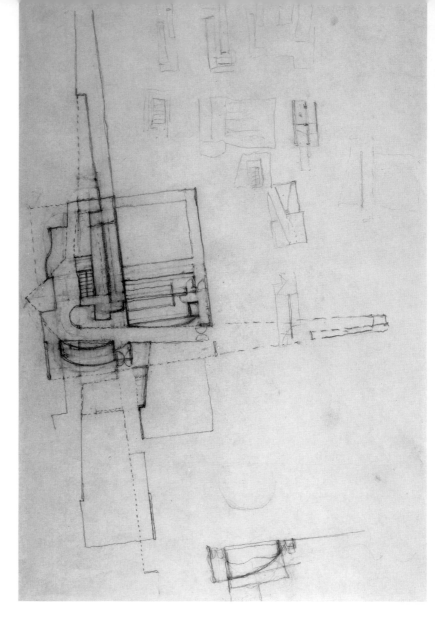

Three architects have dominated the field of contemporary architecture in the twentieth century—Mies van der Rohe, Frank Lloyd Wright, and Le Corbusier. The influence of the latter on Meier is readily acknowledged by him. Meier is that unusual architect who seems to have had a clear and undeviating attitude toward the design of buildings from the moment he established his independent practice in 1963 in New York. His early homes and the most recent projects, while obviously more refined, are clearly by the same hand. There is an awesome consistency in his work, an admirable steadfastness and dedication. The International School, Brutalism, Post-modernism, and other waves of fashion and experimentation of the last twenty years have gone entirely unacknowledged in Meier's work.

Instead there has been the issuance of one striking design after another from the New York office of Richard Meier. Each one white, usually of enameled panels and glass, all of them markedly Neo-Corbusian in form, characterized by the linear play of ramps and handrails. The results are pristine white sculptural pieces accentuated by tables of green lawn, remarkably like one another yet different and never boring—Meier's work is like endless variations on a beautiful theme.

Richard Meier was educated at Cornell University and practiced with a number of capable firms for his apprenticeship, including Skidmore, Owings & Merrill, and Marcel Breuer, but the stamp of individuality on each Meier building is inimitably his own. In 1984, after an exhaustive, painstaking search for an architect for The J. Paul Getty new Art Center in Los Angeles, Meier was selected for this commission of the century—a $500 million cultural campus with an extraordinary mission in the arts, to be located on a commanding promontory above the city. To accomplish this mammoth undertaking of design and engineering Meier has opened a West Coast office and divides his time between the two locations. The Getty project presented a challenge as few others have in this century. Its site is neither urban nor suburban but it is isolated. High above the San Diego freeway it offers unsurpassed views of the city of Los Angeles and on a clear day the Pacific Ocean. The restructured buildable area atop the ridge, the topography, and the access to the site posed problems more common to European monasteries and hill towns than to a campus for a modern urban institution. Meier, working in his characteristic fashion of models at small scale gradually evolving to larger and larger simulations, has successfully brought into equilibrium the forces of site, program, budget, and image.

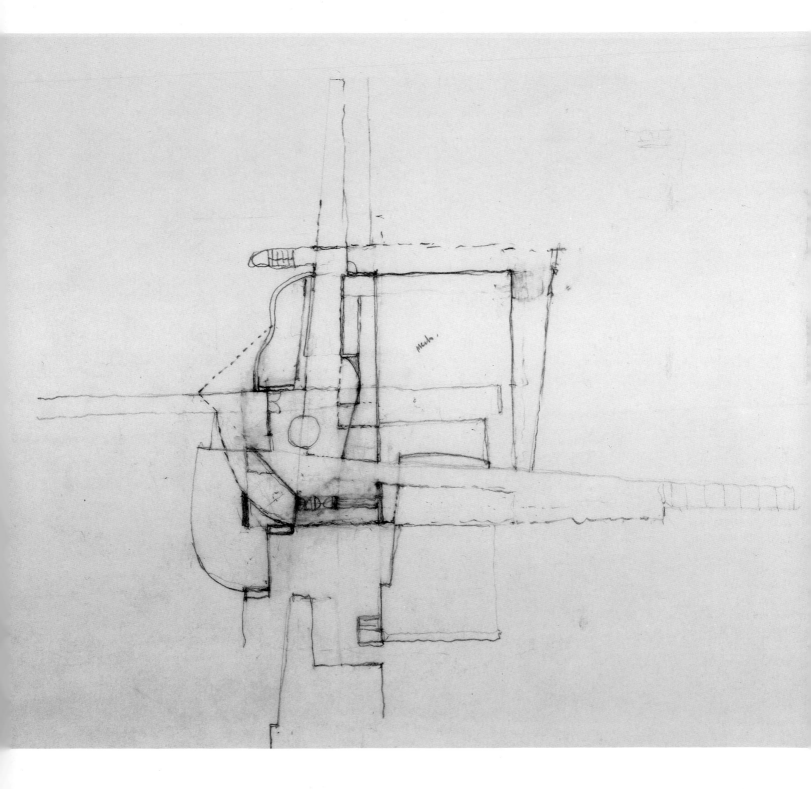

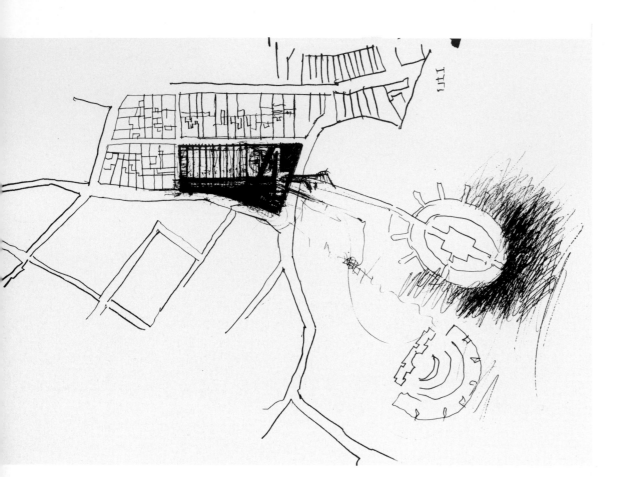

**S**panish architect José Rafael Moneo at the age of fifty-three has reached a pinnacle in his career. He has created a truly magnificent building in Spain, the National Museum of Roman Art, which brings his mature architectural tenets to the fore. He is also deeply involved in the academic world, having been appointed chairman of the Department of Architecture at the Harvard Graduate School of Design. For the National Museum of Roman Art in Mérida, Spain, Moneo has created a building in dialogue with its context and its contents. It is a "building of integrity and presence that will be cherished beyond any changes in its functions or in prevailing fashions," wrote British architecture critic Peter Buchanan.

The museum is sympathetic both to ancient and modern times. Its scale, materials, and construction methods are similar to those of Roman buildings. Yet with three separate zones connected by a longitudinal axis, the building offers contemporary facilities for the museum, auditorium, and administrative offices. At the lowest level are actual Roman ruins that intermix with Moneo's structure, creating a sense of timelessness. On the first level, a corridor of massive arches is flooded with natural light from the monitors set high along one gallery wall.

As an educator, Moneo decries what he calls "ephemeral" architecture. His inaugural speech at Harvard addressed this point:

Is architecture today no longer able to endure as it did in the past? In today's architecture does there exist the sensation that works are perishable? I think these answers must be answered affirmatively. Architects should realize that architecture is a complex reality including many presences. . . . All presences should be acknowledged in the design operation, in order to avoid the reduction that always distorts architectural reality. This should be the key with which the architect condenses disparity into the single self-supported presence of buildings. When architects realize that a building masters its own life, their approach to design is different. It changes radically. Our personal concerns become secondary and the final reality of the building becomes the authentic aim of our work.

13

**NATIONAL MUSEUM OF ROMAN ART,
MÉRIDA, SPAIN. 1980
MEDIUM: PENCIL ON PAPER**

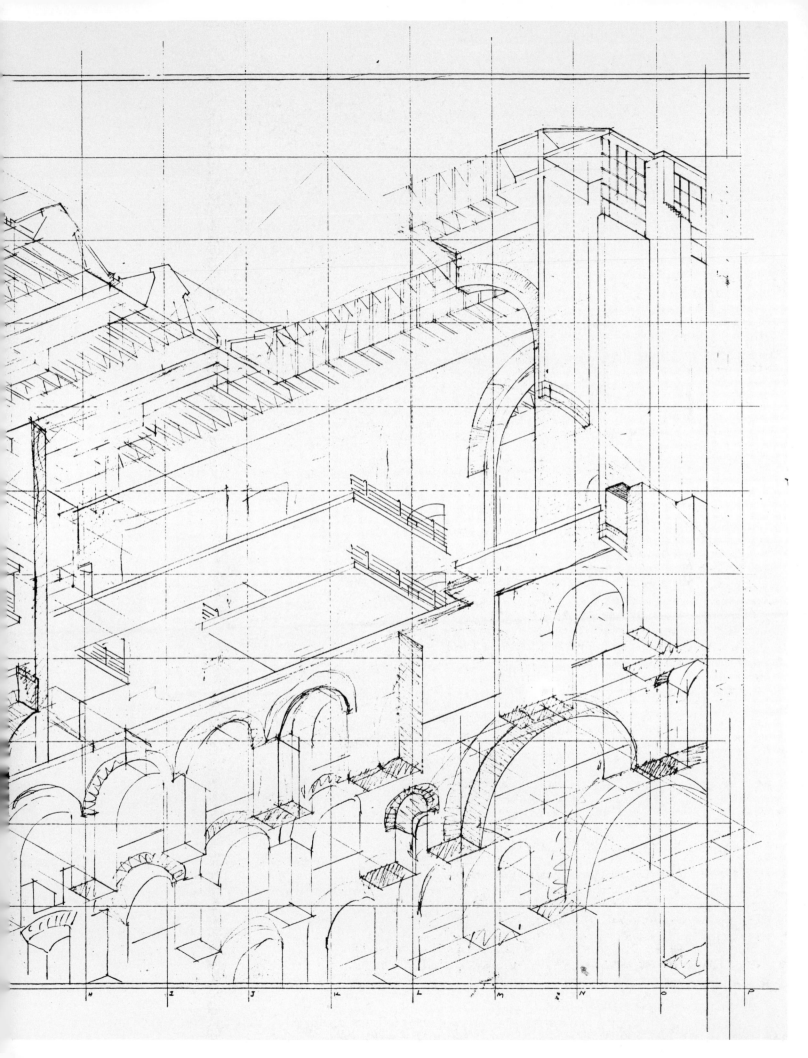

# ARTHUR COTTON MOORE

**S**ome architects become
identified with their hometowns
even though their practices range
considerably beyond those
boundaries. Arthur Cotton
Moore is very involved with the
city in which his offices are
located—Washington, D.C.

Moore has been an active
spokesman in the nation's capital
on behalf of architecture and
urban planning, writing criticism
for both *Washingtonian* magazine
and *The Washington Post* in an
attempt to raise the reading
public's appreciation of the
profession. And he puts the
theories he espouses into
practice as an architect and a
developer. His Canal Square
project transformed colonial and
staid Georgetown, a strategic and
historic Washington district
fronting the Potomac, into a vital
shopping quarter of the city and
set the architectural standard
for the future development of
the area.

While he resists the label of preservationist, his renovation of the Old Post Office on Pennsylvania Avenue is clear evidence of his interest in saving and utilizing older structures in the urban fabric. Now called The Nancy Hanks Center (named for the woman who insisted it be saved, the late Nancy Hanks, chairman of the NEA whose headquarters it now is), this once-decrepit and condemned building is today one of the most vital stones in the necklace of buildings along the nation's "Main Street," which stretches from the White House to the U.S. Capitol. The building's interior with its 12-story-high glass-roofed atrium has been brought to animated new life by Moore and serves as an example for all those who work to give old buildings a purpose in contemporary society.

# CHARLES MOORE

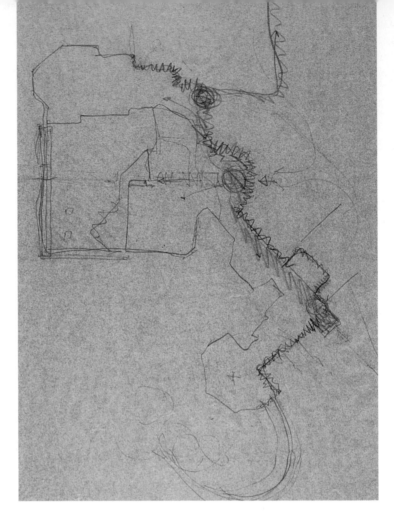

It is a striking characteristic of architects that many of those in the top ranks of the profession feel a need to teach. More than lawyers or doctors, perhaps, full-time practicing architects can be found on faculties of major universities and many of them serve long stints as department chairmen and deans. There is something about the calling to design buildings that is almost religious. This fervent attitude to educate, indoctrinate, "preach," seems to be ingrained in architects. It is observable even in the educational system in the colleges, when senior students teach the initiates and the entire process is modeled after the French atelier or studio tradition where apprentices learn by emulating, being criticized by, and executing designs of the master architects. Among the ranks of revered professors and mentors who have headed schools and who influence

generations of younger architects by their teachings, writings, and examples, no one is more highly regarded than Charles Moore.

Charles Willard Moore stands out even in an increasingly peripatetic profession in terms of the time he spends on airplanes en route to all points of the earth lecturing and tending to his far-flung commissions. He has been a moving target as well in his parallel career in academia, having been a professor at the University of California at Berkeley, Yale University, University of California at Los Angeles, and University of Texas at Austin. His various associations in practice complete the picture of an architect who says yes to almost every opportunity whether it is a building, an exhibition, a book, or a deanship. He has practiced as Moore-Lyndon-Turnbull-Whitaker; Moore Grover Harper, Essex; and Moore Ruble Yudel. Unlike most architects who work hard to establish their name as

the "sole proprietor," Moore has always been willing to share the credit in the interest of getting the job done.

Moore is described by one critic as being the leader of a dissident movement in architecture, and he has been criticized by fellow architects for what they consider a frivolous attitude toward architecture. It is true that he has "incited" several generations of students, beginning with classes at Yale where he was dean in the rebellious 1960s, when he advised them to go forth and build some shocking small-scale projects and bypass the traditional deadening apprenticeship in established architects' offices. But Moore, the architect, author, lecturer, and wry philosopher seems hardly suited for the role of dissident. He resembles more nearly puckish critics whose views of architecture are too limiting and who take themselves and their work too seriously.

Make no mistake, however; Moore is very serious about what he does, even when that seriousness is expressed in a playful manner. He is a thoughtful unreconstructed philosopher whose buildings are informed by an understanding of history. He neither follows tradition nor mocks it, but skillfully incorporates what has gone before into his own special blend of new and engaging design ideas. Although the first twenty years of his practice (1957–77) consisted primarily of residences (including the famous Sea Ranch enclave in California), his commissions now include libraries, museums, and housing developments.

Moore's sketches are fascinating to watch in process, being a kind of nervous squiggling that magically at some point becomes translatable as floor plans, sections cut through a building, or site diagrams. The drawings, like the man, are at once zestful and profound.

**TRINOVA WORLD HEADQUARTERS, TOLEDO, OHIO. 1984**
**MEDIUM: LITHOGRAPH PENCIL AND WATERCOLOR**

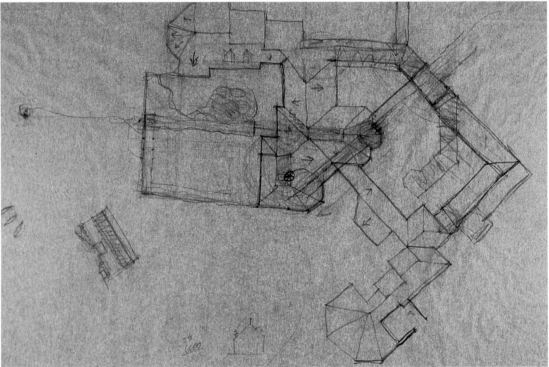

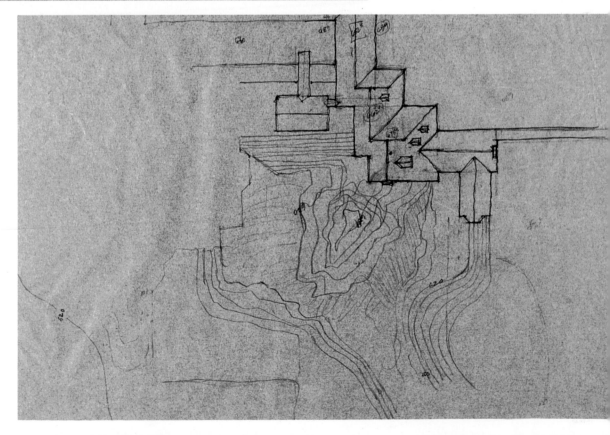

# MORPHOSIS
# THOM MAYNE, MICHAEL ROTONDI

**C**ontemporary architecture on the West Coast of the United States and especially in the Los Angeles area seemed to come of age in the eighties. Whereas before there had only been Frank Gehry and his idiosyncratic work, there now were a number of architects whose work was not just "promising" but had matured into noteworthy, substantial representations of this rich and varied culture. Among them, the firm of Morphosis ("to be in formation") consisting of two partners, Thom Mayne and Michael Rotondi, is the most prominent. Gehry, Morphosis, and others of the LA persuasion sought to make an architecture that was truly representative of their unique, somewhat rootless culture, an architecture that eschewed the normal bounds of traditional forms and materials. Gehry's own house in 1977 became, as Fritz Neumeyer correctly stated, a kind of "architectonic manifesto" outside the "limiting dualism of modern and post modern." And

Morphosis's two restaurants, 72 Market Street and Kate Mantilini, provided an additional page to Gehry's "manifesto."

Their work has been described by them as "concretizing the ephemerality of feeling" and by George Rand as architecture in which "the resultant ensemble has a slightly detached character, like the awkward stance of a body dancing backwards struggling to maintain equilibrium while preventing itself from falling."

Mayne and Rotondi's work is often difficult to decipher and demands dialogue with its users; nowhere is this more evident than in their Golf Club project in Chiba, Japan, which seeks to bring a new dimension to the synthesis of building and the natural landscape incorporating the movements of the sport into the flow of the architectural solution. The basic elements of the scheme—curved wall, secondary circular wall, pavilion, and grounds—are clearly stated in the earliest sketch of the complex.

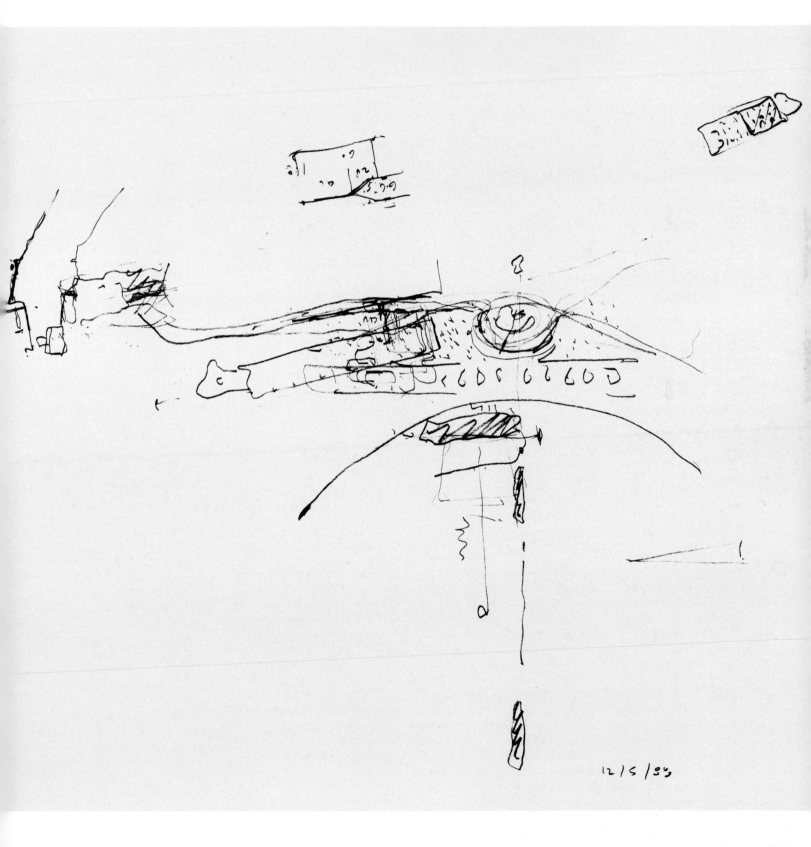

12/5/93

# OSCAR NIEMEYER

Oscar Niemeyer's career spans the twentieth century. He was born in the first decade of the century (1907) and he continues to work productively and creatively into the last with projects on the boards for São Paulo and other locations. His place in history will be forever linked with that of Le Corbusier, the great modern master of France, not because of a long association but because Niemeyer's work seemed to be the will of the master. The major project of his lifetime was Brasilia, the national capital of Brasil, and although it was not Le Corbusier's hand on the drawing board it was clear that his spirit guided its conception and execution. The two met first in 1936 when Niemeyer was a young apprentice architect in the office of the highly respected South American architect and city planner, Lúcio Costa. He was assigned to help the great French architect with the Ministry of Education and Health building in Rio de Janeiro. It was the beginning of a path that would lead to the name of Oscar Niemeyer becoming synonymous with South American contemporary architecture. In 1988 this was confirmed by the Nobel equivalent in architecture, the Pritzker Architecture Prize. In presenting the medal the jury said, "Niemeyer's buildings are the distillation of the colors and light and sensual imagery of his native Brazil. His is an architecture of artistic gesture with underlying logic and substance."

As South America's leading architect, Niemeyer has fulfilled the promise borne from the earlier major commission to design Brasília. In that project, he designed the Supreme Court Building, the presidential offices, the cathedral and the chapel, the Congress Buildings, and the artful Alvorada Palace where the president resides. Niemeyer was a political refuge from the years of 1960 to 1968 after his political patron Kubitschek resigned; he did not see his buildings at Brasília completed until his return to Brazil in 1970.

Although Niemeyer's career was intertwined with Le Corbusier and Kubitschek, the president of Brazil, his one special talent shows through in all his work, nowhere more purely shown than in the early house for himself in Canoas, just outside Rio de Janeiro in 1953. This curvilinear residence set in the dense tropical greenery has become one of the icons of twentieth-century modern architecture. Niemeyer's house could have been done nowhere but in South America and by no one except this extremely talented and visionary architect.

# JEAN NOUVEL

**S**ince the beginning of his architecture career in the 1970s, Frenchman Jean Nouvel has broken the aesthetic of modernism and Post-modernism to create a stylistic language all his own. He places enormous importance on designing a building harmonious with its surroundings. In the end that building's design may borrow from traditional and nontraditional forms, but its presentation is entirely unique.

Context dictates Nouvel's designs. "Nouvel does not make choices or impose a process ahead of time on any project. On the contrary, it is the site, its circumstances, and other givens that will determine the organization of space, the style, and the mode of expression," according to the French critic Alain de Gourcuff. A certain continuity does emerge, however,

due to several devices that Nouvel uses. He consistently presents an interplay of transparency, shadow, and light. This in turn creates a dialogue between interior and exterior spaces. The use of common materials and elements is another Nouvel trademark— garage doors, metal staircases, industrial glass partitions, even photoelectric cells. Generally, these products are incorporated in a simplistic yet bold, manner. Nouvel also borrows techniques from the movie industry such as montage and superimposition.

A building with one facade made entirely of mechanical oculi operated by photoelectric cells is the project that brought Nouvel international recognition, namely the Institut du Monde Arabe in Paris. Here Nouvel masterly set up two large volumes to create a tension with one another—a long, rectangular crystalline shape and a half-curve that

reaches out to meet the street and river beyond. The photoelectric cells activate apparatus in the window units that automatically open and close in response to light levels. The overall effect is at once highly decorative in a Middle Eastern way and projects state-of-the-art electronics.

In another project, a public housing commission in Nîmes, Nouvel designed spaces thirty percent larger than in comparable buildings by simplifying interior spaces and entranceways. The goal was to build homes where the occupants would feel comfortable. "In the case of public housing," Nouvel told *France*, "some architects have seemed content to remain locked into an austere, gloomy, sinister-looking architecture of reinforced concrete. Modernity has grown sad. We must give it a smile again."

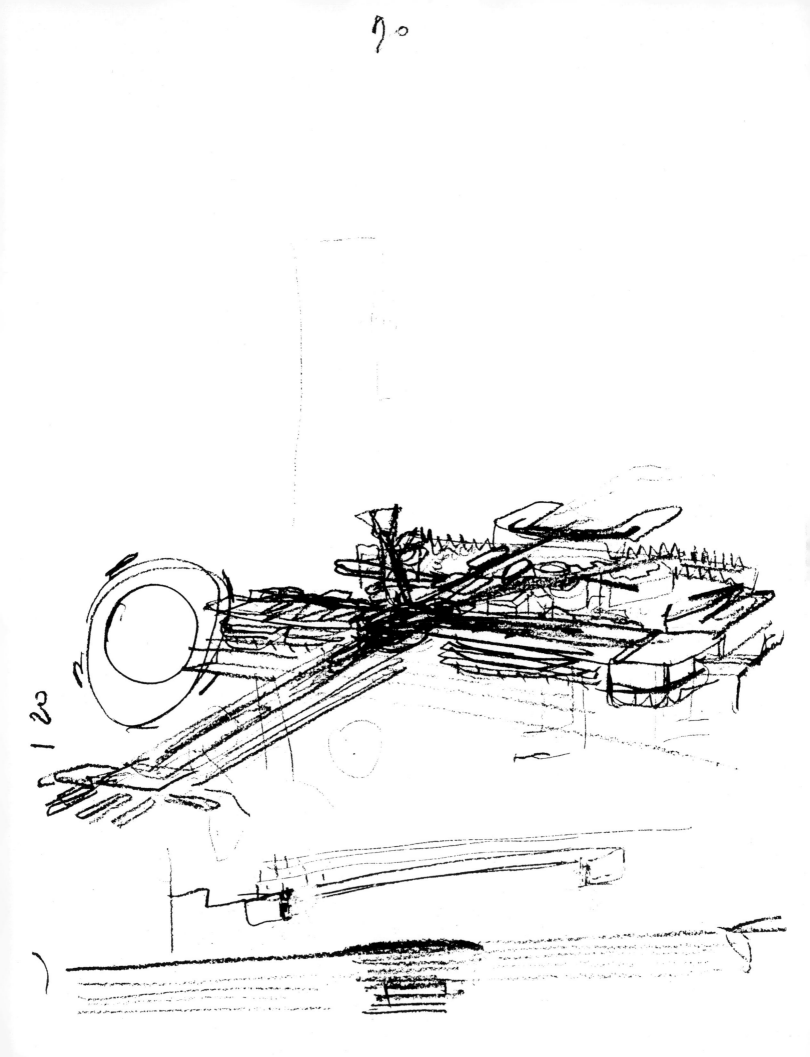

# WILLIAM PEDERSEN

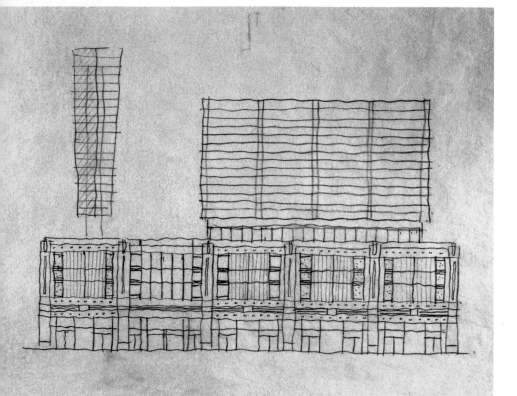

**T**he "P" in KPG (Kohn Pedersen Fox) is William Pedersen, a friendly, unassuming architect from St. Paul, Minnesota. He served an apprenticeship typical of many aspiring, young architects in the 1960s by working in large design firms, including that of I. M. Pei. In 1976, a difficult time for designers, Pedersen took the next step by launching a new firm with partner Eugene Kohn. Pedersen gained almost immediate attention for his design of the studios and offices for ABC television on the west side of Manhattan.

A Post-modernist from the start, Pedersen set the firm's design directions with two widely noticed projects. The first was an office tower at 333 Wacker Drive in Chicago that combines contextualism with theatrical lyricism. The second was the headquarters for Procter & Gamble in Cincinnati, where two octagonal, pyramidally roofed towers and three lower wings perfectly catch the established company's conservative character. Among KPF's current downtown projects is the final, westernmost building for Rockefeller Center in Manhattan. It will be fairly subdued on its Rockefeller Center side, but

pivot in design and display its own decorative lighting on its Times Square side.

KPF's strongly contextual approach tends toward creating literal connections to the past but without relinquishing novelty or intuition. Says Pedersen, "A building can connect to the [urban] fabric, yet have a tremendous individual integrity." As Walter McQuade, formerly of *Fortune*, wrote, KPF "intend their towers to resonate, like Empire State, like Chrysler."

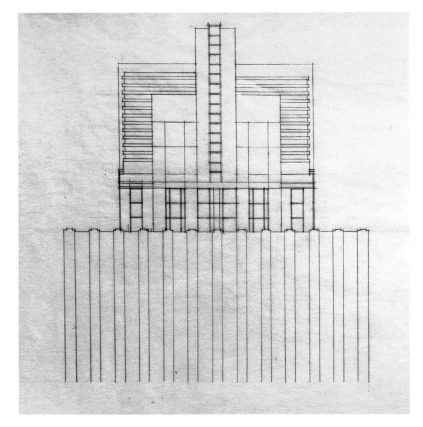

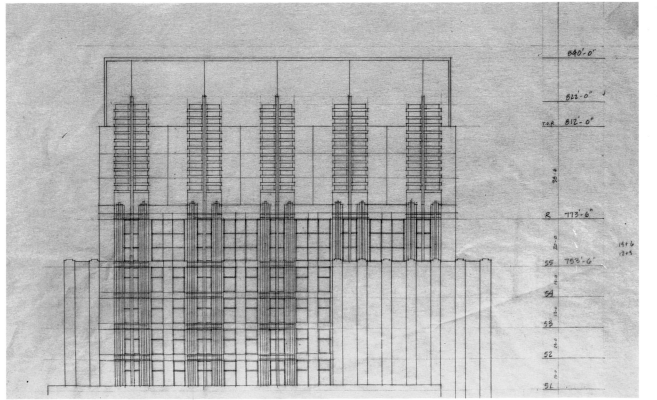

840'-0"

822'-0"

T.O.R. 812'-0"

R 773'-6"

753'-6"

# I. M. PEI

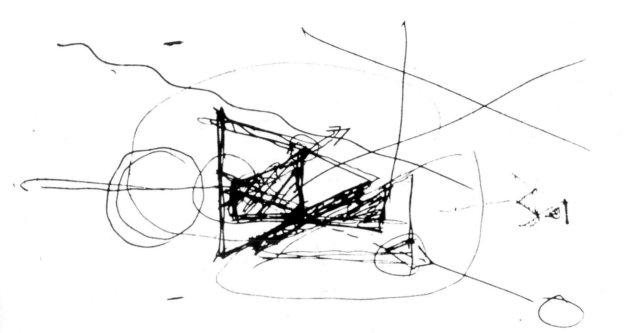

**M**ies van der Rohe, Frank Lloyd Wright, and Le Corbusier dominated the architectural scene for most of this century. The shadow they cast was so great that the idea of successors was rarely raised during their lifetimes. But the mantle must be passed and one of the several architects who moved forcefully into the vacated ranks was Chinese-born I. M. Pei, who studied at MIT and Harvard and went on to become famous for his imaginative design work.

The commencement of World War II was no doubt responsible for the fact that one of this country's naturalized citizens,

and one of the world's greatest architects, did not, upon finishing his studies at MIT in 1940, return to his native China. Instead Ieoh Ming Pei completed his architectural studies at Harvard, studying with two prominent architects—Walter Gropius and Marcel Breuer, both refugees from the war in Europe. It was during these years that Pei's modernist aesthetic sensibilities were formed by exposure to a program that drew heavily on the plain surfaced streamlined dogma of the Bauhaus.

In 1948 Pei left the academic world of Cambridge, Massachusetts, to work as the architect for one of the country's most aggressive and successful real estate developers, William Zeckendorf (the firm name of Webb and Knapp). Pei was thereby able to commence practice designing buildings at a scale few architects beginning their careers could imagine. The chapters of Pei's career are easily categorized. The developer architect of the fifties; the master of concrete forms and composition, expressed most notably in the Everson Museum of Art in Syracuse, New York, and the National Center for

Atmospheric Research in Boulder, Colorado, during the late sixties; and the cultural and corporate architect of choice of the seventies and eighties. Pei was joined by two design partners over time, each to become distinguished architects in his own right—James Freed and Henry Cobb. Eason Leonard, the managing partner, completed the formidable team. The partners could hardly have been more international, or different, in their backgrounds. Pei from China, Leonard from Oklahoma, Freed from Germany, and Cobb from an upper-class Boston family.

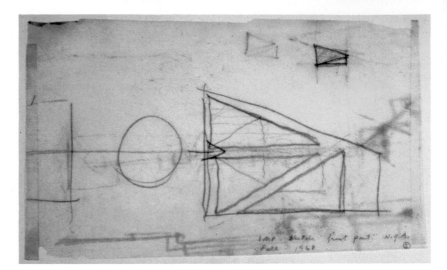

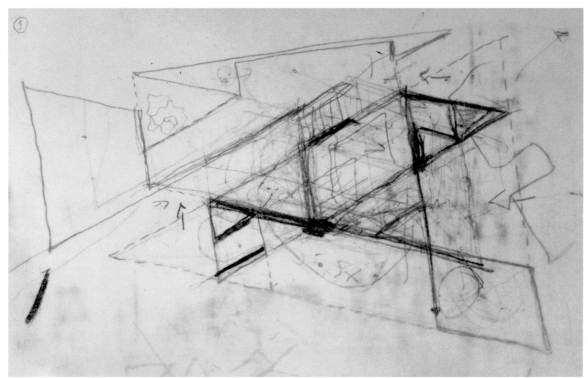

The firm's ascent to their present position as one of the world's most prestigious and successful architectural practices was marred by only one incident, the failure of the curtain wall in Boston's glass-clad John Hancock Tower. The attendant adverse publicity and lawsuits resulting from this event could easily have ended the career of a less dedicated and determined architect. In the end the building proved to be one of the most handsome examples of the art of twentieth-century architecture, and the firm retained its fruitful clientele and hard-won reputation for designing and executing buildings of monumental dignity and precision.

Pei's reputation as the foremost modernist architect of solid, elegant, geometry was further established with the highly acclaimed East Building wing addition to the National Gallery of Art in Washington, D.C., in 1978. With the collaboration of an enlightened client and a prominent site, Pei showed the full range of his artistry in the sensitive use of materials. In a career that seems to accelerate with age, Pei received a cluster of commissions, including the Bank of China Tower in Hong Kong, a 300-room hotel in Beijing, the superb new Morton H. Meyerson Symphony Center in Dallas, and the major renovation of the hallowed Louvre in Paris for the French Government.

It was this latter project with its bold entry pyramid of glass placed squarely in the historic courtyard of the palace that brought Pei forcibly to the attention of the general public. But in some respects the project was in its own way as difficult as the Hancock building. As Pei has said, "My biggest problem was persuading the French public that I was not about to ruin the Louvre museum by constructing a 70-foot-high glass pyramid in the middle of its main square." The pyramid and the expansion of The Louvre is part of an ambitious program of "grand projects" for Paris using architecture as a means for reestablishing the international artistic stature of Paris. President François Mitterand has given France a memorable icon and I. M. Pei a suitable capstone to a brilliant career.

# CESAR PELLI

Though born in Argentina, Cesar Pelli has become fully identified with American architecture. From 1977 to 1984 he was dean of the School of Architecture at Yale University and was winner, in 1988, of the American Institute of Architects Firm Award, the highest prize given by the AIA to an architectural practice. Pelli's firm was selected primarily for its design of the critically acclaimed World Financial Center at Battery Park City, a $4 billion, 92-acre complex of buildings on the southeastern tip of Manhattan.

Pelli's architecture is dignified and substantial-looking, respectful of its surroundings without being conservative; it is friendly, aesthetically pleasing, and precisely executed. For Robert R. Herring Hall and the Ley Student Center, both on the Rice University campus

in Houston, Pelli used contemporary materials, space configurations, and detailing, and still conformed to the tradition of the brick architecture established by Gram Goodhue & Ferguson in the early 1900s. In contrast, at the Pacific Design Center in Los Angeles, Pelli created an audacious urban centerpiece consisting of a glass building, affectionately dubbed the Blue Whale. Used for displaying design products, its commercial success won Pelli the commission for matching green and red "building blocks" to complete the ensemble.

Pelli has said about his approach to urban architecture, "I strongly believe that if we are going to succeed in designing beautiful and coherent cities we, as architects, will have to be able to work within a great variety of design guidelines and constraints, where the individual buildings and vision of each architect will have to yield to the high purpose of the whole and those who are responsible for the whole."

**WORLD FINANCIAL CENTER, NEW YORK CITY. 1987**
**MEDIUM: MARKER ON TRACING PAPER**

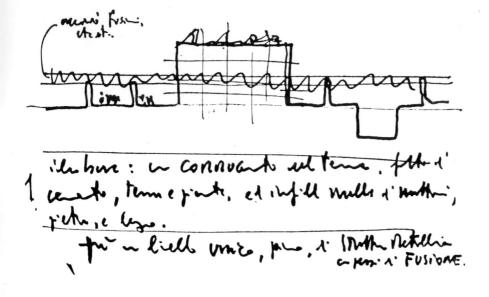

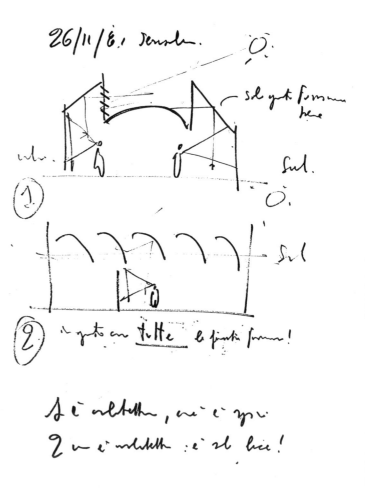

**I**t would be unfair to say that Renzo Piano's reputation was primarily the result of the commission he received from the well-known Houston arts patron Dominique de Menil in 1981 to design the museum for the extensive collections belonging to her and her late husband, industrial magnate John de Menil. It was, however, similar to the commission that a relatively unknown I. M. Pei received from Jacqueline Kennedy to do her slain husband's library; in both instances turning points in the architect's claim on international recognition. Until then Piano was known primarily for his partnership with Richard Rogers and their world-famous design for the Centre Pompidou in Paris in 1978; it was difficult to know precisely the contributions of each to this controversial and successful museum.

The notoriety that attended the opening of the Pompidou tended to blot out Piano's activities immediately following, which included among others, the design of an experimental car for Fiat, a number of housing and urban renewal projects, and large-scale planning exercises. It was the Menil Museum in Houston, however, that brought Piano back to the center stage of architecture and this time, alone.

The de Menils had engaged Louis Kahn to design the museum originally in the 1970s but the deaths of the architect and Mr. de Menil postponed the project for several years during which time Madame de Menil sought the right architect to realize her rather specific goals.

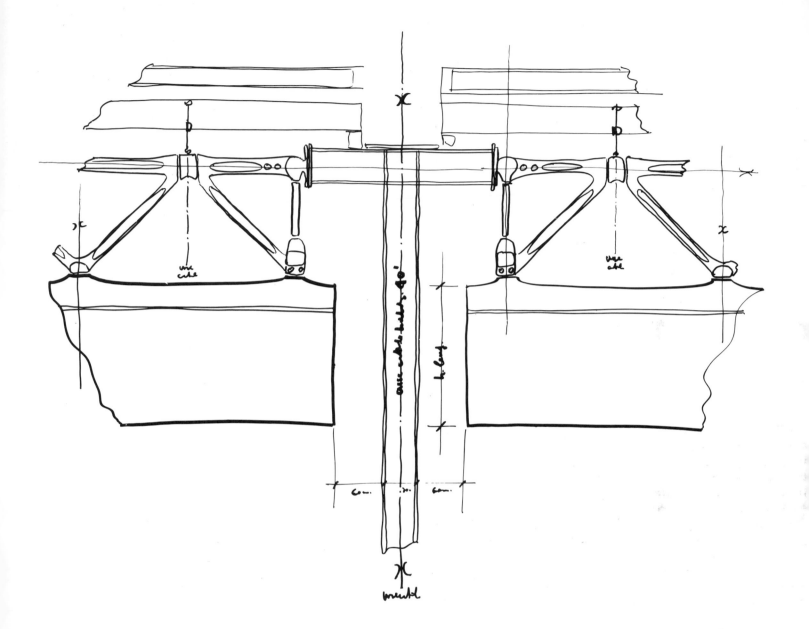

Madame de Menil's influence on the artistic climate of Houston is legendary and encompasses architecture specifically. She lives in an early Philip Johnson house and was responsible for his designing the nearby campus for St. Thomas University and a chapel in collaboration with Howard Barnstone to display fourteen Mark Rothko murals. She developed a media center at Rice University and carried out a modest but inspired "urban renewal" of the frame houses adjacent to and surrounding the museum site. The museum was to be the culmination of her architectural and artistic gifts to the city.

The building is classic and generous in its proportions and elegantly modest in its combination of white steel frame and gray clapboard siding. The simplicity of the structure and its pure geometry is given a dynamic visual counterbalance by a roof plane of reinforced concrete lighting devices that look like a multitude of flaps of a descending jet plane. These "leaves" filter out the hot Texas sun but let in natural light to the galleries, according to the late critic Reyner Barnham, "like no other museum anywhere. The quality of its light may set standards that will make other architects lie awake at night."

Restraint, dignity, beauty, are all words that could aptly be applied to this building which functions precisely for the purposes set down by its remarkable client. According to Barnham, "Renzo Piano has here achieved a building that has put the magic back into Functionalism." Since the Menil Museum opening in 1986, Piano has received numerous important commissions worldwide, including the new airport in Osaka, Japan. Each one demonstrates his ability to work within environmental constraints with technological and artistic sensitivity.

# REIMA PIETILÄ / RAILI PIETILÄ

Most agree that the dominant figure of twentieth-century Scandinavian architecture is Alvar Aalto (1898–1976). Finnish architect Reima Pietilä is considered Aalto's most loyal successor, although Pietilä has achieved international recognition for an architectural vision uniquely his own.

"Pietilä's work represents a continuation of Aalto's spirit of invention, a spirit that thrives on rebellion rather than conformity," critic Malcolm Quantrill proclaimed in his biography of Pietilä, while tagging Pietilä's vision as "an architecture of great complexity and nerve-tingling authenticity." The uniqueness of Pietilä's architecture can be traced to a list of his qualities: his interest in symbolic landscapes; pursuit of underlying contexts for architecture (as distinct from the more obvious physical and visual frameworks of the environment); inclination to overstate an architectural intention in order to increase its imagery and dramatic power; studied plurality in the use of materials, reflecting both the "nature of materials" philosophy and the impact of new technologies on design; and use of light as a material component in the exploration of space and form (firmly within the Finnish tradition and a continuation of Aalto's own preoccupations).

Throughout his career, Pietilä has alternated design activity with long periods of intellectual development. His first commission—and international recognition—came for the design of the Finnish Pavilion for the 1958 World's Fair in Brussels. Since then, his major works have been undertaken with his wife, architect Raili Pietilä, their first products being the Dipoli International Conference Centre for Otaniemi and Kaleva Church in Tempere, both completed in 1966.

Pietilä has called architecture "our basic cultural commodity and as such is original as art. . . . Only as such can architecture help man to experience his environment profoundly and conceive the quality of his own culture. . . . Finnish architecture should be organically one with its own evergreen arctic forest, united with the 'form-language' of the forest. The rhythms of architectural structure and form should be national and characteristic, expressing the shape of space. Colors are to be closely related to nature, providing a strong tie to our cultural heritage."

# JAMES STEWART POLSHEK / JAMES GARRISON

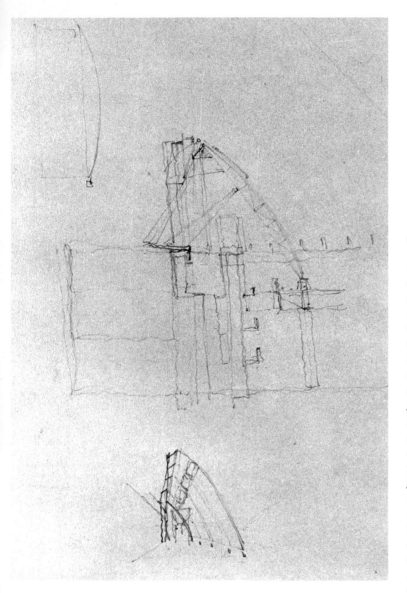

**T**here is a tradition in architectural education of distinguished practitioners serving as deans of colleges of architecture while simultaneously managing thriving practices. In this country since World War II, Gropius and Sert at Harvard, and Pelli and Moore of Yale are among that number, as well as Jim Polshek at Columbia. Polshek began his career in an auspicious manner at the age of thirty-two with a large ($32 million) commission from a Japanese firm in 1962. In 1973 he became the dean of architecture at Columbia University, a post which he held with distinction for many years. Concurrent with his distinguished academic accomplishments he fashioned an office noted for solid, well-designed architecture.

Located in Manhattan, one of the densest enclaves of urban architecture, Polshek's office has been one of the most sympathetic to that context. At Columbia he championed the cause of historic preservation and in his office he hired art historians as well as draftsmen.

His sensitive and talented restoration of Carnegie Hall added luster without egoist intervention to one of the city's cultural treasures and his 50-story high rise at 500 Madison Avenue neatly deferred to the earlier contemporary landmark Pepsi-Cola building without compromising its own integrity. While other architects pay lip service to the fact that there should be foreground buildings (mine) and background buildings (yours), Jim Polshek contends that "There's no such thing as background buildings." In his view all buildings are foreground *and* background and all should be appropriate to their surroundings and their purpose.

Polshek's practice is varied. He seems as comfortable designing high-rise buildings as foreign embassies, and has recently been named architect for the Holocaust Museum in New York City, and co-architect for the new Brooklyn Museum with Arata Isozake. A frequent winner of design competitions, Polshek gives full credit to his design partner, James Garrison, who was primarily responsible for the chosen entry for the National Inventors Hall of Fame in Akron, Ohio.

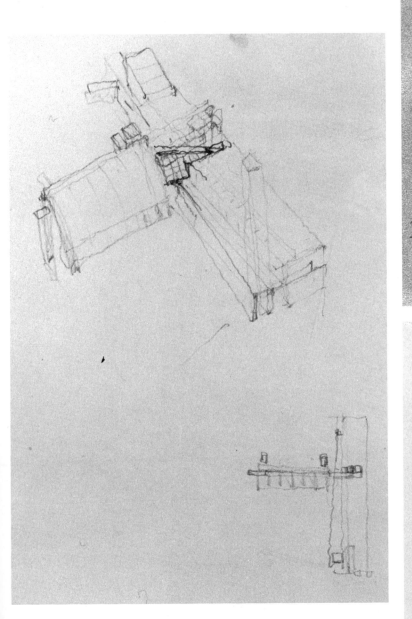

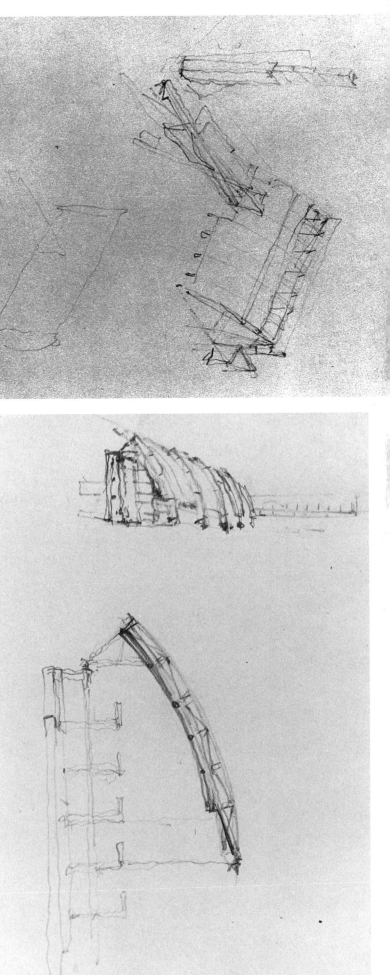

**W**idely respected U.S. architects have tended to cluster on either coast and most often along the eastern shoreline. That didn't deter Midwesterner Frank Lloyd Wright from becoming America's preeminent twentieth-century architect or from eschewing (perhaps loathing is a better word) the skyscraper-crowded cities of the East Coast and the unplanned sprawl of Los Angeles. He created his own communities at Taliesin East (Wisconsin) and Taliesin West (Arizona).

Now a Southwestern architect, Antoine Predock, whose practice is in Albuquerque, New Mexico, is similarly parlaying a reputation for regionally distinctive design into international renown. Though he has won commissions in Florida and in Marne-la-Valle, France, among other locations, Predock is still best known for his buildings in the Southwest, especially his houses and the Fine Arts Center at Arizona State University. Upon giving the Fine Arts Center a national honor award, the AIA described the Center "as romantic and colorful as the desert southwest," a "vibrant city of art [that] awakens the imagination and stirs the senses."

Predock's dun-colored rugged residences in the region tend to be low-slung, stucco-clad adobe, easily nestled among their arid surroundings. Though composed of simple, geometric shapes, Predock's designs are unusually varied. The Fuller house in Scottsdale, Arizona, for instance, is composed mainly of rectangular shapes with deep openings ranged around an outdoor patio with an asymmetrically placed circular swimming pool. But there is also a pyramidal study that rises to a peaked skylight.

The *New York Times* critic Paul Goldberger has written of one Predock building that it "obviously belongs to the southwest, yet it is unlike anything seen before." The same could be said of most of the projects locally that have brought Predock to the attention of the press, a cluster of adobe town houses on a slope overlooking Albuquerque, a downtown condominium outlined in neon tubing, a bloodbank building that looks as if it has been dipped in a bucket of bright red paint.

Predock credits a sojourn at the American Academy in Rome as a pivotal point in his career, a time that allowed him a perspective on history and place that he embodies in all his projects. The common thread running through all of Predock's buildings is their strong association with place, what some have called mystic. To this sense of place Predock incorporates a bold, self-confident handling of forms and a subtle manipulation of colors and textures.

# JAQUELIN T. ROBERTSON

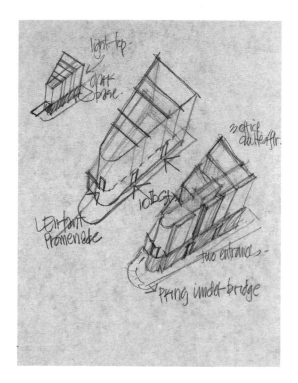

**J**aquelin Robertson's career is filled with paradoxes. He is believable as a southern gentleman, born in Richmond, Virginia, and until quite recently the dean of the graduate school of architecture at the University of Virginia. During this latter academic stint, 1981 to 1988, Robertson seemed to be entirely in his natural milieu, directing a program in the campus setting created by Thomas Jefferson, only a short distance from Monticello.

This sonorous-voiced, pipe-smoking professor of architecture is hardly, however, rural in his attitudes and experiences concerning architecture. He can speak with authority on urban topics, having directed the Office of Midtown Planning and Development in New York City under Mayor John Lindsay. Along with Jonathan Barnett and David Weinstein, Robertson developed conceptual studies and inventive zoning plans that still stand as a high-water mark in that city's planning efforts.

Another paradox is the scale at which Jack Robertson works most effectively. After leaving the midtown Manhattan office it seemed a natural step for him to engage in large-scale urban development projects with Llewelyn-Davies, primarily a new Town Center in Teheran. In recent years, however, while practicing with Peter Eisenman first, and later Alexander Cooper, Robertson has produced a series of extremely creative residential designs. The Rose Barn in Bedford, New York, demonstrates the architect's ability to bring contemporary order to a seventeenth-century barn shell, and in the Rose House in East Hampton he was able to distill the elements of traditional architectural styles historically prevalent in this prestigious summer colony of Long Island, and to do so with distinctive maturity and grace. In keeping with the pendulum swings of Robertson's career, he is once again living and practicing in New York City and one awaits the results of his return to an urban context.

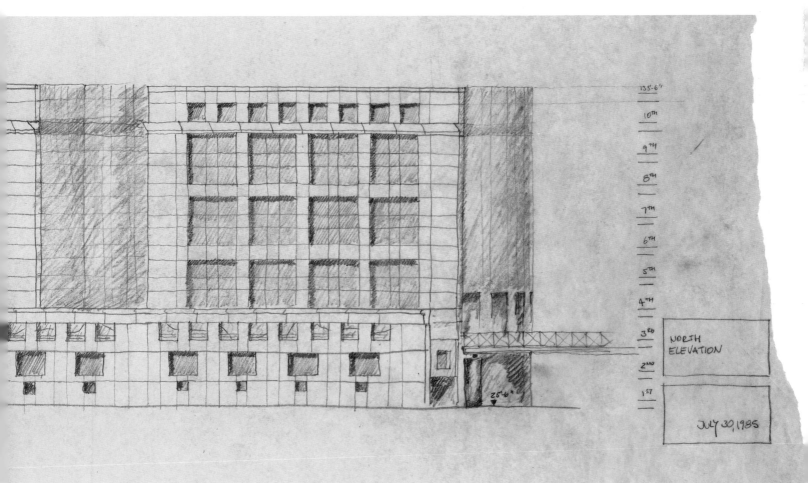

# RICHARD ROGERS

**R**ichard Rogers achieved worldwide recognition when he won the Place Beaubourg Competition in 1971 with the Italian architect Renzo Piano. The prize-winning design was shocking in its bold and colorful forms that denied any connection to the classical or modernist past but embraced unreservedly a technological future and its accompanying aesthetic. Rogers continued for the next decade to produce buildings that were faithful to his belief. He and Foster, with whom he had been a student and produced six projects, were regarded as the High-Tech Twins of Great Britain. To categorize Rogers as a man obsessed with technology and without poetry in his attitude toward architecture, however, is to miss the mark widely. Rogers contends that "Technology cannot be an end in itself but must aim at solving long term social and ecological problems."

If the Centre Pompidou at Beaubourg seemed like an alien spacecraft landed permanently in the heart of Paris, then the Lloyds of London headquarters made that city's downtown seem as if it had come from a "developing" planet. Pompidou is a colorful and playful toy placed in the grayness of Paris while Lloyds, with its shimmering stainless steel towers, is a sophisticated "machine" that makes other architecture around it seem quaint and curious.

The influence of Louis Kahn, who taught Rogers briefly at Yale University as a visiting professor, is evident, as is the fact that in this instance the pupil has seriously challenged the master with a building that must be reckoned with for centuries. The 12-story building, resembling a space launch gantry or an elegant oil refinery as much as a traditional building, is located in a historic district of London. Like Pompidou, the marvel of Lloyds is both in its design and in the astonishing fact that it got built.

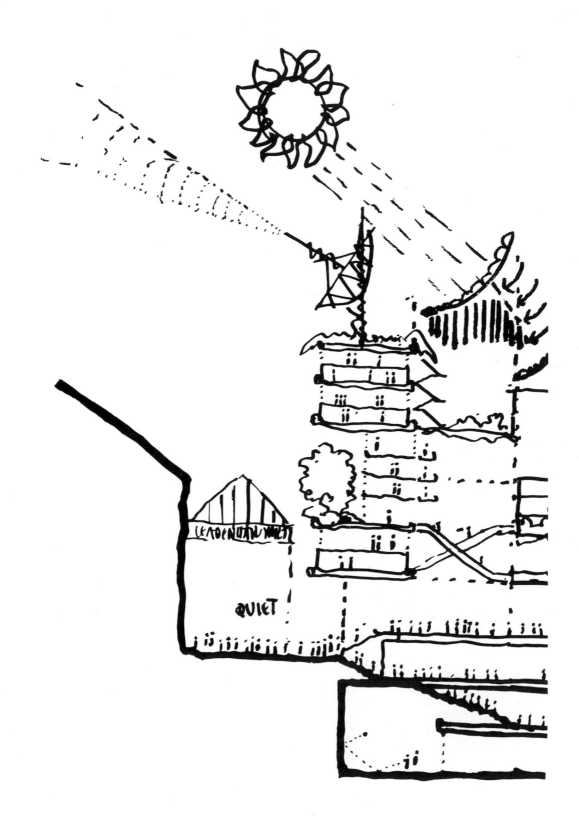

# ALDO ROSSI

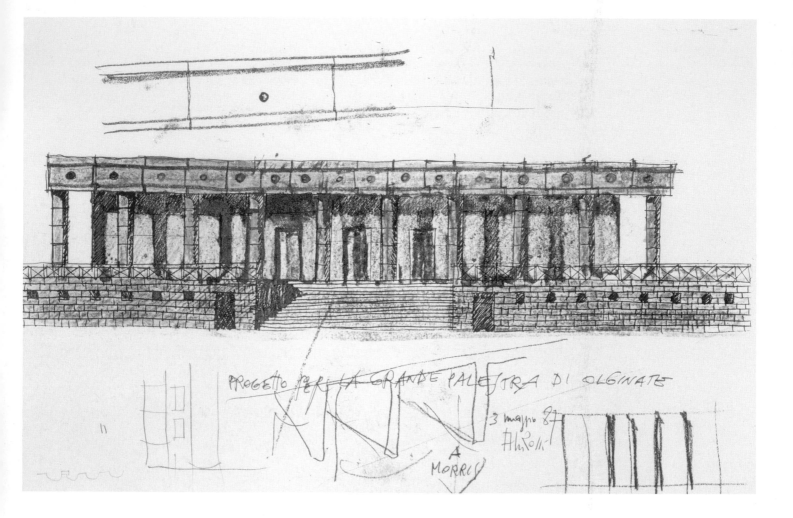

**A**rchitects follow different career paths. For some it is a matter of college, apprenticeship in a respectable office, licensing, and the establishment of an independent office. For others the path is more circuitous and much broader in its scope.

Aldo Rossi is one of the most widely known architects in the world, but that international recognition did not come through a gradually widening audience who became familiar with his buildings. His arrival at this point of acknowledgment by public and peers has come through years of research and publication and through his editorship of *Casabella*, a respected Italian architectural journal. In addition, he has won numerous competitions, including the Venice Biennale, although for the most part his architectural designs were unbuilt. He became as well known for his product designs as for his buildings, in particular the ubiquitous and elegant coffeepot for Alessi, and also for a profusion of drawings which illustrated his artistic sensitivity to architecture. For many years Rossi was known principally as a teacher, lecturer, and theoretician, one whose primary interests were in city planning and the relationship of architecture to urban design. It was clear from his writings and the occasional projects that Rossi was an architect who, when the time was appropriate, would build in a manner that embodied the thoughtfulness of his words and years of preparation.

Rossi's buildings have a kind of stark logic and simplicity to them. There is a steady progress from ground to roof, like the ancient ziggurat form which occurs with frequency in his designs. His architecture is neither modern nor Postmodern, and of such strength that one's attempts to label it seem superfluous. His designs deal with the essence of the problem to be solved in a straightforward and honest manner, deceptively simple yet fraught with ideas and symbolism.

# PAUL RUDOLPH

**DHARMALA SAKTI BUILDING, JAKARTA, INDONESIA. 1988**
**MEDIUM: PENCIL**

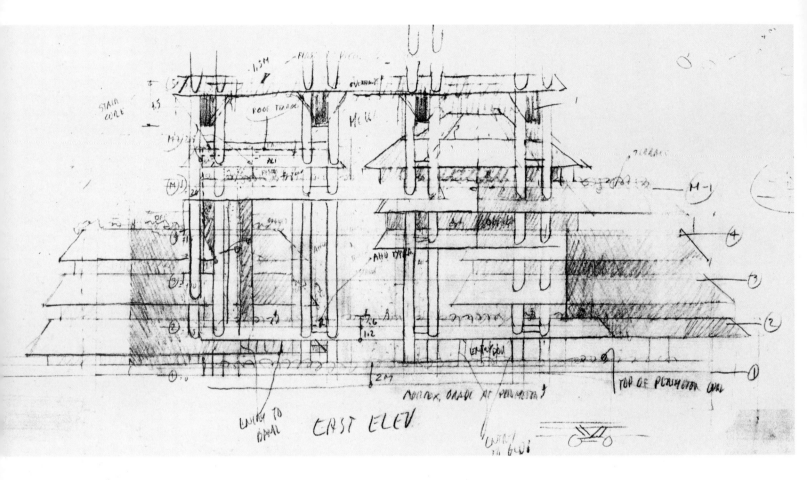

EAST ELEV

There is a certain configuration that seems common to many famous architects' careers in the latter half of the twentieth century. One should have studied at Cranbrook, Yale, or Harvard (preferably with Gropius) or at Pennsylvania (when Kahn was there). One should have worked for a major "name" firm like Skidmore, Owings & Merrill, or I. M. Pei, or Saarinen, and one should have been dean of the school of architecture at one of the above colleges and had a major exhibition at the Museum

of Modern Art. In addition, a book published by Rizzoli, Abrams, or Braziller would be helpful.

Paul Rudolph did not work for Skidmore, Owings & Merrill, but most of the other requisite touchstones of a successful architectural career are included in his resume. He has mainly practiced on his own since 1965 in New York City and earlier in Sarasota, Florida, and New Haven (the latter during a turbulent period when he served as dean at Yale University).

In his nearly forty years of practice Rudolph has built almost every type of building from art center to high-rise office building, private residence to foreign embassy, and each of them since the early days of small-scale houses for a Florida climate has exhibited a bold and assertive kind of architecture that was modernist in its doctrine, but pure Rudolph in the leaps of imagination that resulted in arresting sculptural forms.

# MOSHE SAFDIE

**NATIONAL GALLERY OF CANADA, OTTAWA. 1988
MEDIUM: PEN AND INK, PASTEL**

**A**rchitecture is not a profession one enters if early fame and remuneration are the primary goals. Unlike music and mathematics there are few child prodigies. In point of fact there are few who receive serious recognition before fifty. The exception which proves this particular rule is Moshe Safdie.

Israeli-born Safdie received his architectural education in Canada at McGill University and went on to become their most famous architectural graduate. Three years after graduating he became involved in the 1967 World Exposition in Montreal and built a revolutionary prefabricated housing project as part of the fair's displays and achieved instant world notoriety. The project based in part on his McGill graduate thesis came to be known as "Habitat 67," and while its promise of low-cost, humane housing was not fully realized, it was nevertheless a full-scale demonstration of the possibilities which precast concrete technology afforded. Safdie contended that the high costs which eventually rivaled custom development prices were due to the small number of units (158) produced for the Habitat site and program. This contention was later proven in part by a larger housing project in Puerto Rico, which tended to validate the architect's thesis. Whether it was a success or failure by economic measures can be argued, but there is no question that Habitat 67, a carefully ordered jumble of concrete boxes that formed a new urban silhouette on its spectacular Cité du Havre site, surrounded by water, became an instant symbol throughout the world of modern, advanced technology in architecture.

The early promise of Safdie's talent and energy was borne out by a series of commissions aimed at proving the possibilities that Habitat had barely stated—projects in Israel, Maryland, Puerto Rico, and California quickly followed. None of these achieved the goals of the architect, however, and gradually Safdie's preoccupation with harnessing standardized fabrication to his designs gave way to a series of large-scale urban planning projects for Jerusalem, Senegal, Iran, and Singapore. Safdie complemented his architectural designs with a number of books that paralleled developments in his career: *Beyond Habitat*, 1970, *For Everyone A Garden*, 1974, and *Form and Purpose*, 1982. He lectured extensively on his philosophy of design and joined the Harvard University faculty in 1978, where he served as director of the urban design program for four years.

Safdie's fortunes as an architect plummeted in 1987 with his dismissal from the Columbus Circle project, a major 3-million-square-foot high rise at the southwest corner of Central Park in Manhattan. The Columbus Circle project drew fierce criticism from citizens' groups who protested its environmental impact on Central Park and who filed a lawsuit, and from the New York press for the manner in which the project was chosen by the city. Both groups cited the mass and height of Safdie's prismatic skyscraper, which would cast an objectionably long shadow over the park.

There was little time to dwell on this setback, however, for Safdie received four of the most prestigious commissions available in Canada. One of them, the National Gallery of Canada in 1988, which many consider to be his best work to date, is not only a personal triumph for the architect, but a major architectural achievement for Canada.

# ADÈLE NAUDÉ SANTOS

**A**dèle Naudé Santos is an educator, having been professor at the graduate programs of Harvard University, Rice University, and the University of Pennsylvania, the latter of which she also served as chairman of the Department of Architecture. She is presently dean of the new School of Architecture at the University of California, San Diego. Adèle Naudé Santos is also an architect and urban designer of international scope. In these capacities she has developed over the years a holistic approach to architecture. People need more from the built

environment than accommodation of functional requirements, she maintains. So she seeks to create environments that satisfy the human spirit. As she describes them, some of her ideas and basic principles approaching architecture include:

Architecture is not an art that can be approached abstractly. It has a social reality and comes with some responsibility. It also has a time and place—cultural, physical, political, etc. . . . The pragmatics of architecture are easy. Finding a way to extract the poetic dimension from the problems that are posed is the issue.

We are challenged to intelligently and creatively integrate and synthesize all the circumstantial facts, while developing a formal vocabulary that obeys its own internal esthetic logic and rules.

Architectural form and esthetic vocabulary result out of a quest to find solutions that are appropriate in the widest sense—functionally, psychologically, socially, climatically, contextually, technologically, esthetically.

The resultant architecture should speak of its social basis, its mode of production, its physical context. The language should not be so hermetic or private that it speaks

only to the ones who know. We are dealing with cultural artifacts that have a significance beyond the personal and immediate time frame.

To achieve these goals Santos examines the relationships between "space and experience" and employs techniques that make space seem larger and feel more pleasing. Santos stresses creative use of natural light, interesting volumes and configurations of space, surprising vistas, and connections to the outdoors. Her architecture is also a contextual response to the landscape, whose contours, orientation, and light are essential to the making of form.

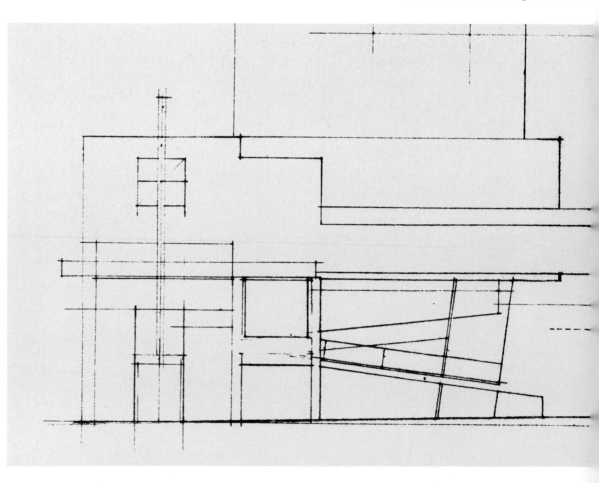

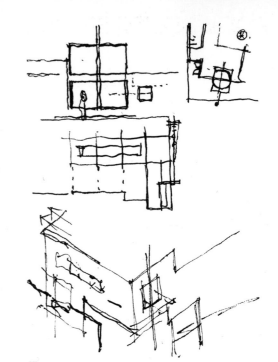

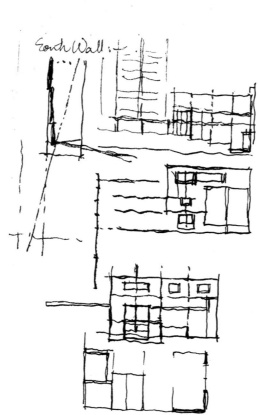

North Wall

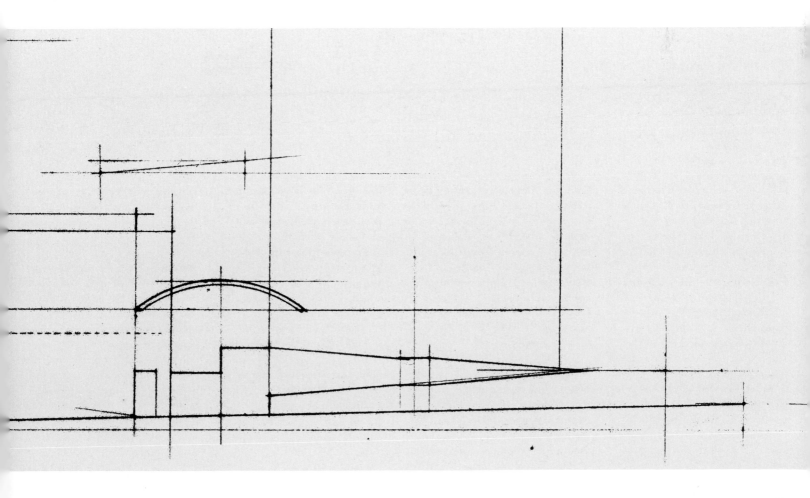

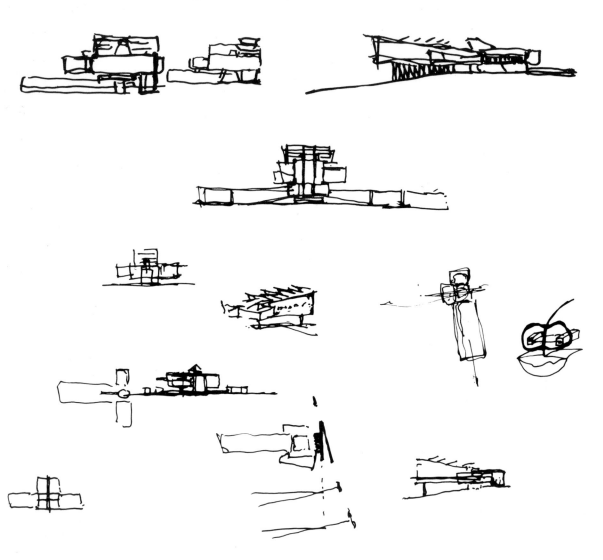

Mack Scogin was born in Atlanta, Georgia, in 1943 and received a bachelor of architecture degree from the Georgia Institute of Technology in 1967. Twenty-three years later he became the chairman of the Department of Architecture at Harvard University, possibly the highest academic post in architectural education in the United States. Prior to assuming this prestigious post Mr. Scogin, in practice as Scogin, Elam and Bray Architects, Inc., had received national recognition from the American Institute of Architects in the form of national and regional awards for his designs. In 1989 the firm won the AIA National Honor Award for their Clayton County Headquarters Library, although another library, the Buckhead Library in Atlanta, sums up more nearly what this brassy firm is about.

Joseph Giovannini, the *New York Times* critic and architectural writer, describes the project as "a porte cochere, an entrance vestibule, a check-out desk, and then a long reading room, that culminates in a view of the Atlanta Skyline . . . but the experience is hardly that of a traditionally planned library—it evokes instead the rare and exhilarating feelings experienced at the prow of an ocean liner, at the foot of a dam, at the top of a ski jump or at the nose of a 737. Both the form and the space lift-off into the view."

Scogin, the subject of this reverie, observes that "architecture has a lot of freedom now. A building doesn't have to tie into the ground. It can soar, cantilever, suspend, hover, float, flow, undulate." And the Buckhead Library does all of these.

Before Scogin, Elam and Bray, and before Harvard, Mack Scogin "paid his dues" in the distinguished firm of Heery and Heery, Architects and Engineers, in Atlanta for seventeen years where he was president and CEO prior to forming his own firm in 1984. In the intervening six short years his firm has claimed a place among the most exciting and promising new offices in architecture.

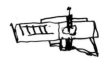

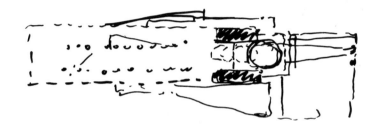

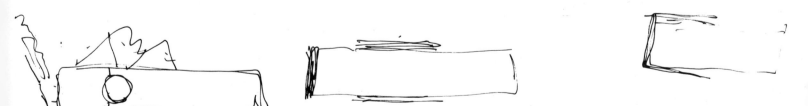

# HARRY SEIDLER

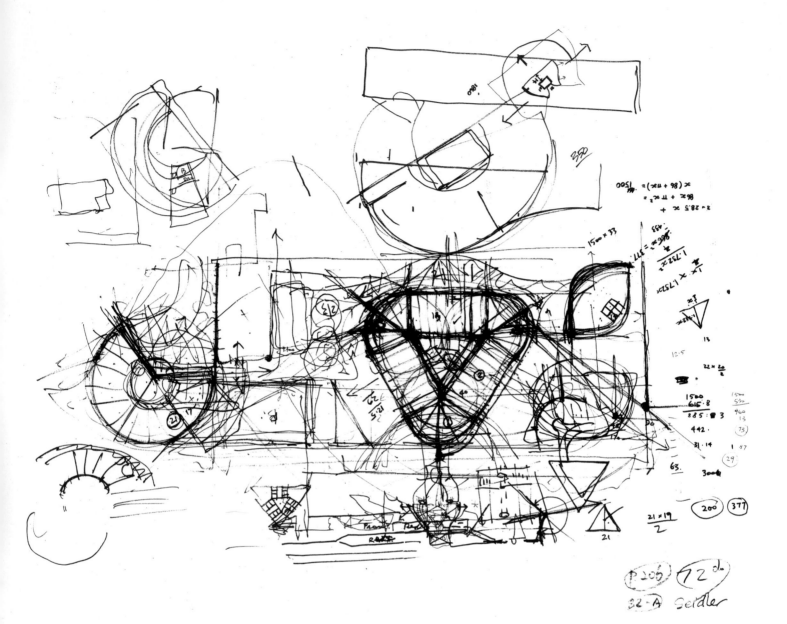

**H**arry Seidler's credentials as a modernist are in perfect order. He received his graduate degree under Gropius at Harvard and worked for Marcel Breuer and Oscar Niemeyer before he established his own practice in Australia in 1948. Since that time he has designed buildings there and throughout the world, many of them as part of large urban complexes. He has won almost all the awards which the profession offers, attesting to the high regard with which his work is held by his peers.

Influences of those for whom one works as an apprentice architect are always evident to some degree or other in future projects, but in Seidler's case it is clearer than most that the concrete structuralism of Breuer and the fluid lyrical forms of Niemeyer still exert a strong influence on his design sensibilities and approach to a problem. Nowhere is this incorporation of the poetic and the engineered more evident than in the 48-story Tower and Riverside Centre in Brisbane built in 1987.

While the Brisbane River is the topographic and scenic feature which dictates the orientation of the Centre, its rationale and realization is based on geometry and structure. The building derives much of its dynamism from its unusual round-ended triangular shape with one bulging side. It is an eccentric shape for a high-rise building that functions amazingly well, giving views in a 360-degree fashion and creating a vortex-like

atrium. This orientation outward from all points on each floor creates solar control problems—solved neatly by adjustable aluminum solar shades. The soft curving continuum of the tower shape is contained at the ground level by flowing landscaped patterns more reminiscent of Rio than Brisbane.

Seidler remains fiercely true to his early modernist training but his variations on that theme have expanded the vocabulary in a way that is at once international and Australian.

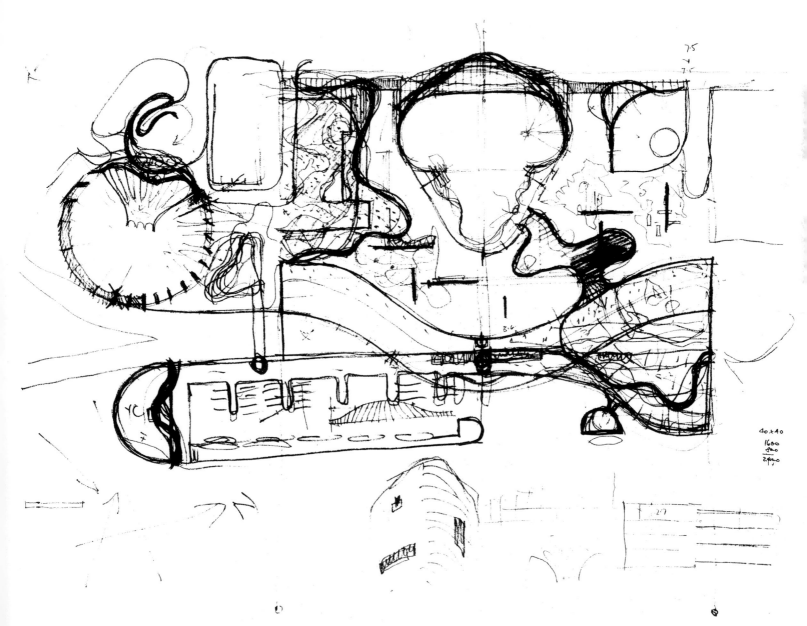

# KAZUO SHINOHARA

Contemporary Japanese architecture relies on traditional design as a starting point, but as Kazuo Shinohara says, "It must be the point to which it returns." Judging by their work, the other "New Wave" architects would agree.

A conspicuous feature of the New Wave is the recurrence of hard-surfaced geometry (thought perhaps to be reminiscent of modern Western architects, and Le Corbusier in particular): the cube, cylinder, trilateral prism, orthogonal grid, or trabeated pergola, to mention a few. These elements are particularly important in Shinohara's architecture, as well as that of Hiromi Fujii, Tadao Ando, Takefumi Aida, and Mayumi Miyawake. For them, the geometry serves to reestablish the genius loci within their structures. The intention is to create the "spirit of places."

Shinohara seeks a rich minimalism. While he shares this quest with Tadao Ando, "Shinohara is an enigma even in today's diverse situation. If the phenomenology of architecture is essential to Ando and his generation in general, it is equally essential to Shinohara. His architecture is a phenomenon in itself. Where the extraordinary in architectural experience leaves off, Shinohara's architecture begins to take shape," writes Botond Bognar in *Contemporary Japanese Architecture: Its Development and Challenge*. Bognar continues: "Shinohara's abstract and 'naked spaces' of transcendent purity are created for reasons beyond easy comprehension. They defy any rational expectation and explanation even if sometimes they are so explained. But while they leave the rational mind stuttering, they 'conform to the deepest levels of human emotions' in Shinohara's words, and promote spiritual purification."

Shinohara acknowledges three stages in his work. The first was steeped in Japanese architectural tradition—lightweight timber construction, beaten earth floors, and what he calls "wasteful," nonfunctioning spaces. In the second phase his work increased in its "savagery," embodied in heavy concrete slanting roofs and large, exposed timber columns. As described by Shinohara, the third phase is a hunt for a "zero-degree machine that will be assembled as the machine used as an architectural analogy in the 1920s, since it will have function as its keyword. But my machine will not be international. It will have a name and nationality clearly indicated."

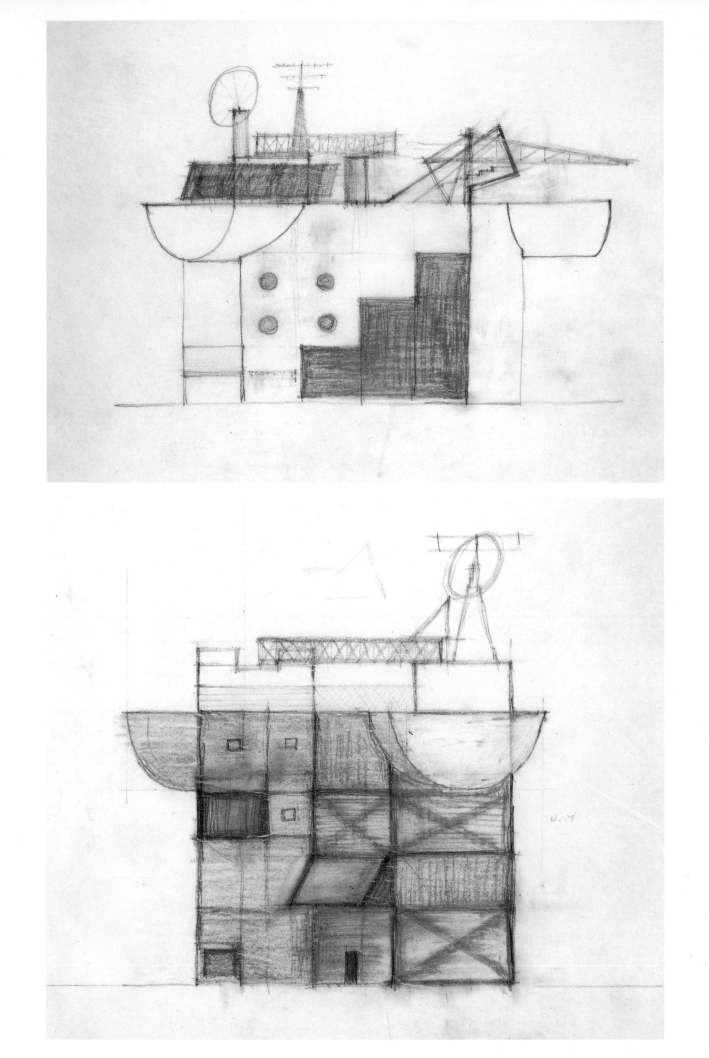

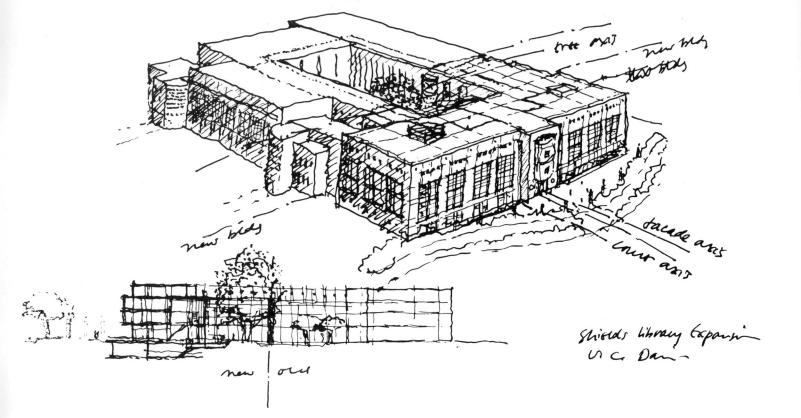

Buildings no longer are evaluated in simple functionalist terms, but instead are judged on their fulfillment of a richer mix of criteria including urban design materials, contextualism, and craft." That statement by San Francisco architect Cathy Simon was written for a ten-year retrospective of her work in *Architecture* magazine in 1987. A quick look at a few buildings designed by Simon—first with Marquis Associates and then with her new firm Simon Martin-Vegue Winkelstein Moris (SMWM)—reveals that these criteria have played a major role in her approach to design.

With Simon as director of architecture, SMWM recently designed a 188,000-square-foot addition to the Peter J. Shields Library at the University of California, Davis, along with alterations to the existing 200,000-square-foot building. The original library is an art deco building of the late 1930s, with two additions made in 1954 and 1969 that are "insensitive to context and human use," Simon reported. The SMWM addition is meant "to relate formally to the context of the adjoining buildings," in Simon's words. "It also creates a new image appropriate to the symbolic importance of the library as the intellectual heart of the university, and expresses openness and accessibility to its broad public." According to Simon, "the three additions relate, respectively, to existing buildings of 60, 40, and 20 years. The circulation network in all three acts as a primary organizing principle and form

determinant. Each makes the analogy between the building's actual use—school, dormitory, music department—and a prototypical pattern—town plan, social and academic community, bridge, and portal. Finally, in an era in which old buildings in established neighborhoods are being added onto instead of razed, the ability to assimilate setting and urban fabric, and the talent to enhance instead of dilute the original design, is becoming more and more important as a design specialty. On the subject of additive architecture Simon says, "the architectural language and imagery of each situation must interpret the architectural context in which it occurs. In a sense, each building is about that context."

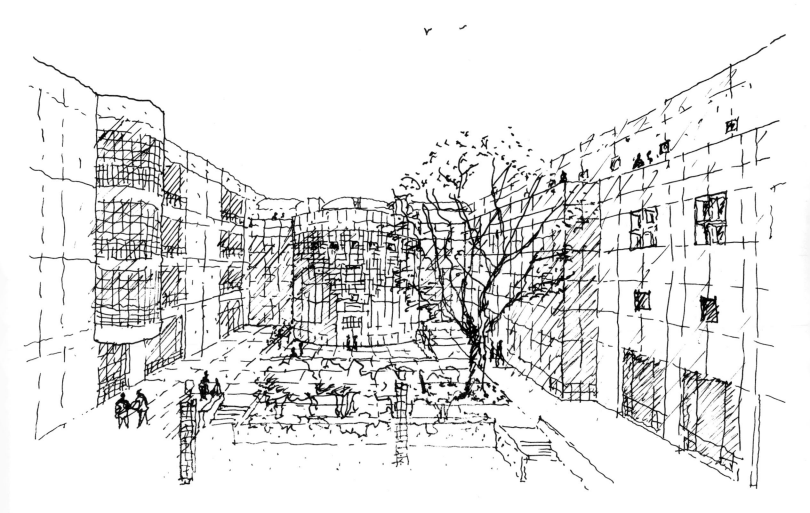

shields courtyard

# SITE
# JAMES WINES, ALISON SKY

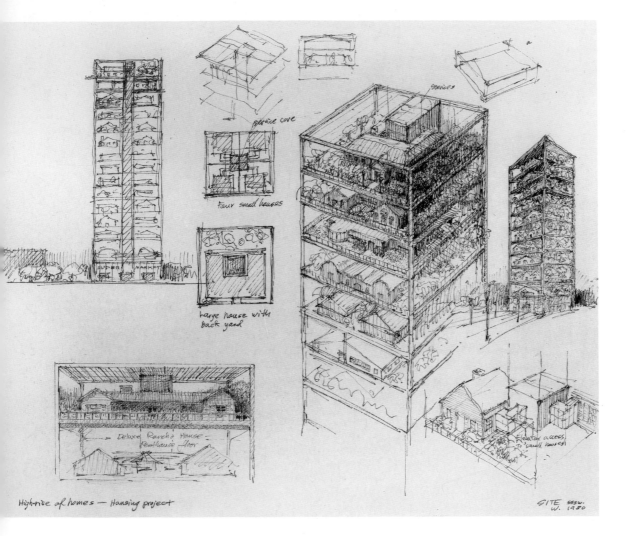

High-rise of homes — Housing project

Looking like a modern-day Moses (with his white beard and long hair) searching for the promised land of a totally integrated world of art and architecture, James Wines, sculptor-cum-architect, and his co-founding partner of SITE, Alison Sky, have been an enigma and often an annoyance to the architecture profession.

Since 1980 when they first began to produce a series of irreverent and highly imaginative solutions to problems that had always defined the domain of the architect, they have been a subject of conjecture in the profession. "Are they architects?

Then why don't they stay out of our business and stick to art?" were the usual complaints which might have been followed by the unvoiced ". . . And why do they get so much publicity?"

Projects for art collectors Sydney and Francis Lewis, who owned a chain of discount stores, were the original source of their notoriety. These projects assailed all the principles architects held sacred. Their stores for Best Products were buildings with brick facades curling at the corners, and buildings with gaping holes in their storefronts and bricks tumbling down, apparently the result of a terrible failure on the part of the architect or engineer. (And SITE

wonders why the profession looks askance?) There is even an "un-enterable" building with a rupture at the corner that opens magically to let in customers. These buildings caused a stir in the press and among the public, which did not subside with ever more daring and perverse incursions into the architects' sanctified realm. "Is there no end to their affront?" was the reaction from the profession. "Or their inventiveness?" was the plaintive echo.

Apparently not. SITE (now joined by the energetic and resourceful Michelle Stone) came up with even more unimaginable

projects that were clearly not sculpture but, with the exception of their own imagination, were dubious architecture. A high-rise building with a grouping of fully grown houses stacked on the floors, instead of the more customary notion of apartments neatly contained, was just too much. But the gambit continues. The SITE group landed the Transportation Pavilion at the Vancouver World's Fair which they solved not with a usual exposition building but with an undulating strip of highway containing all manner of vehicles, frozen in time and concrete, and disappearing, like the Loch Ness Monster, in the water.

**HIGHRISE OF HOMES, PROPOSED FOR A MAJOR U.S. CITY. 1981**
**MEDIUM: PEN AND INK, WASH ON PAPER**

# ALVARO SIZA

From the early 1930s until the Communist revolution of 1974, architecture in Portugal was dictated by the government, particularly under the regime of Premier Antonio de Oliveria Salazar, who died in 1970. This "national" architecture was to be based on vernacular and historical forms. The model was conventional modernism with the addition of vaguely Baroque and classical regional decorative detailing. When the tight dictates of the regime were lifted, Portugal's contemporary architecture changed dramatically. Two main schools emerged: a non-referential modernism that looked primarily to the Tendenze Movement stirring in Italy, led by Alvaro Siza, and Post-modernism, led by Tomas Taveira.

"Siza belongs," characterized architecture critic Kenneth Frampton, "to that generation of modernists who have understood that the liberative legacy of the modern movement resides in its potential for ambiguity and in its capacity for being articulated in terms of spatial fluidity and mechanical transformation." Siza achieved this by using sliding and pivoting elements, such as the mobile, glazed partitions in a 1970 house in Porto. Siza added to that the fan-seam, the use of which can be seen in the rotating and expanding volumes of the banking hall in the Pinto Bank built in the Oliveira de Azemeis in 1974.

By the mid-1980s Siza had added three other characteristics to his work—palladian, interior plan, and collage—all evident in the Duarte House in Ovar. Siza borrows the classic palladian rhythm of ABABA, but omits the last A bay and reduces the adjacent B bay into a single story. The result is an ABA configuration in which the B becomes the main entrance.

Siza looked to Adolf Loos for the *Raumplan*, which is evident in the entrance hall of the Duarte House, where a marble terraced stairway rises. The collage is presented there by placing throughout the house marble identical to the stairway, with particular emphasis placed on the freestanding column and surround to the main living room fireplace. There the marble is treated as a fragment of an eroded archeological stratum.

"The net effect of this tripartite orchestration—palladianism, raumplan, and collage—is to transform a modest suburban house into a 'palazzetta,'" Frampton suggests, "where Siza has conjured up a unique expression, combining the necessary sense of intimacy, with a feeling for high bourgeois, aristocratic grandeur rarely to be found in a contemporary house."

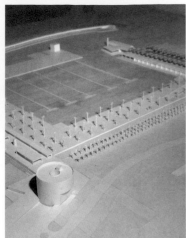

# ETTORE SOTTSASS

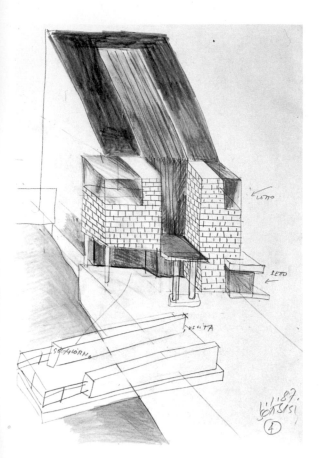

**WOLF RESIDENCE, TELLURIDE, COLORADO. 1990**
**MEDIUM: PEN AND COLORED PENCIL ON PAPER**

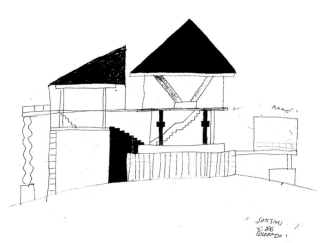

**L**ike many Italian architects and designers, Ettore Sottsass defies neat labeling—designer, author, architect, and philosopher. It is as if there are several Sottsasses. There is the Sottsass who is famous for the many excellently designed products for Olivetti, Alessi, and other product and furniture manufacturers, the Sottsass who sent shock waves through the design world with the founding of the audacious Memphis Group, and finally, the Sottsass who has returned to his earlier training as an architect and is designing buildings.

Born in Innsbruck, Sottsass was graduated in Turin in 1939. In 1946, he started his own architecture practice in Milan but also began designing furniture and objects. Since 1958 he has been Olivetti's chief design consultant and has been responsible for many innovative design concepts in electronics. Most of the pieces designed by Ettore Sottsass have been shown in museums worldwide. He participated in the Museum of Modern Art's exhibition "Italy: A Domestic Landscape" in 1972 and the 1989 International Design Conference in Aspen, "The Italian Manifesto."

Sottsass's work covers many areas—from ceramics to experimental furniture to utopian projects and now

architecture. The Wolf residence in Colorado is designed as a vacation home in the rugged terrain of the western slopes along the Rocky Mountains; the nearest town is the mining village of Telluride. The client, Daniel Wolf, is a discriminating patron of the arts and himself a significant force in the field of photography, having run a New York gallery, published and mounted major exhibitions on the subject, and played a pivotal role in assembling the J. Paul Getty's unequaled photographic archives in Santa Monica. It was not surprising that young Wolf with the connoisseur's eye would seek out an architect of unusual qualifications like Sottsass for his project.

Sottsass is the acknowledged "Dean" of design in Italy and his pronouncements on the subject are highly regarded. In an interview with Alessandro Mendini he was asked about Post-modernism in architecture, to which he responded, ". . . it creates an architectural tradition by manipulating an architectural tradition and never gets into body contact with problems. Of course, I quote, too, but I prefer to quote from traditions that are not systematized to any great degree. I prefer to refer to cultures in a wild state." Perhaps this may have attracted him to build in the American West.

216

3.9.19

# ROBERT A. M. STERN

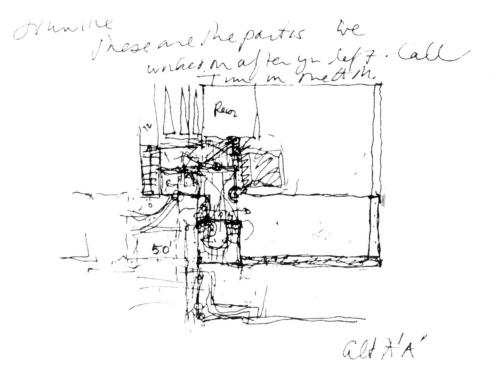

**R**obert Stern is a controversial and sometimes enigmatic architect whose work has been called "slavish copies of the past" by some and "inspired interpretations" by others. There is little argument over Stern's effect on the profession.

Stern is a critic and historian who teaches at Columbia University and was the first director of its Temple Hoyne Buell Center for the Study of American Architecture. A prolific writer, Stern publicized Post-modernism's ideas and positions in articles and in the book *New Directions in American*

*Architecture.* He also earned a box seat among the new media architects in 1986 when he hosted an eight-part public television series elaborating his view of U.S. architectural history, called *Pride of Place: Building the American Dream.*

Stern's designs were among the first examples of Post-modernism to receive attention. But he says, "I am a modern architect, if not necessarily a modernist. . . . For me, the design process is one of emulation: combining imitation and invention. I work with a knowledge and sympathy for the past, but I endeavor not to confuse the circumstances of our era with that of another."

Though Stern is best known for East Coast Shingle-style houses, his recent work includes large commercial and institutional buildings for major clients in countries around the world. Like another American architect, Thomas Jefferson, with whom he welcomes comparison, Stern has sought to, once again, make classical forms a part of the American architectural vocabulary. According to the eminent historian Vincent Scully, Stern's considerable achievement has been to flesh out "a usable late-20th century vernacular."

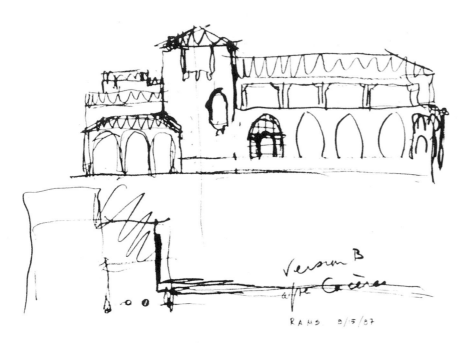

version B
after Gwen

RAMS 9/5/87

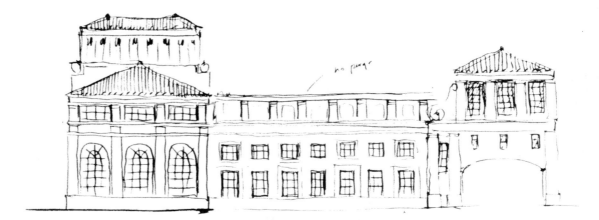

no jungs

# JAMES STIRLING

**F**rom the standpoint of international recognition, the three best-known architects in the United Kingdom are James Stirling, Norman Foster, and Richard Rogers. Foster and Rogers are quite similar in their "high-tech" approach to architecture. Stirling on the other hand has fashioned a career that cannot be categorized easily as either modernist or Post-modernist. His buildings, beginning with the striking and much photographed engineering department project at the University of Leicester in 1963, have marked Stirling as an architect of great talent and singular individuality. His later works have been labeled Post-modern because of their obvious references to the past, but there is a boldness of form and an integrity of structure that moves his architecture into a realm outside that of historical pastiche.

Stirling once wrote, "I ceased to believe in Frank Lloyd Wright's philosophy of 'truth to materials'

when I saw for the first time a building by Palladio, where peeling columns were in fact made of bricks, and not of marble or stone, as I had naively assumed from the books." In keeping with this revelation Stirling shapes his buildings in a straightforward way that solves the client's program of needs. He places a high premium on what he refers to as "functional-symbolic forms" and uses familiar elements like staircases, corridors, windows, rooms, and entrances as his basic design vocabulary, but does so with highly original and provocative assemblages.

In the decade of the 1980s Stirling and his partner, Michael Wilford, completed a trio of building additions to existing major museums in the United States, the United Kingdom, and West Germany that underscored his growing reputation as one of the leading architects practicing today. The projects were the addition to the Tate Gallery in London, called the Clore Gallery, the Arthur M. Sackler Museum, which is an addition to Harvard University's Fogg Museum, and

the Staatsgalerie in Stuttgart, Germany. All three were the subject of great debate and controversy. About the Stuttgart project Stirling has said, "Some think it is too monumental, though I believe that monuments are an essential element in a city. A city without monuments would be no city at all."

Additions to existing buildings, especially ones that are substantial monumental structures and that were designed to be complete at the time they were built, pose difficult design challenges for an architect. Buildings from the previous century were constructed at a time of gradually increasing populations and the need to plan for future growth was not a consideration. To add on in a way that does not detract from the original, but at the same time does not deny the present, is a tricky matter. The decision must be made as to whether the addition will

harmonize or contrast with the old—the question of scale, materials, patterns, and colors must be addressed and always in relation to the existing context. At the Staatsgalerie in Stuttgart, Stirling had a somewhat freer hand because of the museum's sprawling site than what he faced at the Tate when he designed the L-shaped addition to house the Turner collection. The 2-story solution he arrived at there is entirely contemporary in its spaces and decor but it makes the transition from old to new with great sensitivity, without sacrificing the distinct identity of the new Clore Gallery. The early rough sketches show the architect's struggle both with the connection to the older existing building and with the problem of getting natural light to the picture galleries.

Stirling's achievements have been awarded by two of the most sought-after prizes in the profession of architecture, the Pritzker Architecture Prize in 1981 and the Gold Medal of the Royal Institute of British Architects in 1980.

**CLORE GALLERY, TATE MUSEUM, LONDON. 1986**
**MEDIUM: PENCIL AND COLORED PENCIL ON PAPER**

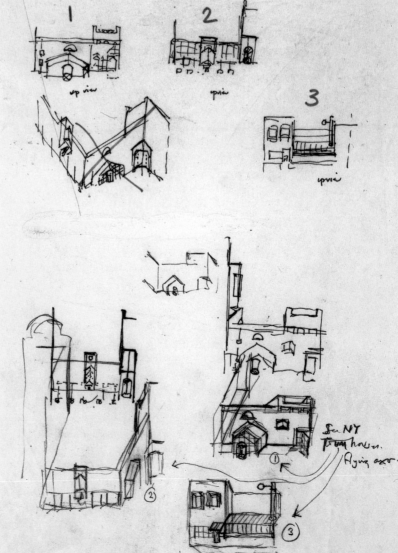

# KENZO TANGE

The prolific career of Kenzo Tange began with the master plan for the rebuilding of Hiroshima in 1946 and has continued unabated to the present. No other architect of the century, with the possible exception of the Greek planner Doxiades, has had such a global practice that ranges from Fort Worth, Texas, to Damascus, from Singapore to Minneapolis. The sheer volume and scale of Tange's work places him in a category which few architects attain in a lifetime.

Tange, born in 1913, has experienced most of this century, and in this time has influenced the physical shape of many of its major cities. His career can be divided into three more or less distinct periods. In the first, following the end of World War II, he attempted to steer Japanese architecture away from the traditional and slavish copying of European and American styles to a more modern architecture that incorporated elements of an earlier Japanese stylistic

vocabulary. This beginning period of his career culminated, and terminated, with the now-famous twin gymnasia for the 1964 Tokyo Olympic Games. These graceful buildings with their sweeping roof lines and artful siting represented a watershed in modern Japanese architecture capturing, as they did, the spirit of the culture in original and contemporary terms.

The second stage of Tange's career seemed propelled by his visionary plan for Tokyo's future growth. In 1960 he proposed a daring overlay of the chaotic existing city plan with his own audacious scheme calling for extending the city into the bay, thereby creating a new system of superhighways and transportation routes. This plan, like Frank Lloyd Wright's proposal for a mile-high skyscraper, quickened the imagination of a new generation of architects and aligned Tange, in particular, with the goals of a group of young architects called Metabolists. Metabolism advocated the organic growth of cities and the recognition of growth, decay, and rebirth in them as it likewise occurred in nature. Like other Utopian

movements, the principal achievement proved not to be the realization of goals but instead the wider recognition of the participants. The Tokyo plan by Tange, however, was such a strong idea that it remains today as an influential factor in city planning.

At a time in most professions when retirement is the natural sequence of events, Tange continues with one remarkable project after another issuing from his office. As he enters the third stage of his career, still innovative, still intellectually curious, he advocates a new "architecture for an advanced information society."

Among his far-flung commissions are a master plan for Place d'Italie in Paris, a major banking plaza in downtown Singapore, the Al'Gassim Campus for King Saud University in Saudi Arabia, the redevelopment of the oldest section of Kuala Lumpur and a new capital there. The primary project in the office which occupies Tange's attention, both from the standpoint of size and national prestige, is the new

Tokyo City Hall, a competition which he won in 1986. This enormous office building and assembly-hall complex will cover a 9-block area with twin towers rising to nearly 500 feet.

In this vast assemblage of spaces for thousands of workers equipped with the latest communications technology, Tange is able to demonstrate his theories of an architecture for an information society, theories which make a distinction between the technical and the social aspects of communication. "The direct communication among men," Tange contends, "cannot be accomplished by electronic communications alone but should be completed with person-to-person communications. The more that indirect communication progresses, the more frequent direct communication becomes necessary!"

Tange has received almost every prize and honor that his chosen profession can offer, including the Pritzker Architecture Prize in 1987, and he can justifiably be proud of his central role in twentieth-century architecture.

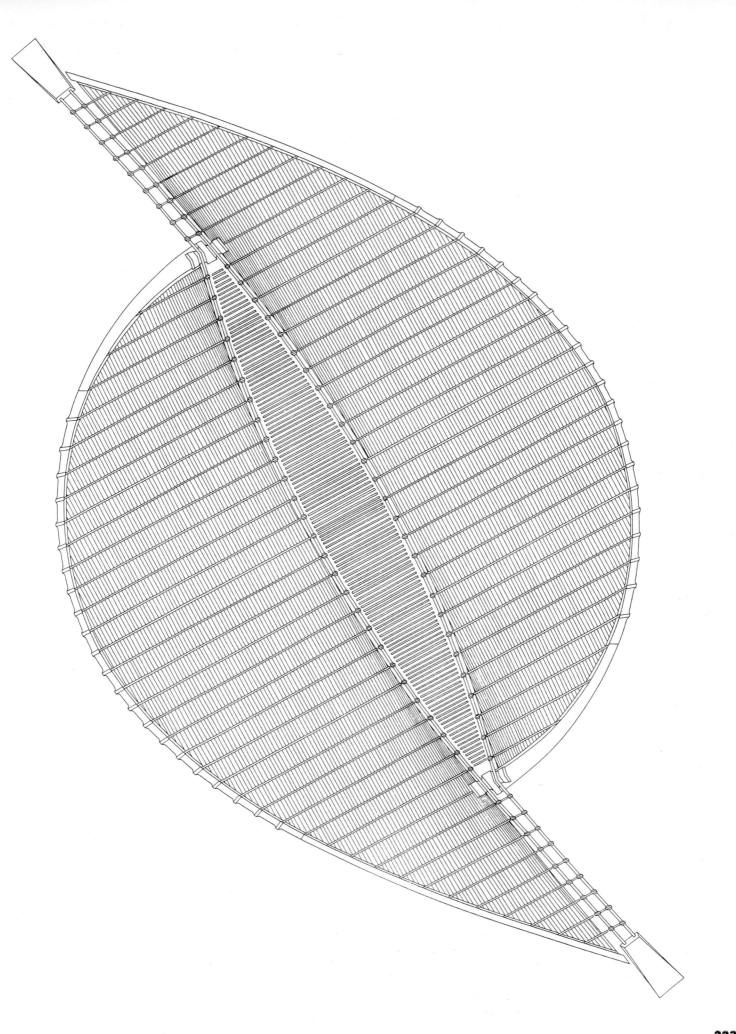

# BENJAMIN THOMPSON

B.T. April 82

No career in architecture is exactly like any other, but Ben Thompson's path to a position of prominence in the profession is probably more varied than any other architect in this century. He graduated from Yale University in 1941 at a time when World War II, not architecture, was on the nation's mind. Thompson spent five years in the navy, but when he returned he more than made up for the missing years by boldly suggesting to the famous refugee architect from Nazi Germany, Walter Gropius (at the time head of the architecture department at Harvard), that they form an architectural practice with some of his Yale classmates.

Gropius, who had founded the historic Bauhaus, accepted and The Architects Collaborative (TAC) was started. It was the first step in a career for Thompson that would set new parameters for the practice of architecture. He has had two extremely successful offices, the first being TAC, the second, Benjamin Thompson Associates. During the period when he was with The Architects Collaborative, Thompson also started a business called Design Research which specialized in products of high design quality, and featured the splashy Scandinavian fabric designs of Marimekko. The success of this venture was enhanced by a building he designed for the outlet that still stands as one of the most effective and outstanding examples of commercial architecture of the century. The 4-story building of concrete frame and sheer glass wall enclosures became a giant display for the merchandise within, both by day and night,

and set a new standard for openness in store designs. It proved the point that the proper display of merchandise is its own best advertisement.

Following the success, and subsequent demise, of Design Research as a showcase for product design (the latter after Thompson's guidance was no longer present), it was a natural next step for him to make use of this interest in the commercial aspects of architecture by applying it to a series of spectacular, large-scale urban shopping districts, beginning with Faneuil Hall in Boston. This was followed by similar acclaim for Harbor Place in Baltimore, South Street Seaport in New York City, and the Union Station redevelopment in Washington,

D.C., Thompson, through his skill in reweaving the contextual fabric of older neighborhoods in choice downtown commercial locations became a successful practitioner of urban renewal with a distinctly pedestrian liveliness.

After fifty years or so of practice, Thompson remains an optimist concerned with the future of architecture and our cities. "We have only begun to recognize architecture's real importance and function in modern life. Architecture should reflect man's hope and faith, interpret life and transmit joy. The very act of building is a symbolic act of confidence. . . . After all, we spend our lives in and around buildings, and, more than we know, our lives are shaped by their qualities—for better or worse."

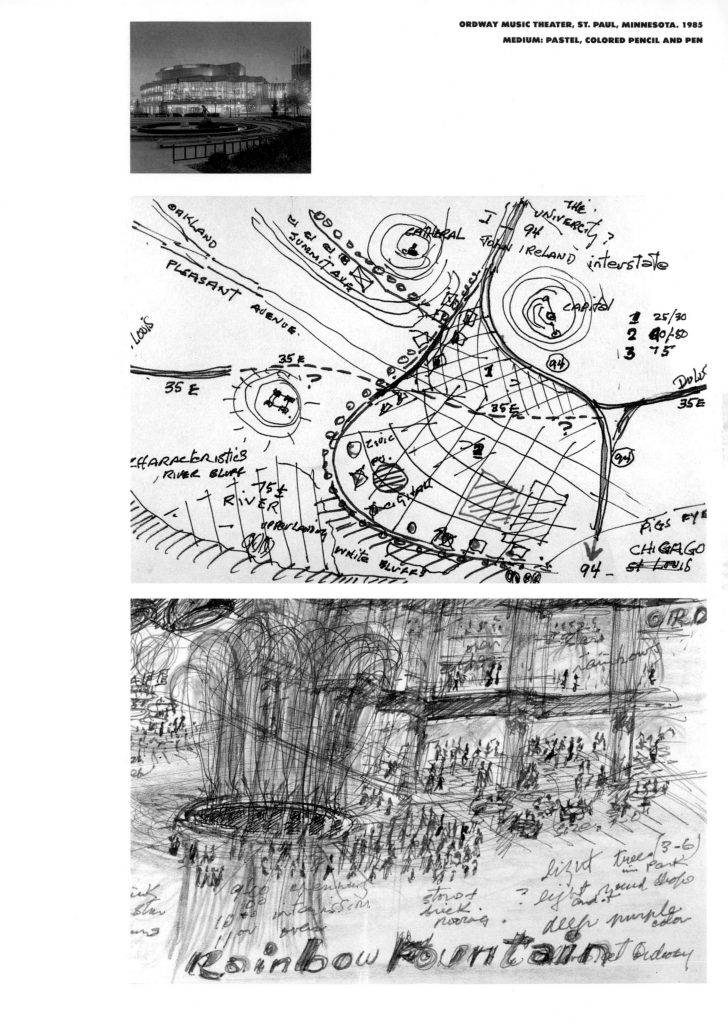

# STANLEY TIGERMAN

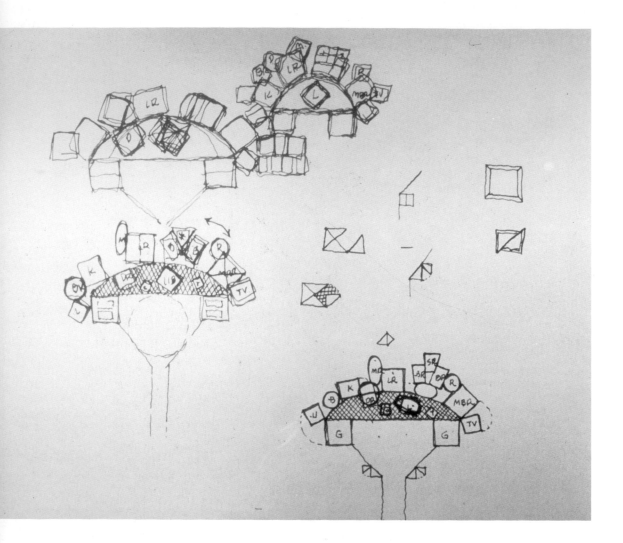

**T**hroughout his career, Stanley Tigerman has stood apart, altering the contemporary design idiom into his own idiosyncratic vision. He admits he never thought any one method necessarily "correct," but borrowed freely from diverse styles to create his own. Highly theoretical, Tigerman describes his work as having progressed through "construction into deconstruction into reconstruction." In a forthcoming book entitled *Failed Attempts at Healing an Irreparable Wound*, Tigerman will address and reinstate the "essential" moral character of architecture.

Tigerman's early works are modernistic—steel and glass taut skins. But there always is a little twist—a curve here, a three-dimensional aspect foreign to modern architecture, an anthropomorphic window, or a strikingly bright facade. He deftly balances attentiveness to detail and sculptural compositions with an eye toward inventiveness and witticism. An imaginative playfulness and wit is seen in the design—as well as the names—of his Hot Dog House, "Animal Crackers," Zipper Townhouses, Dante's Bathroom, "Kosher Kitchen (for a Suburban Jewish-American Princess)," "Tigerman Takes a Bit out of Keck," and more.

During his "deconstruction" phase, Tigerman did just that. The facades of the Hot Dog House, designed in the mid–1970s, explored the "notions of transparency and opacity that were not programmatic in origin," in Tigerman's words. For an apartment building in Chicago, Tigerman designed a modernist elevation on one side and for the other side took that elevation and superimposed upon it decidedly antimodern elements, distorted in scale to "explore issues of displacement."

In the 1980s Tigerman designed buildings in an inclusive state: for a corporate headquarter, a cube in which the ideal solid is destroyed by splitting it open; a butterfly plan house that explores the frail way rectilinear volumes intersect; a residence where like components of the building are disintegrated by rotation.

Tigerman's "failed attempt at healing an irreparable wound" phase aims to reinstate the essential moral character of architecture. The 1990s should be another intriguing episode in the always surprising career of this incorrigible Chicago architect.

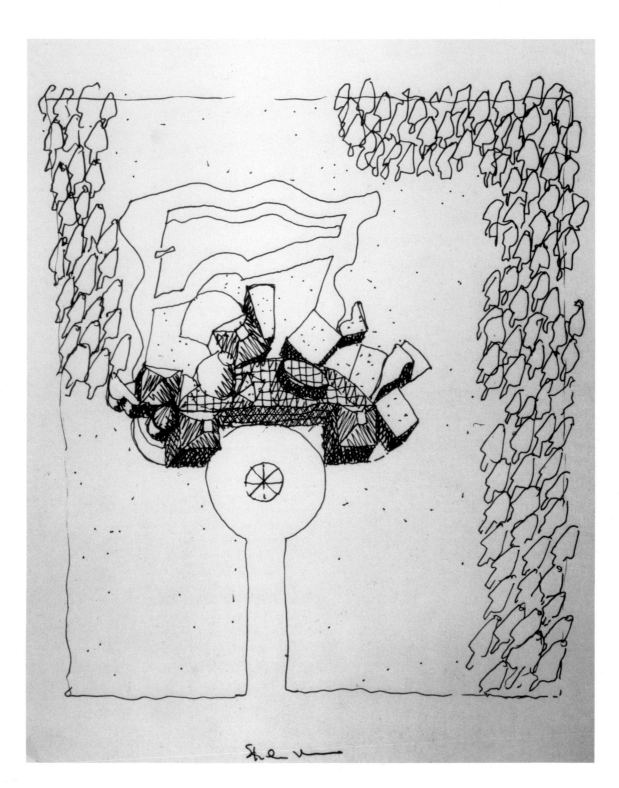

# BERNARD TSCHUMI

**PARC DE LA VILLETTE, PARIS, FRANCE. 1990**
**MEDIUM: PEN AND INK**

If architecture is a great river into which many tributaries of styles and ideas flow to make up the whole, and if, carrying the metaphor further, the course of the river is changed only when some errant current causes the mainstream to overflow its banks and create a slightly different course, then Bernard Tschumi could be that force. If his Parc de la Villette in Paris has not entirely diverted the course of architecture, it has at least caused it to meander outside its normal flow. And in the strictest traditional sense, his design is not quite architecture. It is more aptly described as a composition of intriguing pieces and parts, the pieces and parts being complex red structures called "Follies" by their creator, placed on a green plane like so many extraordinary chess pieces.

For ten years the Swiss-born Tschumi taught at the Architectural Association in London (1970–1980). He has also taught at the Institute for Urban Studies, Cooper Union, and Princeton University. Currently he is dean of the Graduate School of Architecture at Columbia University. In 1983, however, Tschumi was thrust into the international spotlight of instant fame with the announcement that his design had been selected from over 470 submissions for the Parc de la Villette project. Located on one of the last available large sites in Paris (125 acres), the project was, like the Louvre Pyramid, to be one of François Mitterand's "grand projects"—a calculated and ambitious series of public works to restore French prestige internationally by using architecture as the medium. The

Parc was described in the competition program as an "urban park for the 21st century—one that clearly broke with traditional forms of gardens and parks of the past."

In realizing the first phase of the $130 million project, Tschumi will have the opportunity to demonstrate his highly developed theories for a radically new approach to architecture—one that relies on "dis-assembly" of the traditional parts of buildings and takes into account "notations" of movement and activities as opposed to static and axial approaches. Drawing on the early work of Russian Constructivist art, Tschumi's bright red "Follies" will inhabit a park that will indeed be like no other in this century.

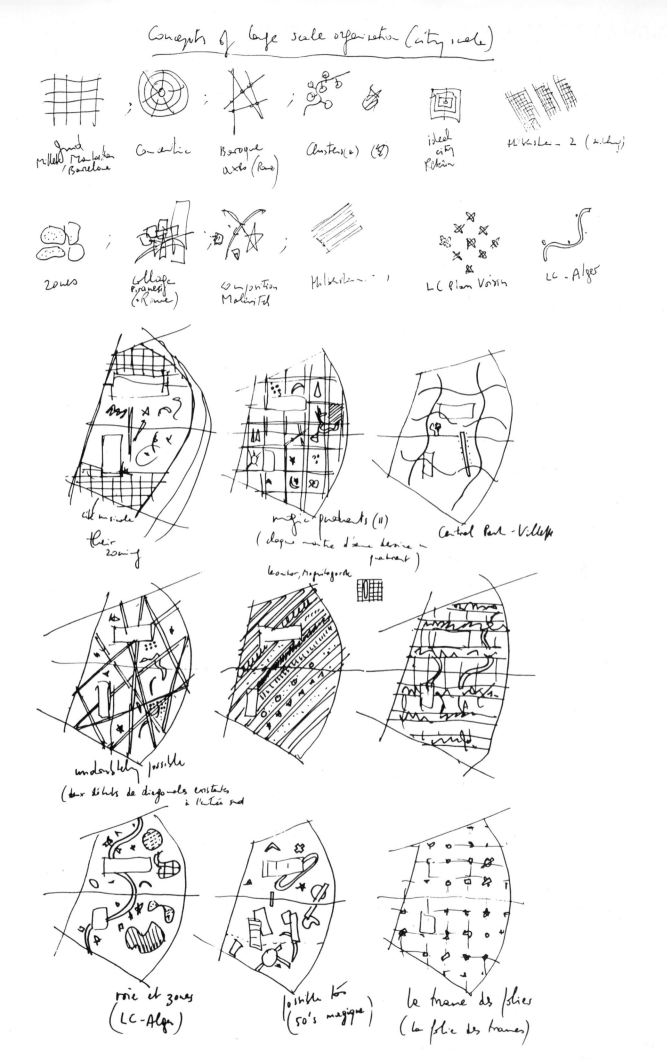

Concepts of large scale organisation (city scale)

millet grid Manhattan / Barcelone
Concentric
Baroque axis (Rome)
Clusters (a) (b)
ideal city Pékin
Hildesheim - 2 (buildings)

zones
collage Piranesif (+ Rome)
composition Malevitch
Hildesheim - 1
LC Plan Voisin
LC - Alger

cité mobile / their zoning
magic products (11) (daque notre d'une dessine = product)
leonhar, Nagdagorsk
Central Park - Villette

undoubtedly possible
(deux débuts de diagonals constates à l'entrée sud

voie et zones (LC-Alger)
possible too (50's magique)
le trame des folies (la folie des trames)

# WILLIAM TURNBULL, JR.

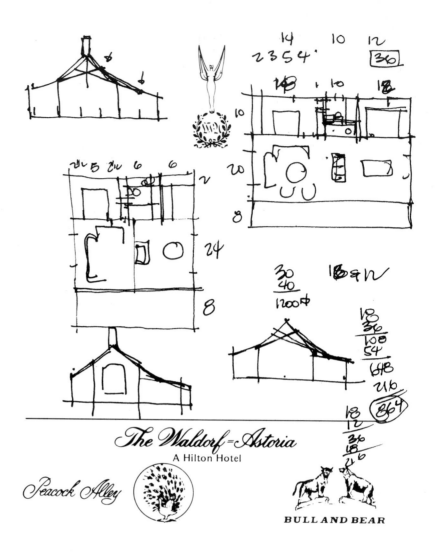

For William Turnbull, Jr., architecture is primarily concerned with establishing a sense of place, one that should be sensitive to the uniqueness of each client and each site. "Since the concept for our buildings is rooted in their environments, we are particularly attentive to topography, microclimate, and vegetation. We listen carefully to the aspirations and requirements of owners and users," Turnbull said of his approach and that of his colleagues at William Turnbull Associates in San Francisco. "Through continual discussions with clients, we seek to make each project compelling and reinforce its contextual setting."

Developing a sense of place emerged early in Turnbull's career—and in a spectacular way. In 1963, along with his partners at the time (Charles Moore, Donlyn Lyndon, and Richard Whitaker as MLTW), Turnbull designed Sea Ranch, a condominium complex for a 5,000-acre site 90 miles north of San Francisco Bay. Other buildings would follow there; the goal was to place them on the seaside meadow and woods in the most environmentally sensitive way possible. A complete analysis of the physical components of the landscape and their interactions by landscape architect Lawrence Halprin was the starting point from which the architects designed redwood cubes (no jarring colors or reflective finishes) that followed ground contours, turned their

backs to the wind, and welcomed sun into the interiors through skylights. Architectural historian David Gebhard called Sea Ranch "the California architectural monument of the 1960s."

Turnbull's work is not restricted to residential architecture, but it is in his houses that his "place making" is readily evident. "Architecture without space and light is devoid of interest. In its making, architecture should delight the mind, respect the purse, and consume the intellect," he said. For example, for their house in Fairfax County, Virginia, the clients, the Zimmermans, had conflicting concerns: he desired a sunny bright house, she wanted a grand porch circling the house.

Turnbull's solution: a skylighted porch. The Davidow vacation house in Hawaii was forced off the ground by the Tsunami wave restrictions. Desiring breeze ventilation, Turnbull transformed the traditional center hallway into a giant outside lanai with rooms clustered around it. Because of excessive summer heat problems in California's Central Valley, Turnbull turned the Allewelt residence there into an inside-outside gazebo with a trellised roof screening the hot sun.

Through many sensitively designed projects since the early fame of Sea Ranch, Turnbull has proven that it is possible, even in a time of media pandering, to develop a solid and respected practice, based on honest and direct solutions to the dictates of clients, site, and local environments.

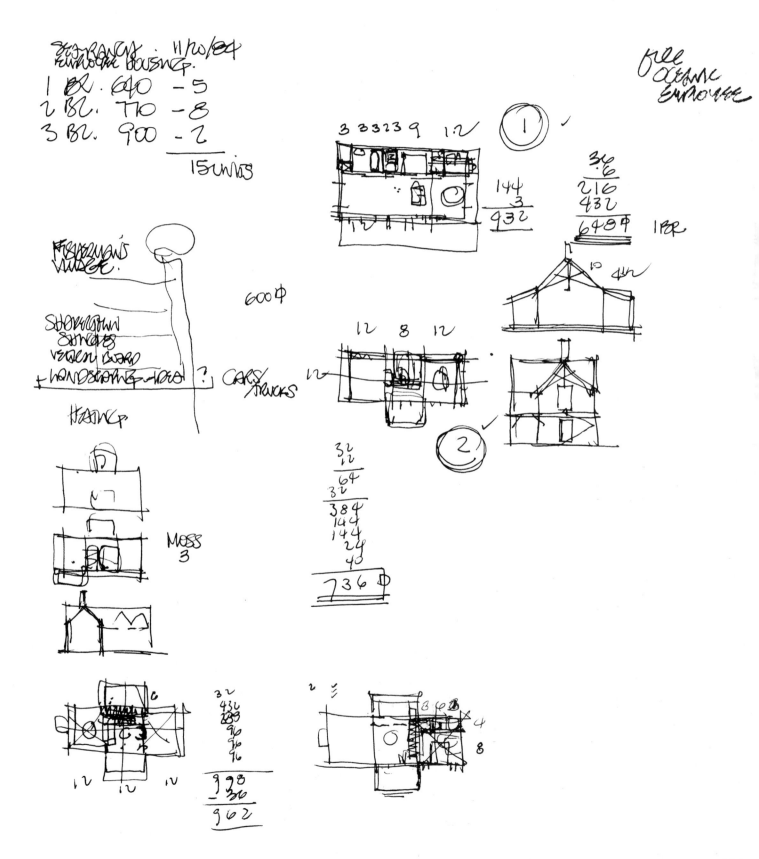

If you want to understand the architecture of Oswald Mathias Ungers through one building, you might choose the Architecture Museum in Frankfurt (1984). On first inspection one sees that the facade of a historical Frankfurt villa was saved and the interior gutted. On closer examination, however, one finds evidence of Ungers's brilliance, for the building is both an architectural monument as well as an architecture museum. Heinrich Klotz, director of the museum when it first opened in a renovated villa, has said, "Oswald Mathias Ungers has found a way from the traditional, multipurpose rooms of these art containers to space where a communication between art and architecture is not only imaginable but really possible. It is important not to have an 'anything-you-want' atmosphere but a specific, individual, and stimulating architecture, that does not destroy art by its emptiness, or its arrogance."

For Ungers, his architectural creations are individual solo performances for which he is totally responsible. He alone must assume the challenges. "Architecture is an analytical discussion with the environment that is developed and stamped by time," Ungers once said. "To accomplish this level of clarity," Ungers added, "the architectural concepts have to be carried through history and seen not as isolated events, as spontaneous inspirations, as clever tricks, or a 'menu of specialties,' but as something that does not change at all, that is permanent, and that only proceeds through continuous stages of transformation."

Ungers labels this philosophy as the "new abstraction"—the transformation of ideas and concepts in the course of history. According to Ungers, new abstraction will revive basic concepts of space that have occurred in all historical periods—for instance, the four-column space, the concept of walls, the courtyard block, the gate, the cruciform building, the square, the circle, the cylinder, the pyramid, and the perfect cube. For it is regular geometrical and volumetric forms that "as universal orders of abstraction represent a quality of permanence," Ungers maintains. "It is not the differentiation of color and form, of material and style, that will be of importance and significance, not the abundance of shapes, volumes, and spaces, but the restriction and economy of means."

Ungers's "house within a house" scheme for the Museum of Architecture in Frankfurt, like all of his works, shows an intellect that is constantly searching for the true meaning behind the apparent meaning. There is a clarity of thought that is refreshing as it is transformed into architectural dimensions.

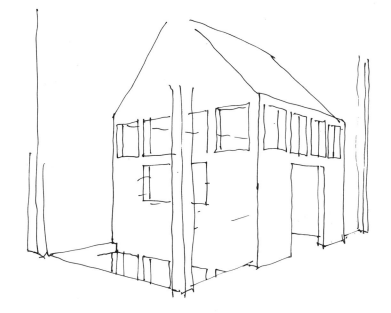

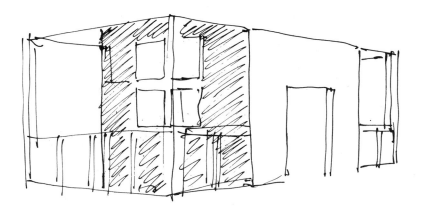

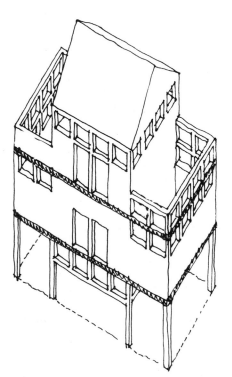

**A**rchitects are known by their buildings, and they are also known for their words. They have a penchant for making manifestos, for creating and publishing magazines, and for writing books that are intended to fully explain their theories and to establish the territory of their ideas. No book in this century, with the possible exception of *Vers Une Architecture* by the French architect Le Corbusier, has had such a visible and profound effect on archiectural thinking as *Complexity and Contradiction in Architecture*, written by Robert Venturi in 1966. This book left a gaping hole in the ship of modern architecture and gave architects the freedom, without guilt, to enjoy vernacular American architecture, to embrace inconsistencies in form and discontinuities in pattern.

Venturi made the vulgar acceptable and celebrated the ordinary. In the book that followed six years later, with Denise Scott Brown and Steven Izenour, *Learning From Las Vegas*, he expanded his revolutionary ideas to include that reviled consequence of cars and commerce, the "strip development," and cited its glittering zenith in Las Vegas, Nevada, as the model to study.

Venturi's early houses—one for his mother in 1961 and summer houses in Massachusetts—gave form to some of his theories. At the time they confounded critics and angered his peers. Subsequently he has produced a consistent body of ever more thoughtful and refined architecture. Among the premier commissions of recent years has been the much-sought-after commission to design a major wing to the National Gallery of Art in London, and the major disappointment, the postponement of the firm's grand plan for the western boundary of Manhattan called Westway. Robert Venturi's considerable impact on architects and architecture in the twentieth century was recognized in 1991 by his selection as the Pritzker Architecture Prize recipient.

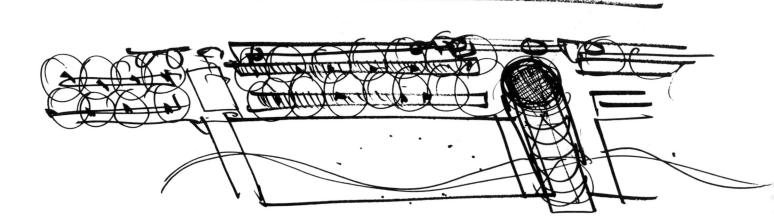

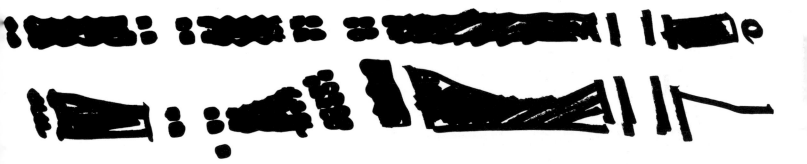

Side Sec

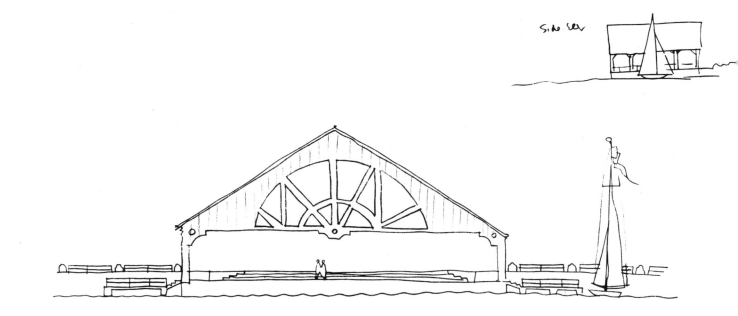

# HARRY M. WEESE

**A**rchitects, like writers who become known for a single book or poets for the one great poem, often are identified, fairly or unfairly, with the building that receives that much desired "recognition" factor which in modern marketing parlance makes the product memorable. In Harry Weese's case, after a career of award-winning buildings which included the Arena Stage Theater II in Washington, D.C., the Federal Correction Center in Chicago, and the First Baptist Church in Columbus, Indiana, he became singularly known and identified with the design of the subway system in the nation's capital.

Weese's choice for this commission was an especially appropriate one, since he was one of the earliest of modernist architects to include in his practice a sincere respect for the past. He had proven this in many historic preservation battles in his native Chicago and with his own notable restoration of the impressive Chicago Auditorium theater by Louis Sullivan and Dankmar Adler in 1967, well before the general movement took hold in the United States. In the Washington, D.C., urban transit project Weese solved the problem of a unifying framework by using a giant coffered ceiling structure that arched over each stop and allowed for individual design diversity within each one. As a result there was no loss of orientation or distortion of the overall conceptual theme.

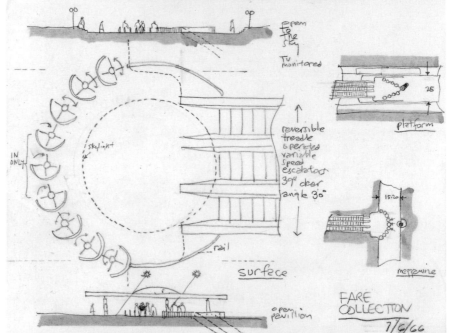

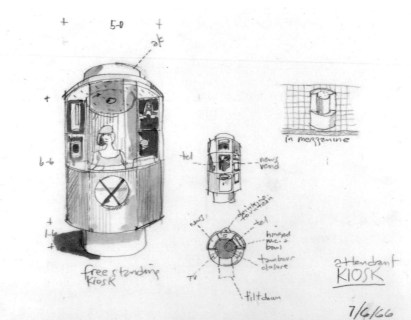

**METRO STATION SYSTEM, WASHINGTON, D.C. 1977**
**MEDIUM: COLORED PENCIL AND MARKER**

Weese is a passionate reformer and a visionary. He has been engaged in many civic battles in Chicago to make it the city he envisions. In his optimistic view of the future city he sees one that will be "denser, greener, more permanent, and more responsive to human needs and individual creativity," a city where people will live in town and go to work on the fringes "rather than the other way around" because the city should be "throbbing with the ongathering of institutions, culture, circus and commerce. . . ."

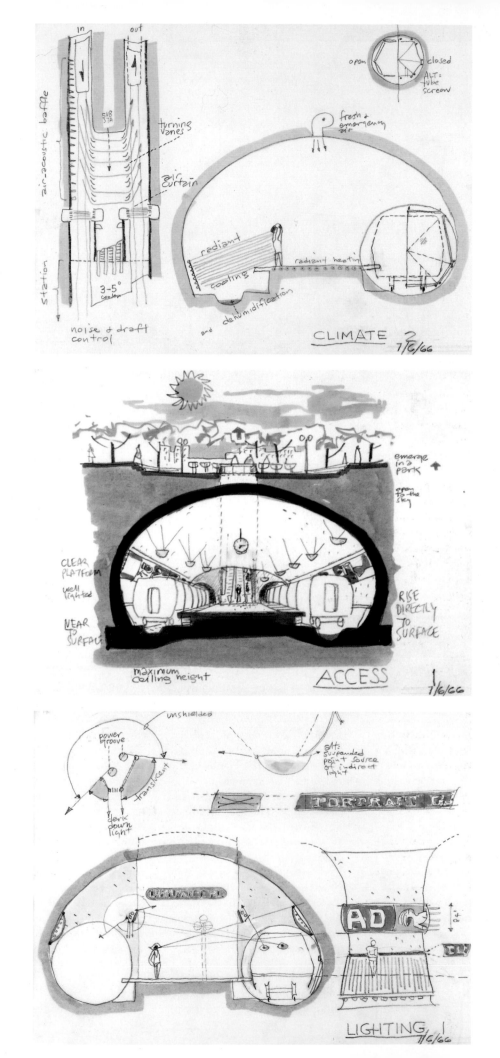

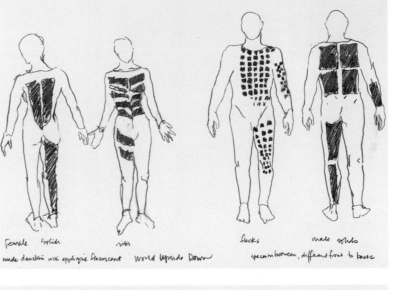

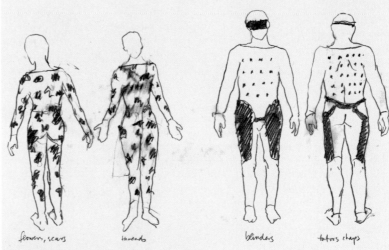

It would be easy to describe Williams and Tsien simply as a couple like Charles and Ray Eames or Denise Scott Brown and Robert Venturi, who have combined professional and personal lives, but that would tell too little of these two remarkable talents.

Tod Williams graduated from Princeton, Billie Tsien from Yale and UCLA. Mr. Williams worked with the firm of Richard Meier for six years and on his own for seventeen years before forming the current partnership with Billie Tsien in 1986 in New York City. Williams and Tsien have lectured at many major universities, have exhibited their special brand of architectural ideas at the principal showcases for such works, and have executed a number of award-winning commissions. Among this latter group is the Feinberg Hall Dormitory at Princeton University in 1988. They have been the recipient of a number of awards from the American Institute of Architects, and grants from the National Endowment for the Arts and the New York State Arts Council. Tsien was included in the notable "40 Under 40" list by *Interiors* magazine in 1986, and both Williams and Tsien have been widely recognized for their special creative talents and ability to meet the needs of the client and the dictates of the site.

In 1989 Williams and Tsien achieved another level of notoriety with their provocative show called "Domestic Arrangements," which opened at The Walker Art Center in Minneapolis, Minnesota. Using the most obvious and ubiquitous design example, the house, Williams and Tsien expanded the limits of domestic design. They tackled the problem of contemporary living arrangements using innovative ideas such as an oversize table which also served as a bed, and explored the use of ordinary materials used in plain and straightforward ways, always with their unique blend of forward-looking modernism. Their designs move toward an architectural style that fits current fashion, but is thoughtful and original stemming as it does from the problem to be solved and their aesthetic response.

This versatile, inventive, and artistic pair have not limited their practice to buildings only. Their most recent incursion into the related arts, with Kathy Inukai, has been the design of dance costumes and sets for a work called "The World Upside Down," performed by the Elisa Monte Dance Company, which premiered in Amsterdam in 1990.

"WORLD UPSIDE DOWN" DANCE PROJECT,
HET MUZIEK THEATER, AMSTERDAM. 1990
MEDIUM: PENCIL, OPPOSITE
MEDIUM: PEN AND INK

# HARRY C. WOLF

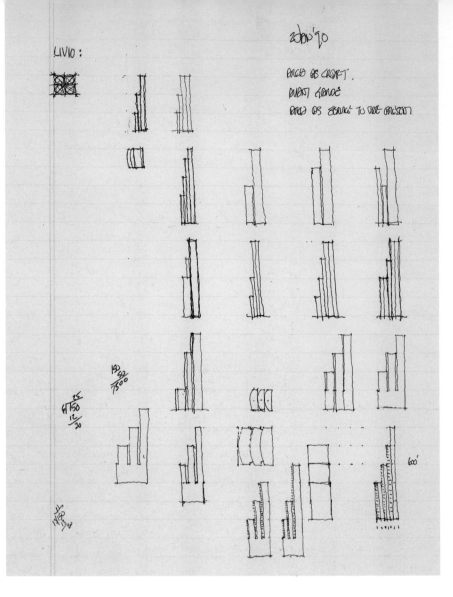

The design process in architecture is centered around the search for an organizing principle—a set of conditions or an understanding of the problem that allows an architect to apply his or her particular experience and talent to its solution. In Harry Wolf's case, the focus in arriving at a design is dictated in large part by a strong belief in the beauty and order of geometry. While other architects might let the procession of spaces or the dictates of imagery shape their building, Wolf, like Mies ("I do not want to invent a new architecture every Monday"), proceeds from one geometric analysis to the next. Also like Mies, his buildings show this willing conformity to the constraints of a mathematical

order that is as old as the art of building. The larger forms are a consequence of the details, and when analyzed the details are an integral replication of the larger design, not unlike our universe in which the microscopic and the cosmic are all part of the same larger fabric.

Wolf, a North Carolinian, received his formal education at the Massachusetts Institute for Technology, graduating in 1960. Six years later he started his own firm in Charlotte, North Carolina, and quickly gained recognition regionally and nationally for his innovative work in restoring that city's urban vitality. Since that time Wolf's career has proceeded through various partnerships and associations in different locations, first in New York City

and now in Los Angeles, where his firm is called Wolf +. The one consistency in these different affiliations and changing addresses has been the string of outstanding projects that prompted critic Kenneth Frampton to call him "one of the most sensitive practicing architects in America today."

Work such as the pure cylindrical bank headquarters building in Tampa, Florida, elicited another critical assessment calling it "a completely fresh architecture created out of a Miesian genre" that is "poetic and elegant in its understatement." For the bank, Wolf used The Fibbonacci series (1,2,3,5,8,13 . . .) to arrive at its near perfect form and proportions.

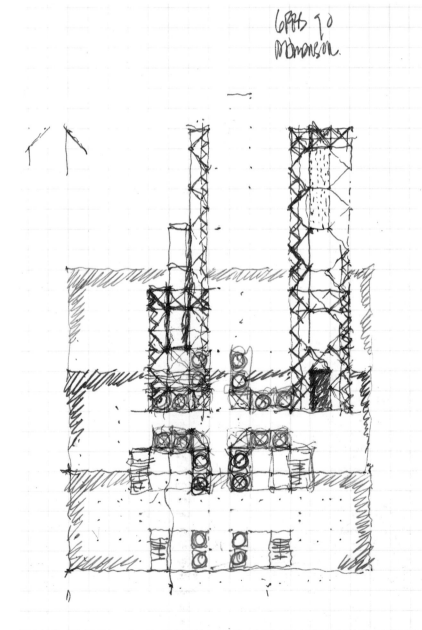

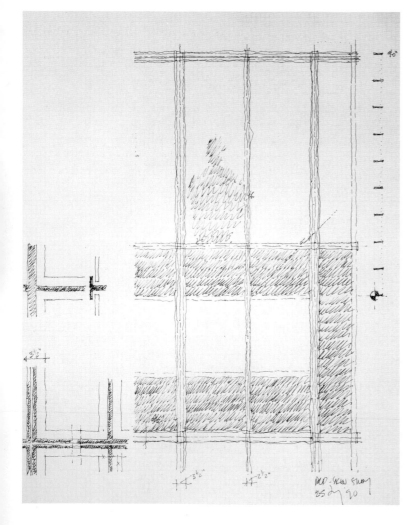

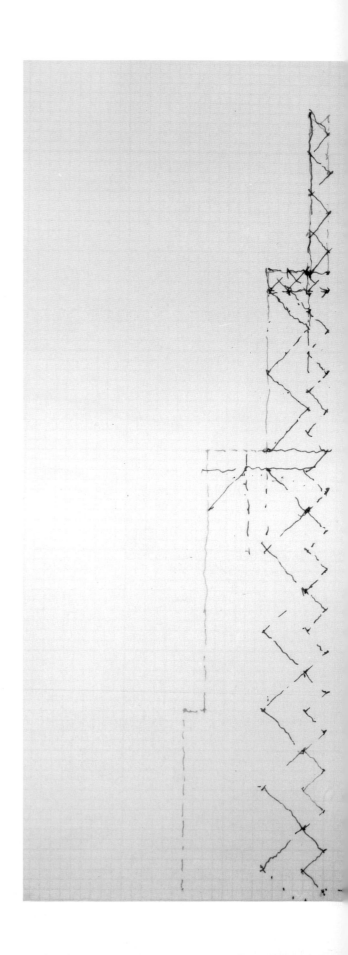

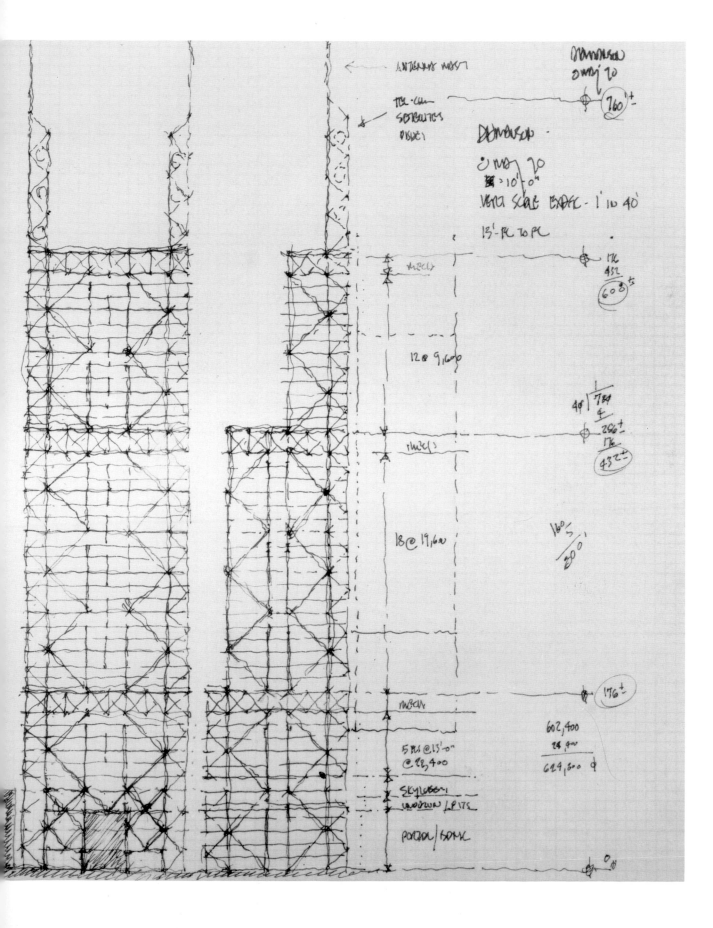

# LEBBEUS WOODS

Andres RIN. — 29 400. 6
N EVE CENTRUM — BERLIN.

**W**ith the inevitable and seemingly irresistible incursion of electronic media into all art forms, the notion of hand-drawn lines on paper as a part of the architectural design process seems relegated to an era of ground ink and crow quill pens. Images of sepia line renderings of capitals and columns, not contemporary architecture, seem more congruent with this approach.

The drawings of Lebbeus Woods give lie to that impression in the most dramatic way. The skill of Woods's commanding draftsmanship matches a vision usually reserved for great masters of painting and a finished drawing by Woods (if there can be such a thing) is an awesome realization in line. Like Duchamp's revolutionary *Nude Descending A Staircase*, he sets free one's imagination, destroys preconceptions of how architecture should properly look or be presented, and draws the viewer into the author's fantasy of a future time and place.

Described by Christian Thomsen as "one of the most exotic birds of the international architectural scene," Woods founded a nonprofit institution in New York City whose goals are to advance architecture through experimentation and research. His work is widely exhibited abroad and he is generally recognized not only as one of the finest draftsmen in the classical sense of architecture but also as one of its most intriguing philosophers.

Woods's attitude about architecture and his daring approach is summed up in his statement that "'architectural beauty cannot exist without the beauty of ideas." No project to date of Woods's exemplifies this thesis more than his "Berlin-Free-Zone." Here the center of a united Berlin is intended as giant "heterarchy or network" of individuals equipped with the latest telecommunication equipment whose community activities give shape to the area. One senses in Woods's drawings the genesis of a new architecture that once realized will make these drawings, now shocking, seem inevitable and familiar.

'BERLIN-FREE-ZONE' PROJECT, BERLIN, GERMANY. 1990
MEDIUM: PEN AND INK, COLORED PENCIL

'BERLIN-FREE-ZONE' PROJECT, BERLIN, GERMANY. 1990
MEDIUM: PEN AND INK, COLORED PENCIL

# BIOGRAPHIES

## ANTHONY AMES

**Born 1944, United States**

**Residence: United States**

**Education: Georgia Tech, Atlanta; Harvard University, Graduate School of Design, Cambridge, Massachusetts**

**Principal Honors: Fellow, American Academy in Rome, 1983; Fellow, American Institute of Architects, 1989**

## RAIMUND ABRAHAM

**Born 1933, Austria**

**Residence: United States**

**Education: Technische Universitaet, Graz, Austria**

**Principal Honors: Fellowship, Deutscher Akademischer Austausch-Doenst, 1981**

## TADAO ANDO

**Born 1941, Japan**

**Residence: Japan**

**Education: Self-educated**

**Principal Honors: Annual Prize, Architectural Institute of Japan, 1979; Japanese Cultural Design Prize, 1983; Alvar Aalto Medal, 1985; Annual Award, Japanese Ministry of Education, 1986; The Mainichi Art Prize, 1987; Isoya Yoshida Award, 1988; Gold Medal, Académie d'Architecture, Paris, 1989**

## EMILIO AMBASZ

**Born 1943, Argentina**

**Residence: United States**

**Education: Princeton University, New Jersey**

**Principal Honors: U.S. Representative at Venice Biennale, 1976; *Progressive Architecture* Award, 1976, 1980, 1985; Compasso d'Oro, Italy, 1981; Industrial Design Excellence Award, Industrial Designers Society of America, 1983, 1987, 1988; Quarternario Award, 1990**

## GAETANA AULENTI

**Born 1927, Italy**

**Residence: Italy**

**Education: Milan Polytechnic School of Architecture**

**Principal Honors: Grand International Prize, Triennale, Milan, 1960–64; Honorary Member, Italian National Society of Interior Designers, 1967; Honorary Member, American Society of Interior Designers, 1976**

## JOHN ANDREWS

**Born 1933, Australia**

**Residence: Australia**

**Education: University of Sydney, Australia; Harvard University, Cambridge, Massachusetts**

**Principal Honors: Associate, Royal Institute of British Architects, 1959; Fellow, Royal Architectural Institute of Canada, 1967; Centennial Medal, Canada, 1967; Massey Medal, Canada, 1967; Arnold W. Brunner Memorial Prize in Architecture, American Academy and Institute of Arts and Letters, 1971; Fellow, Royal Australian Institute of Architects, 1972; Bronze Medal, Queensland Institute of Architects, 1976; Gold Medal, 1980, Royal Australian Institute of Architects; Honor Award, American Institute of Architects, 1983**

## EDWARD LARRABEE BARNES

**Born 1915, United States**

**Residence: United States**

**Education: Harvard University, Cambridge, Massachusetts**

**Principal Honors: Arnold W. Brunner Memorial Prize in Architecture, American Academy and Institute of Arts and Letters, 1959; Fellow, American Institute of Architects, 1966; Fellow, American Academy of Arts and Sciences, 1978; Louis Sullivan Award, American Institute of Architects, 1979; Firm Award, American Institute of Architects, 1980; Thomas Jefferson Medal in Architecture, University of Virginia, 1981**

## ARQUITECTONICA

**Bernardo Fort-Brescia**

**Born 1951, Peru**

**Residence: United States**

**Education: Harvard University, Cambridge, Massachusetts; Princeton University, New Jersey**

**Laurinda Spear**

**Born 1951, United States**

**Residence: United States**

**Education: Columbia University, New York; Brown University, Providence, Rhode Island**

**Principal Honors: Fellow, American Academy in Rome, 1978**

## KAREN BAUSMAN / LESLIE GILL

**Karen Bausman**

**Born 1958, United States**

**Residence: United States**

**Education: The Cooper Union for the Advancement of Science and Art, New York**

**Leslie Gill**

**Born 1957, United States**

**Residence: United States**

**Education: The Cooper Union for the Advancement of Science and Art, New York**

## GUNNAR BIRKERTS

**Born 1925, Latvia**

**Residence: United States**

**Education: Technische Hochschule, Stuttgart**

**Principal Honors: Honor Award, American Institute of Architects, 1962, 1970, 1973; Fellow, American Institute of Architects, 1970; Fellow, Latvian Architects Association, 1971; Fellowship, Graham Foundation, 1971; Arnold W. Brunner Memorial Prize in Architecture, American Academy and Institute of Arts and Letters, 1981**

## THOMAS BEEBY

**Born 1941, United States**

**Residence: United States**

**Education: Cornell University, Ithaca, New York; Yale University School of Architecture, New Haven, Connecticut**

**Principal Honors: Honor Award, American Institute of Architects, 1984, 1986**

## RICARDO BOFILL

**Born 1939, Spain**

**Residence: Spain**

**Education: French Institute of Barcelona; Escuela Tecnica Superior de Arquitectura, Barcelona; Architecture University of Geneva**

**Principal Honors: International Design Award, American Society of Interior Designers, 1978; Gold Medal, Académie d'Architecture Paris, 1983; Honorary Fellow, American Institute of Architecture, 1983**

## GOTTFRIED BÖHM

**Born 1929, Germany**

**Residence: Germany**

**Education: Apostein-Gymnasium, Cologne; Technische Hochschule, Munich; Academy of Sculptural Art, Munich**

**Principal Honors: Gold Medal, Académie d'Architecture, Paris, 1983; Honorary Fellow, American Institute of Architects, 1983; Pritzker Architecture Prize, 1986**

## JEAN PAUL CARLHIAN

**Born 1919, France**

**Residence: United States**

**Education: University of Paris; Ecole Nationale Supérieure des Beaux-Arts, Paris and Marseille; Harvard University, Graduate School of Design, Cambridge, Massachusetts**

**Principal Honors: Wheelwright Fellow, Harvard University, 1947; Fellow, American Institute of Architects, 1973; Fellow, Royal Society of Artists, London, 1980; Edward C. Kemper Award, American Institute of Architects, 1989**

## MARIO BOTTA

**Born 1943, Switzerland**

**Residence: Switzerland**

**Education: Instituto Universitario di Architettura, Venice**

**Principal Honors: Honorary Fellow, Bund Deutscher Architekten, 1983; Honorary Fellow, American Institute of Architects, 1984**

## PETER CHERMAYEFF

**Born 1936, United States**

**Residence: United States**

**Education: Harvard University, Cambridge, Massachusetts; Harvard University, Graduate School of Design**

**Principal Honors: Design Award, American Institute of Architects, 1967; American Institute of Architects/American Library Association Award, 1970; Fellow, American Institute of Architects, 1983**

## DAVID CHILDS

**Born 1941, United States**

**Residence: United States**

**Education: Yale University, New Haven, Connecticut**

**Principal Honors: Federal Design Achievement Award, 1984; Excellence Award, International Masonry Award, 1987**

## COOP HIMMELBLAU

**Wolf D. Prix**

**Born 1942, Austria**

**Residence: Austria**

**Education: Technical University of Vienna**

**Helmut Swiczinsky**

**Born 1944, Poland**

**Residence: Austria**

**Education: Technical University of Vienna**

**Principal Honors: (Firm Awards) Berliner Forderungspreis für Baukunst Award, 1982; Award of the City of Vienna for Architecture, 1988; Honorary Membership, Bund Deutscher Architekten, Germany, 1989; League of Austrian Architects Special Award, 1989; State of Carinthia Superior Architecture Prize, 1989**

## HENRY N. COBB

**Born 1926, United States**

**Residence: United States**

**Education: Harvard University, Cambridge, Massachusetts; Harvard University, Graduate School of Design**

**Principal Honors: Fellow, American Institute of Architects, 1959; Arnold W. Brunner Memorial Prize in Architecture, American Academy and Institute of Arts and Letters, 1977; Fellow, American Academy of Arts and Sciences, 1984**

## CHARLES CORREA

**Born 1930, India**

**Residence: India**

**Education: St. Xavier's College, Bombay; University of Michigan, Ann Arbor; Massachusetts Institute of Technology, Cambridge**

**Principal Honors: Fellow, Indian Institute of Architects, 1964; Padma Shri Award, Government of India, 1972; Honorary Fellow, American Institute of Architects, 1979; Gold Medal, Royal Institute of British Architects, 1984; Gold Medal, The International Union of Architects, 1990**

## BALKRISHNA VITHALDAS DOSHI

**Born 1927, India**

**Residence: India**

**Education: Fergusson College, Poona; J. J. School of Art, Bombay**

**Principal Honors: Associate Member, Royal Institute of British Architects, 1954; Fellowship, Graham Foundation, 1958; Honorary Fellow, American Institute of Architects, 1971; Fellow, Indian Institute of Architects, 1971; Padma Shri Award, Government of India, 1976**

## PETER EISENMAN

**Born 1932, United States**

**Residence: United States**

**Education: Cornell University, Ithaca, New York; Columbia University, New York; Cambridge University, England**

**Principal Honors: Fellowship, Graham Foundation, 1966; Fellowship, Guggenheim Foundation, 1976; Arnold W. Brunner Memorial Prize in Architecture, American Academy and Institute of Arts and Letters, 1984**

## ANDRES DUANY/ ELIZABETH PLATER-ZYBERK

**Andres Duany**

**Born 1949, Cuba**

**Residence: United States**

**Education: Princeton University, New Jersey; Yale University School of Architecture, New Haven, Connecticut**

**Elizabeth Plater-Zyberk**

**Born 1950, United States**

**Residence: United States**

**Education: Princeton University, New Jersey; Yale University School of Architecture, New Haven, Connecticut**

**Principal Honors: (Firm Awards) Honor Award, American Institute of Architects, 1987**

## ARTHUR ERICKSON

**Born 1924, Canada**

**Residence: Canada**

**Education: University of British Columbia, Vancouver; McGill University, Montreal**

**Principal Honors: Fellow, Architectural Institute of Canada, 1953; Massey Medal, 1955, 1958, 1967; Molson Prize, Canada Council, 1967; Architectural Institute of Japan Award, 1970; Auguste Perret Prize, International Union of Architects, 1974; Honorary Fellow, American Institute of Architects, 1978; Gold Medal, Royal Institute of Canada, 1984; Gold Medal, Académie d'Architecture, Paris, 1984**

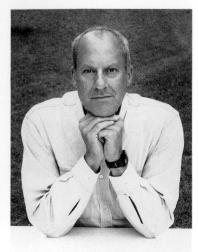

## NORMAN FOSTER

**Born 1935, England**

**Residence: England**

**Education: University of Manchester, School of Architecture and Department of Town and Country Planning; Yale University School of Architecture, New Haven, Connecticut**

**Principal Honors: Royal Institute of British Architects Award, 1969, 1972, 1977, 1978, and Gold Medal, 1983; R. S. Reynolds Memorial Award, American Institute of Architects, 1976, 1979; 6th International Prize for Architecture, Brussels, 1980; Premier Architectural Award, Royal Academy, London, 1983**

## JAMES INGO FREED

**Born 1930, Germany**

**Residence: United States**

**Education: Illinois Institute of Technology, Chicago**

**Principal Honors: R. S. Reynolds Memorial Award for Excellence in Architecture, 1975; Fellow, American Institute of Architecture, 1977; Arnold W. Brunner Memorial Prize in Architecture, American Academy and Institute of Arts and Letters, 1987; Honor Award, American Institute of Architects, 1988**

## ULRICH FRANZEN

**Born 1936, Germany**

**Residence: United States**

**Education: Williams College, Williamstown, Massachusetts; Harvard University, Graduate School of Design, Cambridge, Massachusetts**

**Principal Honors: Arnold W. Brunner Memorial Prize in Architecture, National Institute of Arts and Letters, 1962; Louis Sullivan Award, American Institute of Architects, 1970; Fellow, American Institute of Architects, 1970; Thomas Jefferson Medal in Architecture, American Institute of Architects and the Masonry Institute, 1971; Honor Award, American Institute of Architects, 1971, 1972**

## FRANK GEHRY

**Born 1929, Canada**

**Residence: United States**

**Education: University of Southern California, Los Angeles; Harvard University, Cambridge, Massachusetts**

**Principal Honors: Fellow, American Institute of Architects, 1974; Arnold W. Brunner Memorial Prize in Architecture, American Academy and Institute of Arts and Letters, 1977; Fellow, American Academy and Institute of Arts and Letters, 1987; Pritzker Architecture Prize, 1989**

## ROMALDO GIURGOLA

**Born 1920, Italy**

**Residence: Australia**

**Education: Master of Science in Architecture, Columbia University, New York; University of Rome, Italy**

**Principal Honors: Arnold W. Brunner Memorial Prize in Architecture, National Institute of Arts and Letters, 1966; Commendatore of the Order of the Republic of Italy, Italian Government, 1972; Fellow, American Institute of Architects, 1975; Institute Member, American Academy and Institute of Arts and Letters, 1977; Member, Accademia Nazionale di San Luca, Rome, 1980; Gold Medal, American Institute of Architects, 1982; Thomas Jefferson Medal in Architecture, University of Virginia, 1987; Gold Medal, The Royal Australian Institute of Architects, 1988**

## MICHAEL GRAVES

**Born 1934, United States**

**Residence: United States**

**Education: University of Cincinnati, Ohio; Harvard University, Cambridge, Massachusetts**

**Principal Honors: Fellow, American Academy in Rome, 1960; Honor Award, American Institute of Architects, 1975, 1985; Fellow, American Institute of Architects, 1979; Arnold W. Brunner Memorial Prize in Architecture, American Academy and Institute of Arts and Letters, 1980**

## CHARLES GRAVES

**Born 1927, United States**

**Residence: United States**

**Education: Georgia Institute of Technology; University of Pennsylvania**

**Principal Honors: Fellow, American Institute of Architects, 1983**

## ALLAN GREENBERG

**Born 1938, South Africa**

**Residence: United States**

**Education: University of the Witwatersrand, Johannesburg; Yale University, New Haven, Connecticut**

## CHARLES GWATHMEY

Born 1938, United States

Residence: United States

Education: University of
Pennsylvania School of
Architecture, Philadelphia; Yale
University School of Architecture,
New Haven, Connecticut

Principal Honors: William Wirt
Winchester Travelling Fellowship,
1962; Fulbright Fellowship,
France, 1962–63; Arnold W.
Brunner Memorial Prize in
Architecture, American Academy
and Institute of Arts and Letters,
1970; Bard Award, City Club of
New York, 1977; Fellow,
American Institute of Architects,
1981; National Firm Award,
American Institute of Architects,
1982

## HUGH HARDY

Born 1932, Spain

Residence: United States

Education: Princeton University,
New Jersey

Principal Honors: Arnold W.
Brunner Memorial Prize in
Architecture, American Institute
of Arts and Letters, 1974; Fellow,
American Institute of Architects,
1976; Bard Award, City Club of
New York, 1977; Honor Award,
American Institute of Architects,
1977, 1983; Architecture Firm
Award, American Institute of
Architects, 1981

## ZAHA HADID

Born Iraq

Residence: England

Education: The American
University, Beirut; Architectural
Association of Architecture,
London

Principal Honors: British
Architectural Awards Gold Medal,
1982

## GEORGE HARTMAN/
WARREN COX

George Hartman

Born 1936, United States

Residence: United States

Education: Princeton University,
New Jersey

Principal Honors: Honor Award,
American Institute of Architects,
1970, 1971, 1981, 1983; Louis
Sullivan Prize, American Institute
of Architects, 1972; Fellow,
American Institute of Architects,
1975

Warren Jacob Cox

Born 1935, United States

Residence: United States

Education: Yale University, New
Haven, Connecticut

Principal Honors: Honor Award,
American Institute of
Architecture, 1970, 1971, 1981,
1983; Louis Sullivan Prize,
American Institute of Architects,
1972; Honor Award, American
Institute of Architects, 1977;
Fellow, American Institute of
Architects, 1977

## STEVEN HOLL

**Born 1948, United States**

**Residence: United States**

**Education: University of Washington, Seattle; Architectural Association School of Architecture, London**

**Principal Honors: Honor Award, American Institute of Architecture, 1989; Arnold W. Brunner Memorial Prize in Architecture, American Academy and Institute of Arts and Letters, 1990**

## JOHN HEJDUK

**Born 1929, United States**

**Residence: United States**

**Education: The Cooper Union for the Advancement of Science and Art, New York; University of Cincinnati, Ohio; Harvard University, Graduate School of Design, Cambridge, Massachusetts**

**Principal Honors: Fulbright Scholarship, Italy, 1953; Fellow, American Institute of Architects, 1979; Arnold W. Brunner Memorial Prize in Architecture, American Academy and Institute of Arts and Letters, 1986; Topaz Medallion for Excellence in Architectural Education, American Institute of Architecture and Association of Collegiate Schools of Architecture, 1988**

## HANS HOLLEIN

**Born 1934, Austria**

**Residence: Austria**

**Education: Department of Civil Engineering, Bundesgewerbeschule, Vienna; Academy of Fine Arts, School of Architecture, Vienna; Illinois Institute of Technology, Chicago; University of California, College of Environmental Design, Berkeley**

**Principal Honors: R. S. Reynolds Memorial Award, American Institute of Architects, 1966, 1984; Austrian State Award, 1968, 1983; Bard Award, City Club of New York, 1970; City of Vienna Prize, 1974; Industrial Design Excellence Award, Industrial Designers Society of America, 1977; Honorary Fellow, American Institute of Architects, 1981; German Architecture Award, 1983; Pritzker Architecture Prize, 1985**

## HERMAN HERTZBERGER

**Born 1932, The Netherlands**

**Residence: The Netherlands**

**Education: Technical University, Delft, The Netherlands**

**Principal Honors: Amsterdam Architectural Award, 1968; Eternit Award, 1974; Fritz Schumacher Award, 1974; A. J. van Eck Award, 1980**

## MICHAEL HOPKINS

**Born 1935, England**

**Residence: England**

**Education: Bournemouth Art School, Sherbourne School, Architectural Association School of Architecture, London**

**Principal Honors: Royal Institute of British Architects, 1988, 1989**

## ARATA ISOZAKI

**Born 1931, Japan**

**Residence: Japan**

**Education: University of Tokyo**

**Principal Honors: Annual Prize, 1967, 1975 and Special Expo Prize, 1970, Architectural Institute of Japan; Honorary Fellow, American Institute of Architects, 1983; Honorary Member, Bund Deutscher Architekten, West Germany, 1983; The Mainichi Art Prize, Tokyo, 1983**

## HELMUT JAHN

**Born 1940, Germany**

**Residence: United States**

**Education: Technische Hochschule, Munich; Illinois Institute of Technology, Chicago**

**Principal Honors: Honor Award, American Institute of Architects, 1975, 1979, 1987; Arnold W. Brunner Memorial Prize in Architecture, American Academy and Institute of Arts and Letters, 1982; Presidential Design Award, National Endowment for the Arts, 1988; R. S. Reynolds Memorial Award, American Institute of Architects, 1988; Chevalier dans l'Ordre des Arts et des Lettres, Ministry of Culture, France, 1988**

## HUGH NEWELL JACOBSEN

**Born 1929, United States**

**Residence: United States**

**Education: University of Maryland, College Park; Architectural Association School of Architecture, London; Yale University, New Haven, Connecticut**

**Principal Honors: Fellow, American Institute of Architects, 1971; John Fitzgerald Kennedy Memorial Fellowship, New Zealand, 1971; Associate, National Academy of Design, 1988**

## CARLOS JIMENEZ

**Born 1959, Costa Rica**

**Residence: United States**

**Education: University of Houston, Texas; University of Tennessee, Knoxville**

## JOHN JOHANSEN

**Born 1916, United States**

**Residence: United States**

**Education: Harvard University, Cambridge, Massachusetts; Harvard University, Graduate School of Design**

**Principal Honors: Arnold W. Brunner Memorial Prize in Architecture, American Academy and Institute of Arts and Letters, 1968; Fellow, American Institute of Architects, 1969; Honor Award, American Institute of Architects, 1972; Bard Award, City Club of New York, 1977**

## E. FAY JONES

**Born 1921, United States**

**Residence: United States**

**Education: University of Arkansas, Fayetteville; Rice University, Houston, Texas**

**Principal Honors: Fellow, American Institute of Architects, 1979; Fellow, American Academy in Rome, 1980; Gold Medal, American Institute of Architects, 1990**

## PHILIP JOHNSON

**Born 1906, United States**

**Residence: United States**

**Education: Harvard University, Cambridge, Massachusetts**

**Principal Honors: Silver Medal of Honor, Architectural League of New York, 1950; First Prize, Bienal, São Paulo, 1954; Fellow, American Academy and Institute of Arts and Letters, 1963; Fellow, American Institute of Architects, 1965; Twenty-Five Year Award, 1975, and Gold Medal, 1978, American Institute of Architects; R. S. Reynolds Memorial Award, American Institute of Architects, 1978; Thomas Jefferson Medal, University of Virginia, 1978; Pritzker Architecture Prize, 1979**

## SUMET JUMSAI

**Born 1939, Thailand**

**Residence: Thailand**

**Education: Cambridge University, England**

# GERHARD KALLMANN / NOEL MCKINNELL

**Gerhard Kallmann**

Born 1915, Germany

Residence: United States

Education: Architectural Association School of Architecture, London

Principal Honors: Fellow, American Academy of Arts and Sciences, 1985

**Noel McKinnell**

Born 1935, England

Residence: United States

Education: University of Manchester, London; Columbia University, New York

Principal Honors: Silver Medal, Royal Manchester Institute, 1960; Arnold W. Brunner Memorial Prize in Architecture, American Academy and Institute of Arts and Letters, 1969; Fellow, American Academy of Arts and Sciences, 1985

Principal Honors: (Firm Awards) Honor Award, American Institute of Architects, 1969, 1982, 1990; Firm of the Year Award, American Institute of Architecture, 1984

## JOSEF PAUL KLEIHUES

Born 1933, Germany

Residence: Germany

Education: Technical University, West Berlin; Ecole Nationale Supérieure des Beaux-Arts, Paris

Principal Honors: Berlin Art Prize, 1967; Berliatlas zu Stadtbild und Stradtraum, Berlin, 1974; Honorary Fellow, American Institute of Architects, 1989

# RAM KARMI / ADA KARMI-MELAMEDE

**Ram Karmi**

Born 1931, Israel

Residence: Israel

Education: The Technion, Israel Institute of Technology, School of Architecture, Haifa; Architectural Association School of Architecture, London

Principal Honors: Rokach Prize, Tel Aviv, 1965, 1970; Rechter Prize, Tel Aviv, 1967; Reinholds Prize, Tel Aviv, 1969; Associate, Royal Institute of British Architects, 1973

**Ada Karmi-Melamede**

Born 1936, Israel

Residence: Israel

Education: The Technion, Israel Institute of Technology, School of Architecture, Haifa, Israel; Architectural Association School of Architecture, London

## REM KOOLHAAS

Born 1944, The Netherlands

Residence: The Netherlands

Education: Architectural Association School of Architecture, London

## KISHO KUROKAWA

**Born 1934, Japan**

**Residence: Japan**

**Education: Kyoto University; Tokyo University**

**Principal Honors: The Mainichi Art Prize, 1978; Honorary Fellow, American Institute of Architects, 1982; Honorary Member, Union of Architects of Bulgaria, 1982; Life Fellow, Royal Society of Arts, London**

## WILLIAM S. W. LIM

**Born 1932, Hong Kong**

**Residence: Singapore**

**Education: Architectural Association School of Architecture, London; Harvard University, Cambridge, Massachusetts**

## RICARDO LEGORRETA

**Born 1931, Mexico**

**Residence: Mexico**

**Education: Universidad Nacional Autonoma de Mexico, Mexico City**

**Principal Honors: Distinguished Honorary Fellow, Mexican Society of Architects, 1978; Honorary Fellow, American Institute of Architects, 1979**

## MARK MACK

**Born 1949, Austria**

**Residence: United States**

**Education: Academy of Fine Arts, Vienna, Austria**

## DANIEL LIBESKIND

**Born 1946, Poland**

**Residence: Germany**

**Education: The Cooper Union for the Advancement of Science and Art, New York; Essex University, England**

**Principal Honors: Fellowship, Graham Foundation, 1983; Fulbright Fellowship, 1985; First Prize, Leone di Pietra, Venice Bienale, 1985**

## RICHARD MEIER

**Born 1934, United States**

**Residence: United States**

**Education: Cornell University, Ithaca, New York**

**Principal Honors: National Honor Award, American Institute of Architects, 1969, 1971, 1974, 1977; Arnold W. Brunner Memorial Prize in Architecture, American Academy and Institute of Arts and Letters, 1972; Bard Award, City Club of New York, 1973, 1977; Fellow, American Institute of Architects, 1976; R. S. Reynolds Memorial Award, American Institute of Architects, 1977; Architectural Award of Excellence, American Institute of Steel Construction, 1978; Pritzker Architecture Prize, 1984**

## FUMIHIKO MAKI

**Born 1928, Japan**

**Residence: Japan**

**Education: University of Tokyo; Cranbrook Academy of Art, Bloomfield Hills, Michigan; Harvard University, Graduate School of Design, Cambridge, Massachusetts**

**Principal Honors: Japan Institute of Architects Award, 1963; The Mainichi Art Prize, Tokyo, 1969; Honorary Fellow, American Institute of Architects, 1980; 12th Japan Art Prize, Tokyo, 1980**

## RAFAEL MONEO

**Born 1937, Spain**

**Residence: Spain**

**Education: Escuela de Arquitectura, Madrid**

**Principal Honors: Premio de Roma, 1962**

## IMRE MAKOVECZ

**Born 1935, Hungary**

**Residence: Hungary**

**Education: Technical University, Budapest, Hungary**

## ARTHUR COTTON MOORE

**Born 1935, United States**

**Residence: United States**

**Education: Princeton University, New Jersey**

**Principal Honors: Honor Award, American Institute of Architects, 1977; Fellow, American Institute of Architects, 1979**

## OSCAR NIEMEYER

Born 1907, Brazil

Residence: Brazil

Education: Escola Nacional de Belas Artes, Rio de Janeiro

Principal Honors: Prix Joliet-Curie, Paris, 1956; Work Medal, Brazil, 1959; Lenin Award of the USSR, 1963; Benito Juarez Award, Mexico City, 1964; Gold Medal, American Institute of Architects, 1970; Gold Medal, Académie d'Architecture, Paris, 1982; Pritzker Architecture Prize, 1988

## CHARLES MOORE

Born 1925, United States

Residence: United States

Education: University of Michigan, Ann Arbor; Princeton University, New Jersey

Principal Honors: Honor Award, American Institute of Architects, 1965, 1966; Fellow, American Institute of Architects, 1970; Fellowship, Guggenheim Foundation, 1976; Topaz Medallion for Excellence in Architectural Education, American Institute of Architecture and Association of Collegiate Schools of Architecture, 1989; Gold Medal, American Institute of Architects, 1991

## JEAN NOUVEL

Born 1945, France

Residence: France

Education: Ecole Nationale Supérieure des Beaux-Arts, Paris

Principal Honors: Equerre d'Argent, 1987; Grand Prix d'Architecture, 1987

## MORPHOSIS

Thom Mayne

Born 1944, United States

Residence: United States

Education: Harvard University, Cambridge, Massachusetts

Michael Rotondi

Born 1949, United States

Residence: United States

Education: Southern California Institute of Architecture, Santa Monica

Principal Awards: (Firm Awards) Honor Award, American Institute of Architects, 1986, 1988

## WILLIAM PEDERSEN

Born 1938, United States

Residence: United States

Education: University of Minnesota, Minneapolis; Massachusetts Institute of Technology, Cambridge, Massachusetts

Principal Honors: Rome Fellow, American Academy in Rome, 1965; Honor Award, American Institute of Architects, 1984; Arnold W. Brunner Memorial Prize in Architecture, American Academy and Institute of Arts and Letters, 1985; Architecture Firm Award, American Institute of Architects, 1990

# IEOH MING PEI

**Born 1917, China**

**Residence: United States**

**Education: Massachusetts Institute of Technology, Cambridge, Massachusetts; Harvard University, Graduate School of Design**

**Principal Honors: Arnold W. Brunner Memorial Prize in Architecture, American Academy and Institute of Arts and Letters, 1961; Fellow, American Institute of Architects, 1964; Thomas Jefferson Medal in Architecture, University of Virginia, 1976; Gold Medal, American Institute of Architects, 1979; Gold Medal, Académie d'Architecture, Paris, 1981; Pritzker Architecture Prize, 1983; Praemium Imperiale, 1989**

# RENZO PIANO

**Born 1937, Italy**

**Residence: Italy**

**Education: Polytechnic, Milan, Italy**

**Principal Honors: Auguste Perret Prize, International Union of Architects, 1978; Compasso d'Oro Award, Milan, 1981; Honorary Fellow, American Institute of Architects, 1981; Commandeur des Arts et des Lettres, 1985; Legion d'Honneur, 1985; Honorary Fellow, Royal Institute of British Architects, 1986**

# CESAR PELLI

**Born 1926, Argentina**

**Residence: United States**

**Education: University of Tueuman, Buenos Aires; University of Illinois, Champaign-Urbana**

**Principal Honors: Arnold W. Brunner Memorial Prize in Architecture, National Institute of Arts and Letters, 1978; Fellow, American Institute of Architects, 1980**

# REIMA PIETILÄ / RAILI PIETILÄ

**Reima Pietilä**

**Born 1923, Finland**

**Residence: Finland**

**Education: Institute of Technology, Helsinki**

**Principal Honors: Honorary Foreign Member, Swedish Royal Academy of Liberal Arts, 1969; Prince Eugene Medal, Sweden, 1981; Honorary Member, League of German Architects, 1983**

**Raili Pietilä**

**Born 1926, Finland**

**Residence: Finland**

**Education: Institute of Technology, Helsinki**

## JAMES STEWART POLSHEK/ JAMES GARRISON

**James Stewart Polshek**

Born 1930, United States

Residence: United States

Education: Case Western Reserve University, Cleveland, Ohio; Yale University, New Haven, Connecticut

Principal Honors: Fulbright Fellowship, 1956; Osaka Prefecture Architecture Prize, Japan 1965; Gold Medal, Architectural League of New York, 1965; Fellow, American Institute of Architects, 1972; Honor Award, American Institute of Architects, 1972, 1988; Bard Award, City Club of New York, 1988

**James Garrison**

Born 1953, United States

Residence: United States

Education: Syracuse University, New York

## JAQUELIN T. ROBERTSON

Born 1933, United States

Residence: United States

Education: Yale University, New Haven, Connecticut; Magdalen College, Oxford, England

Principal Honors: Bard Award, City Club of New York, 1970; Fellow, American Institute of Architects, 1979

## ANTOINE PREDOCK

Born 1936, United States

Residence: United States

Education: Columbia University, New York

Principal Honors: Fellow, American Institute of Architects, 1981; Fellow, American Academy in Rome, 1985; Honor Award, American Institute of Architects, 1987; Gran Premio Internacional de la Bienal Internacional de Arquitectura de Buenos Aires, 1989

## RICHARD ROGERS

Born 1933, Italy

Residence: England

Education: Architectural Association School of Architecture, London; Yale University, New Haven, Connecticut

Principal Honors: Auguste Perret Prize, International Union of Architects, 1978; Honorary Fellow, American Institute of Architects, 1981; Honorary Fellow, Royal Academy of Art, The Hague, 1981; The Royal Gold Medal for Architecture, 1985; Chevalier, l'Ordre National de la Légion d'Honneur, 1986

## ALDO ROSSI

**Born 1931, Italy**

**Residence: Italy**

**Education: Milan Polytechnic**

**Principal Honors: Pritzker Architecture Prize, 1990**

## MOSHE SAFDIE

**Born 1938, Israel**

**Residence: United States**

**Education: McGill University, Montreal**

**Principal Honors: Massey Medal for Architecture, Canada, 1968; The Order of Canada, 1986; Le Prix d'Excellence in Architecture of the Quebec Order of Architects, 1988**

## PAUL RUDOLPH

**Born 1981, United States**

**Residence: United States**

**Education: Alabama Polytechnic Institute, Auburn; Harvard University Graduate School of Design, Cambridge, Massachusetts**

**Principal Honors: Arnold W. Brunner Memorial Prize in Architecture, American Academy and Institute of Arts and Letters, 1958; Honor Award, 1964, American Institute of Architects; Fellow, American Institute of Arts and Letters, 1971; Honorary Member, Instituto de Arquitectos de Puerto Rico, 1975; Fellow, American Society of Interior Designers, 1976**

## ADÈLE NAUDÉ SANTOS

**Born 1938, South Africa**

**Residence: United States**

**Education: Architectural Association School of Architecture, London; Harvard University, Cambridge, Massachusetts**

**Principal Honors: Bronze Medal of the Cape Institute of South African Architects, 1967; Wheelwright Traveling Fellowship, Harvard University, 1968**

## MACK SCOGIN

**Born 1943, United States**

**Residence: United States**

**Education: Georgia Institute of Technology, Atlanta**

**Principal Honors: Honor Award, American Institute of Architects, 1988, 1989**

## KAZUO SHINOHARA

**Born 1925, Japan**

**Residence: Japan**

**Education: Institute of Technology, Tokyo**

**Principal Honors: Architectural Institute of Japan Prize, 1972; Honorary Fellow, American Institute of Architects, 1988**

## HARRY SEIDLER

**Born 1923, Austria**

**Residence: Australia**

**Education: University of Manitoba, Canada; Harvard University, Cambridge, Massachusetts; Black Mountain College, Berea, North Carolina**

**Principal Honors: Sir John Sulman Medal, Royal Australian Institute of Architects, 1951, 1976, 1981, 1983; Wilkinson Award, Royal Australian Institute of Architects, 1965, 1966, 1967; Honorary Fellow, American Institute of Architects, 1966; Order of the British Empire, 1972; Gold Medal, Royal Australian Institute of Architects, 1976; Honorary Member, Académie d'Architecture, 1982; Companion of the Order of Australia, 1987**

## CATHY SIMON

**Born 1943, United States**

**Residence: United States**

**Education: Wellesley College, Massachusetts; Harvard University, Cambridge, Massachusetts**

**Principal Honors: Canadian Architect Award, 1986; Fellow, American Institute of Architects, 1986**

## SITE

**James Wines**

**Born 1932, United States**

**Residence: United States**

**Education: Syracuse University, New York**

**Principal Honors: Fellow, American Academy in Rome, 1956; Fellowship, Guggenheim Foundation, 1962; Fellowship, Graham Foundation, 1974**

**Alison Sky**

**Born 1946, United States**

**Residence: United States**

**Education: Adelphi University, New York; Columbia University, New York**

## ETTORE SOTTSASS

**Born 1917, Austria**

**Residence: Italy**

**Education: Polytechnic, Turin**

**Principal Honors: Premio Compasso d'Oro, Milan, 1959**

## ALVARO SIZA

**Born 1933, Portugal**

**Residence: Portugal**

**Education: Escola Superior de Belas Artes do Porto**

## ROBERT A. M. STERN

**Born 1939, United States**

**Residence: United States**

**Education: Columbia University, New York; Yale University, New Haven, Connecticut**

**Principal Honors: Honor Award, American Institute of Architects, 1980, 1985; Fellow, American Institute of Architects, 1984**

## JAMES STIRLING

**Born 1926, Scotland**

**Residence: England**

**Education: Liverpool University, England; School of Town Planning and Regional Research, London**

**Principal Honors: Honorary Member, Akademie der Kunste, Berlin, 1969; Honorary Fellow, American Institute of Architects, 1976; Arnold W. Brunner Memorial Prize in Architecture, American Academy and Institute of Arts and Letters, 1976; Alvar Aalto Award, Helsinki, 1977; Honorary Member, Accademia Nazionale di San Luca, Rome, 1979; Fellow, Royal Society of Arts, London, 1979; Royal Gold Medal for Architecture, Royal Institute of British Architects London, 1980; Pritzker Architecture Prize, 1981; Honorary Member, Bund Deutscher Architekten, 1983; Thomas Jefferson Medal in Architecture, University of Virginia School of Architecture, 1986; Hugh Haring Prize, 1988**

## BENJAMIN THOMPSON

**Born 1918, United States**

**Residence: United States**

**Education: Yale University, New Haven, Connecticut**

**Principal Honors: Honor Award, American Institute of Architecture, 1968, 1971, 1978; Firm of the Year Award, American Institute of Architecture, 1987**

## KENZO TANGE

**Born 1913, Japan**

**Residence: Japan**

**Education: University of Tokyo**

**Principal Honors: Annual Prize, Architectural Institute of Japan, 1954, 1955, 1958; Honorary Member, Academie der Kunste,Germany, 1962; Gold Medal, Royal Institute of British Architects, 1965; Honorary Fellow, American Institute of Architects, 1966; Honorary Member, American Academy of Arts and Letters, 1966; Gold Medal, American Institute of Architects, 1966; Thomas Jefferson Medal in Architecture, University of Virginia, 1970; Gold Medal of the President of Italy, 1970; Gold Medal, Académie d'Architecture, France, 1973; Commander, National Order of Merit, France, 1977; Order of Merit, Republic of Italy, 1979; Associate, Institut de France Académie des Beaux-Arts, Paris, 1983; Gran Oficial de la Orden El Sol del Peru, 1983**

## STANLEY TIGERMAN

**Born 1930, United States**

**Residence: United States**

**Education: Massachusetts Institute of Technology, Cambridge; Institute of Design, Chicago; Yale University, New Haven, Connecticut**

**Principal Honors: Honor Award, American Institute of Architects, 1982; Masonry Institute Award, 1982**

# BERNARD TSCHUMI

**Born 1944, Switzerland**

**Residence: United States**

**Education: Federal Institute of Technology, Zurich, Switzerland**

# O. M. UNGERS

**Born 1926, Germany**

**Residence: Germany**

**Education: Technische Hochschule, Karlsruhe**

# WILLIAM TURNBULL, JR.

**Born 1935, United States**

**Residence: United States**

**Education: Princeton University New Jersey; Ecole des Beaux-Arts**

**Principal Honors: Honor Award, 1963, 1967, 1968, 1973, 1976, Merit Award, 1966, 1970, American Institute of Architects; Fellow, American Institute of Architects, 1976**

# ROBERT VENTURI

**Born 1925, United States**

**Residence: United States**

**Education: Princeton University, New Jersey**

**Principal Honors: Rome Fellow, 1954; Fellowship, Graham Foundation, 1963; Arnold W. Brunner Memorial Prize in Architecture, American Academy and Institute of Arts and Letters, 1973; Honor Award, American Institute of Architects, 1977; Fellow, American Institute of Architects, 1978; Thomas Jefferson Medal in Architecture, University of Virginia, 1983; Fellow, Accademia Nazionale di San Luca, Rome, 1983; Commendatore of the Order of Merit, Republic of Italy, 1986; Pritzer Architecture Prize, 1991**

## HARRY WEESE

**Born 1915, United States**

**Residence: United States**

**Education: Massachusetts Institute of Technology, Cambridge; Yale University, New Haven, Connecticut; Cranbrook Academy of Art, Bloomfield Hills, Michigan**

**Principal Honors: Fellow, American Institute of Architects, 1961; Arnold W. Brunner Memorial Prize in Architecture, American Academy and Institute of Arts and Letters, 1964; Merit Award for Design Excellence, 1965, Honor Award, 1969, 1970, 1973, 1977, 1983, and Firm of the Year Award, 1978, American Institute of Architects; Union of Polish Architects Award, Second World Biennale of Architecture, 1983**

## HARRY C. WOLF

**Born 1935, United States**

**Residence: United States**

**Education: Massachusetts Institute of Technology, Cambridge; Georgia Institute of Technology, Atlanta**

**Principal Honors: Honor Award, American Institute of Architects, 1971, 1974, 1980, 1983; Fellow, American Institute of Architects, 1976**

## TOD WILLIAMS / BILLIE TSIEN

**Tod Williams**

**Born 1943, United States**

**Residence: United States**

**Education: Princeton University, New Jersey**

**Principal Honors: Fellow, American Academy in Rome**

**Billie Tsien**

**Born 1949, United States**

**Residence: United States**

**Education: Yale University, New Haven Connecticut; University of California at Los Angeles**

**Principal Honors: (Firm Awards) Honor Award, American Institute of Architects, 1988, 1989; three distinguished Architecture Awards, 1989**

## LEBBEUS WOODS

**Born 1940, United States**

**Residence: United States**

**Education: Purdue University School of Engineering; University of Illinois, Champaign-Urbana**